Simple Models of Income Redistribution

András Simonovits

Simple Models of Income Redistribution

palgrave
macmillan

András Simonovits
Hungarian Academy of Sciences
Budapest, Hungary

ISBN 978-3-030-10214-2 ISBN 978-3-319-72502-4 (eBook)
https://doi.org/10.1007/978-3-319-72502-4

Softcover re-print of the Hardcover 1st edition 2018

Cover design: Akihiro Nakayama

Printed on acid-free paper

This Palgrave Macmillan imprint is published by the registered company Springer International Publishing AG part of Springer Nature
The registered company address is: Gewerbestrasse 11, 6330 Cham, Switzerland

Preface

With the emergence of the modern economy and the general elections, in developed countries the government had to help the old-aged and the working poor. The required inter- and intragenerational *income redistribution* was served by the introduction of public and private pension systems and of personal income taxation. After the Second World War, the extension of social protection and especially the public pension system (Social Security in the United States) has led to the creation of the welfare state.

To understand the functioning of the income redistribution and its tool, the transfer system, modern economics uses *models*. A model is a simplified description of the reality and its application makes the analysis easier and more transparent. There are classic books (e.g., Atkinson and Stiglitz 1980; Auerbach and Kotlikoff 1987; Atkinson and Bourguignon 2006; Salanié 2011 and Stiglitz 2000) on the topic, but they worked with rather complex models. Other books (e.g., Verbon 1988; Simonovits 2003) used simple models but confining attention to pensions.

The present book discusses about two-dozen simple models of these transfer systems in a self-contained structure. It is written to students and researchers, who are interested in the logic of transfer systems. To those who are ready to go into details of simple models, where everything can and should be understood. (This is almost impossible in sophisticated models.) In principle, it is sufficient if the Reader knows the basics of economics and calculus. In practice, occasionally the analysis is quite involved and requires some persistence from the Reader.

The Introduction contains a detailed outline of the book, here I only sketch the book's most important characteristics.

The models are not only simple but mostly *minimal*: by leaving out further elements, the given model loses its very interest. Two examples on minimalism in our pension models: (a) Typically there are only two time-periods: in period 1 the employee works and in period 2 she is retired. (b) Frequently there are only two types of workers: the high-earners who are farsighted and the low-earners who are shortsighted. Removing any of these simplifications, the means-tested or the voluntary pension systems could not be analyzed.

Though the models are neither econometrically verified, nor calibrated, they can be filled with meaningful numbers and *run* on a computer (even with Excel or Basic).

In our typical models, the benevolent government offers the citizens a transfer scheme and the citizens optimize their behavior under the scheme. Anticipating these individual reactions, the government maximizes a social welfare function (cf. Feldstein 1985). The practice of malevolent government is also important but lies out of the scope the book.

The government's transfers have various *functions*: to counteract the myopia of workers concerning their old-age, to redistribute from the rich to the poor, to give insurance on longevity risk, etc. but occasionally simply to maximize the revenues.

The book is mostly *theoretical* but with an eye on transfer policies rather than a theory for its own sake. Sporadically one can find empirical material and the quite mixed Hungarian practice appears at a number of places.

In addition to well-known results, the book contains a couple of new results. To mention few of them: (i) If financing pension contributions from loans is excluded (contrary to Feldstein 1985), then the relative ranking of the public pension system with respect to the private one improves. (ii) The strong and increasing positive correlation between lifetime income and life expectancy at retirement suggests some redistribution even in otherwise proportional (defined contribution) pension systems. (iii) The widespread presence of fragmented labor careers calls into question the usefulness of seniority pensions.

I express my debt to those who helped me writing the papers underlying the present book. First of all, thanks to my co-authors of several related papers: T. Czeglédi, P. Eső, B. Garay, E. Granseth, W. Keck, Zs. Méder, W. Nagl, E. Szabó, M. Tir, J. Tóth, and J. Vincze. I am also obliged to other persons, namely J. Banyár, H. Fehr, and R. I. Gál for their permanent constructive criticism. Occasionally, I was able to ask the advice of the late M. Augusztinovics, N. Barr, I. Bessenyei, P. A. Diamond, L. Halpern, E. Kovács, E. Krajcsovicz, F. Legros, M. C. Lovell, B. Muraközy, Á. Reiff, E. Sőregi, and I. Gy. Tóth. The anonymous referees of earlier versions of the underlying papers have contributed to the improvement of the models. Last but not least, I thank T. Bakó, Á. Drabancz, J. Köllő, M. T. Kurbucz, Yali Liu, T. Pintér, A. Rácz, B. Szabó, J. Szabó, and E. Szobonya for careful checking parts of the various versions of the typescript.

I am indebted to my past and present work places: the Institute of Economics, CERS Hungarian Academy of Sciences, the Mathematical Institute of Budapest University of Technology, the Economics Department of Central European University, and the Department of Mathematical Economics and Quantitative Analysis at Budapest Corvinus University. I acknowledge the support of the Hungarian Science Research Foundation's projects K 81482 and 108668.

Budapest, Hungary
October 2017

András Simonovits

References

Atkinson, B. A., & Stiglitz, J. E. (1980). *Lectures on Public Economics.* New York: McGraw-Hill.

Atkinson, B. A., & Bourguignon, F. (Eds.). (2006). *Handbook of Income Distribution.* Amsterdam, Elsevier.

Auerbach, A. J., & Kotlikoff, L. J. (1987). *Dynamic Fiscal Policy.* Cambridge, Cambridge University Press.

Feldstein, M. S. (1985). The optimal level of social security benefits, *Quarterly Journal of Economics, 100,* 302–320.

Salanié, B. (2011): *The Economics of Taxation* (2nd ed.). Cambridge, MA: MIT Press.

Simonovits, A. (2003). *Modeling Pension Systems.* Houndsmill, Basingstoke, Palgrave, Macmillan.

Stiglitz, J. E. (2000). *Economics of Public Sector* (3rd ed.). New York: W. W. Norton & Company.

Verbon, H. (1988). *The Evolution of Public Pension Schemes.* Berlin: Springer.

Contents

List of Tables

1
Introduction

During the last decade, I analyzed about a dozen *simple* models on income redistribution achieved through transfer (tax and benefit) systems. The adjective simple means that I neglected everything in creating the given model which could be neglected without destroying the basic insights. To defend this minimalism and relying on Rubinstein's essay (2017), I cite two observations from Rodrik (2015): (i) "Relevance does not require complexity and complexity may impede relevance" (p. 44). (ii) "What matters to the empirical relevance of a model is the realism of the *critical* assumptions" (p. 94).

Constructing simple public pension (and other transfer) models, I followed the basic idea of Feldstein (1985) (as a precursor, see Samuelson 1975; as a follower, see Cremer and Pestieau 2011): The *paternalistic* government overwrites its citizens' excessive discounting while designing the intergenerational transfer system. He made, however, two unrealistic critical assumptions (cf. Andersen and Bhattacharya 2011): (i) the representative worker can always pay the contributions from bank credits; (ii) though the public system is sustainable, the worker only expects a small share of the true benefits. On such a shaky basis, Feldstein proved that public pensions are only needed if the bulk of the workers are very myopic (see Appendix D), suggesting the eventual replacement by

A. Simonovits, *Simple Models of Income Redistribution*,
https://doi.org/10.1007/978-3-319-72502-4_1

a private system. Note also that to consumption smoothing, Barr and Diamond's (2008) added three further criteria: insurance, poverty relief and redistribution.

Originally, I had studied only pension systems exclusively based on the *intergenerational* redistribution (summarized in Simonovits 2003) but later, I realized that one needs to extend the analysis to *intragenerational* redistribution. Indeed, Feldstein (1987) already combined the two when he compared flat systems with means-tested ones. The basic idea of Feldstein's approach is that private saving is so much more efficient than the public one that the government intervention can only make things worse. Since this problem is a central topic of the book, I make four remarks on it right now.

(i) When I also assume that private saving is more efficient than the public one, apart from Sect. 3.3, I deliberately neglect the other important aspect of Social Security: delivering unisex and indexed life annuities (cf. Barr and Diamond 2008; Banyár 2016). (ii) Even if the higher efficiency were true, replacing the unfunded system with a funded one would require a complex transition process which may eliminate the prospective gains (cf. Geanakoplos et al. 1998; Simonovits 2003, Chapter 15). (iii) Apart from mortgages, poorer workers are generally credit-constrained and this should be taken into account, even if this complicates the analysis. (iv) As the contribution rate rises, the welfare decreases until the savings become zero. To have a socially useful pension system, the contribution rate should be high enough to ensure higher welfare than the original no-pension system does. Figuratively speaking, the transfers should "the gap" created by the inefficiency of the public system with respect to the private one.

In the remainder of the Introduction, we present the empirical background (Sect. 1.1), the specifics (Sect. 1.2) and the outline of the book (Sect. 1.3).

1.1 Empirical Background

Since this is a theoretical book, I only mention few empirical data on transfers; Salanié (2011) and especially Atkinson and Bourgignon (2006) particularly Boadway and Keen (2006); Scheve and Stasavage (2016) contain rich material on the historical development of intragenerational transfers. The Mirrlees Report (edited by Mirrlees et al. 2010, 2011) gives a state of the art of the tax and benefit systems. Concerning intergenerational data, World Bank (1994), Simonovits (2003) and Barr and Diamond's (2008) are recommended.

Progressive income taxation is a powerful tool of income redistribution. Table 1.1 shows the role of World War I in the spread of progressive income taxation, contrasting mobilization and nonmobilization countries (entering and not entering the war) and confining attention to the top earners. The role of mobilization is obvious.

Table 1.2 reports the spread of taxation in general and progressive income taxation in particular in the United Kingdom around World Wars I and II. The estimate measures the direct and indirect taxes as a percent of income. Note the increase of taxation between 1903 and 1913 and its acceleration during the wars.

Moving ahead in time, Table 1.3 displays recent values of three income inequality indicators of several Organization of Economic and Development (OECD) countries: the deciles' gross income ratio (the ratio of the gross incomes of the richest to the poorest deciles), the Gini coefficients and the ratio of median to mean wage. (The third indicator will play a leading role in our theoretical analysis in the whole book.) (i) Denmark has the lowest decile ratio of 5.2, the OECD average is 9.6, while the

Table 1.1 World War I and progressive income taxation

Annual income	Prewar	Postwar	Difference
90th percentile			
Mobilization countries	0.0	4.3	4.3
Nonmobilization countries	2.8	3.3	0.5
Difference in difference			3.8
99th percentile			
Mobilization countries	1.4	12.1	10.7
Nonmobilization countries	3.7	5.0	1.3
Difference in difference			9.4

Source. Based on Scheve and Stasavage (2016, Table 3.1, p. 82). Average marginal tax rates, four mobilization and four nonmobilization countries, prewar (1913), postwar (1920)

United States (US) has the highest ratio of 18.8. (ii) The country order of the Gini coefficients is the same, starting from 0.25 and ending with 0.40. (iii) The ratio of median to mean net income drops from 0.95 (Denmark) to 0.82 (US) for net rather than gross wage. (The respective figure for gross income was about 0.715 in the US household income in 2014.)

Table 1.4 compares income inequality before and after taxes and benefits in selected European Union (EU) countries between 2001 and 2005. As is to be expected, the net Gini is lower than the gross Gini, but their relation varies across countries.

Turning to pension issues, demographic data will be useful. Table 1.5 displays the total fertility rate (approximately, the standardized number of children born by a woman during her whole life) between 1970 and 2010 for a couple of countries. For their special past and overwhelming weights, China and India are also selected. (Since in 1970, the infant mortality indicators in these countries were relatively high, the number of surviving children was much lower.) Note that a number of countries have declining trend and most of the displayed countries have ups and downs in their fertility indices.

Table 1.6 presents the population shares of the youngest and the oldest age-groups in selected countries in 2010. Concerning its population, India is still a young country, where children and old-aged comprise 28.5 and 5.8% of the population, respectively. China has recently become older, with the corresponding indicators being 17.1 and 9.6%, respectively. The United States is older than China; and Germany is the oldest among the mentioned countries. The world average is close to India. Roughly speaking, decades ago the older countries had similar age structures than younger countries have now.

Table 1.2 Total burden of taxation in the United Kingdom, 1903–1941, %

Annual income (Pound)	1903	1913	1918	1937	1941
100	5.6	5.4	9.9	10.4	19.1
1000	6.1	5.2	16.9	12.8	32.2
10,000	5.0	8.0	42.5	39.1	68.3
50,000	4.8	8.4	50.6	56.7	90.7

Source. Based on Scheve and Stasavage (2016, Table 5.1, p. 122)

Table 1.3 Decile ratio, Gini coefficient and median/mean wage, 2012/2013

Country	Gross		Net median/mean wage
	Decile ratio	Gini-coefficient	
Denmark	5.2	0.25	0.95
Germany	6.6	0.29	0.93
Poland	7.4	0.30	0.88
OECD average	9.6	0.32	0.85
United Kingdom	10.5	0.35	0.82
United States	18.8	0.40	0.82

Source. OECD 2014

Table 1.4 Gini coefficients before and after taxes and benefits

Country	Denmark	Germany	Hungary	UK	Poland
Gross income	0.30	0.33	0.35	0.35	0.35
Net income	0.23	0.25	0.23	0.25	0.33

Source. Figure 7.1 of Paulus et al. (2009, p. 155). Gross income contains public pensions

Table 1.5 Total fertility rates in selected countries, 1970–2010

Country	1970	1980	1990	2000	2010
China	5.51	2.63	2.34	1.74	1.60
France	2.47	1.95	1.78	1.89	2.01
Germany	2.03	1.56	1.45	1.38	1.39
Great Britain	2.43	1.89	1.83	1.64	1.98
Hungary	1.97	1.92	1.84	1.33	1.25
India	5.49	4.68	3.92	3.12	2.63
The Netherlands	2.57	1.60	1.62	1.72	1.79
Sweden	1.92	1.68	2.13	1.54	1.98
United States	2.44	1.84	2.08	2.06	1.93

Table 1.7 displays certain key numbers on taxation in Sweden, Germany and the United States, representing strongly, typically and moderately redistributive countries, respectively. The first row displays the tax revenue–GDP-ratio (GDP stands for Gross Domestic Product): declining from 46 through 36 to 25%. The next three rows present the structure of the tax revenues. The middle row is the most interesting: the property taxes being low in Sweden and Germany and high in the United States.

Table 1.6 Population shares of the youngest and the oldest age-groups, %

Country	Population shares of	
	Below 14	Above 64
India	28.5	5.8
China	17.1	9.6
United States	19.4	14.5
Germany	13.0	21.1
World	25.8	8.3

Source. Central Intelligence Agency (CIA) Fact Book 2010

Table 1.7 Taxation in Sweden, Germany and the United States, %

Country	Sweden	Germany	United States
Tax revenue/GDP	45.8	36.3	24.8
Share of tax revenue			
Income taxes	68.4	68.7	70.0
Property taxes	2.4	2.4	11.8
Consumption taxes	28.8	28.4	17.9
Income tax distortions			
Top marginal tax rate	73.6	59.3	43.3
Participation tax rate	76.7	63.0	36.6

Source. From Kleven (2014, Table 1, p. 78), around 2012

Turning to the last block, the top marginal rate declines from 74 through 59 to 43%. The last row needs an explanation: the *participation tax rate* shows the combined effect of all taxes and contributions paid by a wage earner. This index diminishes from 77 through 63 to 37%.

Table 1.8 presents the dramatic changes in the gross government debt in terms of the GDP before and after the Great Recession of selected countries. Note that in the majority of countries presented, the foregoing ratio drastically increased (either by increasing the debt like in Ireland or letting the GDP to drop like in Greece). There were other countries (e.g., Germany) where the debt ratio remained stable. Even there is a small country, Estonia which preserves its indicator as one-digit. Note, however, that this indicator sensitively depends on the current status of the mandatory funded pension system. For example, in Hungary, the so-called second pillar was nationalized in 2010, decreasing the debt ratio by

Table 1.8 The government debt–GDP ratio for selected countries, 2007–2016, %

Country	Debt ratio		Change in GDP
	2007	2016	
Japan	183.0	250.4	2.1
Greece	103.1	183.4	–21.0
United States	64.0	108.2	11.2
Spain	35.5	101.1	–3.0
France	64.4	97.1	3.2
Great Britain	42.2	89.0	4.6
Hungary	65.6	75.3	0.9
Ireland	23.9	74.6	–0.4
Germany	63.5	68.2	7.2
Slovakia	29.9	52.8	16.7
China	29.0	46.3	92.7
Latvia	7.2	35.1	–3.5
Estonia	3.7	9.5	1.2

Source. International Monetary Fund, GDP index calculated at constant prices

Table 1.9 Wealth distribution in Sweden and the US: actual, estimated and desired

Share	Sweden		US wealth	
	Wealth	Actual	Estimated	Desired
Upper	36	84	59	32
Second	21	11	20	22
Third	18	4	10	20
Fourth	15	0.2	8	15
Lowest	11	0.1	3	11

Source. Norton and Ariely (2011, Figures 1 and 2, pp. 10–11)

10% points in itself with respect to the no nationalization and 'saving' the annual transaction cost for the coming years.

Next, we transform two related figures from Norton and Ariely (2011) into Table 1.9, showing the wealth distribution among the five quintiles in Sweden and the United States, respectively. (Unfortunately, the Swedish data are mixed up in the original figure and refer to incomes rather than wealth.) The last but one and the last columns show the estimation and the Rawlsian desired values of a random sample of US citizens, respectively. Note the huge differences between the last three categories.

Turning to pension data, Table 1.10 characterizes the redistribution and (for later use) the size of the public system in a few mandatory public

Table 1.10 Size and redistribution of public pension systems in OECD countries, cc. 2000, %

Country	Replacement rate for earnings			Type	Aggregate pension per GDP
	Half	Average	Double		
France	84	84	73	Proportional	12.5
Hungary (2000)	78	79	73	Proportional	9.5
Germany	76	72	75	Proportional	12.8
Unite States	65	55	32	Progressive	4.6
Great Britain	72	50	35	Progressive	4.4
Czechia	81	49	28	Progressive	9.6
The Netherlands	73	43	25	Flat	5.2

Source. Simonovits (2003, Table 4.5, p. 48)

systems around 2000. Obviously, in France, Hungary and Germany, the replacement ratio is basically independent of the earning: proportional (earning-related) systems; while in the United States and Czechia, the ratio decreases: progressive systems, ending with the Dutch flat system. As expected, the more progressive the system, the smaller its size (except for Czechia which is an outlier). Recent data for much more countries are presented in OECD (2015, p. 147, Table 6.15).

We continue the presentation with a couple of shortened tables from OECD (2011, 2015). We start the presentation with the early and normal male and female retirement ages of several OECD countries in 2014. Note that France still has a very low normal retirement age and some countries have lower female than male retirement ages. Hungary and the Netherlands stand out with their rigid system, the early and the normal retirement ages are the same, 62.5 and 65, respectively. It would be useful to learn more about the effective retirement ages (Table 1.11).

Consulting OECD (2011, 25–26, Tables 1.1 and 1.2), we see that in those countries where the normal retirement ages are low, they were higher in the past and will be higher in the future.

Tables 1.12 and 1.13 contain past, present and future data on life expectancy at normal retirement age. Note that each of the foregoing countries has a much lower male than female life expectancy at any adult age and the countries also differ in their male and female indicators,

Table 1.11 Early and normal retirement ages of several OECD countries, 2014

Country	Male		Female	
	Early	Normal	Early	Normal
Czehia	60.0	62.67	60.0	61.33
France	61.2	61.2	60.0	61.2
Germany	63	65	63	65
Great Britain	65	65	62.5	62.5
Hungary	62.5	62.5	62.5[a]	62.5
The Netherlands	65	65	65	65
Sweden	61	65	61	65
Switzerland	63	65	62	64
United States	62	66	62	66

[a]Except for those with 40 years of eligibility
Source. OECD (2015, Table 5.7, p. 131)

Table 1.12 Life expectancy at normal retirement age, selected countries: males

Country	1993	2010	2050[a]
Czechia	15.7	17.0	18.1
France	19.4	21.7	24.8
Germany	16.5	17.0	20.3
Great Britain	14.2	16.9	16.9
Hungary	14.5	14.0	16.3
The Netherlands	14.4	17.3	20.6
Sweden	15.5	17.9	21.1
Switzerland	15.9	16.9	22.4
United States	15.3	16.8	17.7

[a]Forecast
Source. OECD (2011, p. 29, Table 1.3)

respectively. Therefore, the life expectancy at the normal retirement age has a special importance. (Since the source gave the normal Hungarian retirement age in 2010 as 65 rather than 62, we corrected the corresponding numbers: male and female numbers are changed from 16.5 to 14.0 and 22.6 to 20.0.) Note the striking difference between French male indicator of 24.8 years and the US counterpart: 17.7 years. Note that the normal retirement age rises so much (by 5 year) in Great Britain that the corresponding female life expectancy will drop between 2010 and 2050. The stagnation of the male counterpart is difficult to rationalize.

Table 1.13 Life expectancy at normal retirement age, selected countries: females

Country	1993	2010	2050[a]
Czechia	23.0	23.8	22.5
France	24.6	26.5	29.5
Germany	22.5	20.7	24.4
Great Britain	21.9	24.5	21.9
Hungary	24.2	20.0	21.1
The Netherlands	18.8	20.4	23.5
Sweden	19.1	21.1	24.2
Switzerland	22.6	24.1	26.6
United States	18.9	19.3	21.9

[a]Forecast
Source. OECD (2011, p. 30, Table 1.4)

Table 1.14 Changes in gross pension wealth for different working age 60–65, males

Country	Individual earning level (% of average)		
	Low (50%)	Average (100%)	High (150%)
Czechia	30.3	22.9	18.3
France	8.3	9.5	–0.1
Germany	–16.3	13.9	13.9
Great Britain	3.5	2.9	1.9
Hungary	9.5	9.5	9.5
The Netherlands	14.1	24.0	27.3
Sweden	–10.5	4.2	4.3
Switzerland	13.4	12.1	8.5
United States	–1.2	–1.2	0.4

Source. OECD (2011, p. 57, Table 3.2)

Table 1.14 displays a very important indicator: the change in gross pension wealth for working age 60–65 and different relative earnings levels. In an actuarially fair system, there is no change; positive (negative) change signals the presence of incentives for late (early) retirement. Note how few countries have indicators close to zero!

Until now we have not discussed the changing structure of social expenditures. Table 1.15 displays the growing share of social expenditures and changing weights of four important parts in Great Britain, between 1950 and 2010. Within the growing share of social expenditures (from 11.8 to

Table 1.15 The GDP-share of four important programs, Great Britain, 1950–2010, %

Year	Education	Social welfare	Health expenditures	Public pensions	Total
1950	4.2	3.0	2.6	2.0	11.8
1970	4.1	5.4	4.0	3.8	18.6
1990	4.3	6.4	4.3	4.2	19.2
2010	5.9	7.4	7.8	7.8	28.9

Source. www.ukpublicspending.co.uk/past-spending

Table 1.16 Social protection and government expenditures for selected countries, 1960–1980, %

Country	Social protection/GDP		Government/GDP	
	1960	1980	1960	1980
Australia	7.4	12.8	22.7	30.6
Germany	18.1	25.7	31.4	46.6
Great Britain	10.2	16.4	33.0	44.4
Japan	4.1	11.9	17.0	30.1
The Netherlands	11.7	28.3	30.0	56.9
Sweden	10.8	25.9	31.3	61.1
United States	7.3	15.0	28.1	35.4

Source. OECD (1985, Appendix C)

28.9%), the most spectacular rise occurred with health and public pensions.

As a summary, in Table 1.16 we display the social welfare and total government expenditures between 1960 and 1980 for selected OECD countries, a period, when the most spectacular rise occurred. The initial intercountry differences remained, but the share of the public sector steeply increased in every country.

A similar summary is given in Table 1.17 for a longer period, also containing separated pension expenditures (Laps 2015). Note the persistent intercountry differences, the US being at the end, while France, Germany and Sweden the leaders.

We could continue the presentation of data but probably the data displayed are sufficient to inform the Reader about the general features of the transfer systems.

Table 1.17 The relative size of social protection and especially of pensions, 1960–2010, %

Country	1960		1980		2010	
	Pension	Soc. Prot.	Pension	Soc. Prot.	Pension	Soc. Prot.
France	4.7	12.4	9.5	20.8	13.3	32.1
Germany	8.4	15.3	10.4	22.1	11.5	27.3
Great Britain	4.0	–	4.2	16.3	6.1	22.8
Japan	1.2	–	3.0	10.3	10.2	22.1
The Netherlands	3.0	10.1	6.4	24.8	7.0	23.5
Sweden	3.9	10.1	7.1	27.1	9.6	28.3
United States	3.9	7.2	6.2	13.2	6.8	19.2

Remark. Laps (2015, p. 4, Table 1.1)

1.2 Specifics of the Book

Having presented some basic facts about income redistribution through transfer systems for selected countries and periods, we move to the discussion of our models. The tools applied in the book are very simple: the population often consists of only one type or two types whose decisions (saving, working, reporting earning, giving birth to children) maximize their subjective utility functions. Typically, the utility function is additive in age or across labor disutility or tax morale. For example, in the intergenerational models, a worker's lifetime utility function is the sum of his young- and old-age utility function, the second is discounted (cf. Samuelson 1937). To simplify the calculations, the terms are frequently logarithmic or linear-quadratic.

Most tax systems have a number of tax subsystems: personal income tax, value-added tax, capital tax, corporate tax, excise tax; and they finance public goods and direct income redistribution (and achieve macroeconomic stabilization). Concentrating on the personal income tax system (cf. Mirrlees 1971), one also gets simpler models, shedding more light on certain aspects of the problems like flexible labor supply (caused by high taxes) and tax evasion (caused by low tax morale). (Stiglitz 2000 and Salanié 2011 discussed other taxes as well.) These systems are typically progressive and have more than one marginal rate, but again for simplicity, we shall only consider a flat (single) rate income tax, financing basic income. (Though

Mankiw et al. (2009) argued for the flat-rate tax's optimality and Appendix A constructs a similar example, Diamond and Saez (2011) convincingly showed that *in general* this is far from the social optimum, especially for Pareto wage distributions.) Sometimes we also investigate means-tested, capped or pension credit systems which are nonlinear.

The paternalistic government maximizes a social welfare function which is a function of the modified individual utility functions (e.g., in the intergenerational models, the government replaces the discounted utility functions with undiscounted ones). Sometimes we use pure utilitarian social welfare functions, other occasions we apply Rawlsian ones. When applying the political economy framework, the social welfare function is replaced by the median voter's utility function.

We shall not bother too much with the problem of sufficiency of the first-order conditions of the optimum except for the case of having more than one stationary point; especially the phenomenon of jumping the gap, when in addition to maxima, minima also appear.

A further specific feature of these models is that the theoretical analysis is always supplemented by *numerical* illustrations. Though the models are not calibrated, the numbers may help the Reader to get a feeling for the order of magnitudes. The models are presented more or less independently of each other but by their structure, the chapters also form a book.

Though I have always had strong reservations on the central role of utility maximization, for pedagogical reasons the present book as a rule follows the traditional utility maximization framework. (Nevertheless, Sect. 6.2 and Chapter 14 lack any optimization.) At least at this place, however, I call attention to alternatives like *behavioral economics* (cf. Kőszegi 2014; Rabin 1998; Chetty 2015). This approach has already been applied in many fields, e.g., the explanation of voluntary pensions studied in Chapter 8 in a traditional framework. Finally, I mainly study such governments which maximize *paternalistic* social welfare, but Appendix A's criterion is the tax revenue and Chapter 12 analyzes the transfer systems' problems in the framework of political economy rather than social welfare.

1.3 Outline of the Book

The book starts with Chapter 2 which presents the simplest *tax* models: (i) taxpayers restrain their labor supply (due to labor disutility) and (ii) hide only part of their incomes (due to tax morale). The socially optimal tax rate is a decreasing function of the minimum wage in (i)–(ii) and an increasing function of the tax morale in (ii).

Chapter 3 presents three simple *pension* models: (i) Depending on the parameter values of the economy, a public pension system can be more efficient than a private saving scheme to provide old-age security to a myopic worker. Note a key feature of that model (and the whole book): the worker cannot finance his/her pension contribution from bank loan. (ii) Longevity risk can only covered by public life annuity. (iii) A redistributive public pension system socially insures risky old-age income (Varian 1980).

In Chapter 4, we recalculate Feldstein's two-type models (1985 and 1987) with heterogeneous wages, while uniform public pensions are replaced by proportional ones. The favorable results on proportional system are preserved. Following Feldstein (1987), we prove that the proportional system can be further improved by means-testing. Other variants are obtained by imposing a cap on the contributions or completing mandatory public pensions with voluntary pensions.

In Chapters 5–8, we generalize the two-type pension models of Chapter 4 to multitype models, where the discount factor is an increasing function of the wage. (Except for Chapter 6, wages have a Pareto distribution.)

Chapter 5 considers a proportional pension system, and presents the dependence of the socially optimal contribution rate on the distribution of myopia and on the interest rate.

Not all public pension systems are proportional. We have already met the simplest nonproportional system, namely the *means-tested* one in Sect. 4.3. In Chapter 6, we consider progressive transfer systems. For example, we generalize the means-tested and the basic *plus* systems and study the *pension credit*, where the basic pension is tapered off, as the savings and proportional pensions increase. This generalization improves the efficiency of the system.

Another nonproportional or semi-proportional pension system is the *capped* one (Chapter 7). In most pension systems, there is a cap on the pension contribution base, above which the worker does not pay additional contribution and does not receive an additional pension. Generalizing Chapter 5, the cap (as well as the contribution rate) is designed optimally: the lower-paid and myopic workers obtain a relatively high replacement, while the others enjoy the enlarged possibilities of the more efficient private savings.

The *voluntary* pension system (Chapter 8) differs from the previous ones: in addition to the public one (in our case, the proportional one), the government matches the private savings by collecting earmarked taxes. The dependence of socially optimal outcomes on parameter values is complex; but higher matching rates and lower caps are socially preferable.

Chapter 9 introduces *flexible (variable) retirement*, where workers can choose their retirement age. For the nonfinancial defined contribution (NDC) system, we determine the optimal retirement age of a representative worker. If the life expectancies are heterogeneous, the NDC has a pitfall: it redistributes from the ex ante short-lived to the ex ante long-lived. Introducing *fragmented* (incomplete) work careers (studied by Augusztinovics and Köllő 2008, 2009), we are able to discuss the *pros* and *cons* of seniority retirement.

Chapters 10 and 11 move to a rather controversial field: how does the *fertility* depend on the child support and its Siamese twin, namely the public pension system (van Groezen et al. 2003)? In Chapter 10, there are heterogeneous parents with different wages and, young- and old-age workers are distinguished but pensioners are excluded. We show that positive child benefits are socially optimal when the past average fertility is below 1. In Chapter 11, we give up wage and age heterogeneity (among workers) but introduce old-age with saving and pensions. As it turns out, the child support and the pension systems suppose each other, and the phenomenon jumping the gap appears again.

Chapter 12 discusses a well-known alternative to social welfare maximization, namely Political Economy in general and the *theory of median voter* in particular. Concerning intragenerational transfers (Sect. 12.2), it can be shown that the higher the relative median wage or the lower the tax morale, the lower the median voter's tax rate. Extending the analysis to intergenerational transfers as well (Sect. 12.3), we modify Razin et al. (2002), and expose how strong and implausible assumptions are needed to obtain their paradox and erroneous conclusion: the older the population, the smaller the welfare state.

Chapter 13 analyzes the consequences of *imperfect knowledge* of the tax and the pension rules: workers overestimate the efficiency of the private pillar and their future pensions, while underestimating the actuarial adjustment rate.

Chapter 14 considers the case when the longevity is an increasing function of wage. First, we present three adjustments to the basic NDC to diminish income redistribution. Second, we show that making the adult retirement ages proportional to the adult life expectancies, the redistribution becomes even stronger (cf. Chapter 9 above). Third, we consider the impact of diminishing the *wage share in pension indexation.*

Chapter 15 studies *dynamic* extensions arising in transfer models: (i) government debt dynamics; (ii) the dynamics of propagation of tax reduction in a pension system; (iii) the leading model of modern economics, namely *overlapping generations,* where the interest rate is not given but determined endogenously (Samuelson 1958).

Chapter 16 concludes but then ten Appendices (denoted by A,..., J) complement certain chapters of the book. Appendix A (to Chapter 2) shows an example when the socially optimal quadratic income tax schedule is linear. Appendix B (to Chapter 3) demonstrates the special features of Cobb–Douglas utility functions within the family of constant relative risk aversion (CRRA) utility functions. Appendix C (to Chapter 3) presents some simple mathematical methods to find numerically and efficiently the roots of nonlinear equations. Appendix D (to Chapter 3) outlines how Feldstein undervalued the optimal Social Security. (Notwithstanding its errors, this seminal paper was the starting point of the whole book.) Appendix E (to Chapter 4) quantifies the error of approximating $40 + 20 = 60$ years of adult saving/dissaving path by a two-period model. Appendix F (to Chapter 4) extends the analysis from homogeneous life spans to heterogeneous ones. Appendix G (to Chapter 9) generalizes the traditional NDC into two directions: modeling realistic survival curve and fragmented labor careers. Appendix H (to Chapter 10) exposes the nature of approximating the child raising cost function of Chapter 10 by that of

Chapter 11. Appendix I (to Chapter 11) explains the phenomenon jump the welfare gap: some transfer programs are only advantageous if they pass a critical value. Appendix J (to Chapter 15) presents the dynamics of pension expenditures when the benefits in progress are indexed.

A Thesaurus contains the short definitions of key concepts of the book. The references are placed at the end of each chapter, including the Appendices.

The following models (written by me or with coauthors) appearing or at least mentioned in the book have already seen print: Simonovits (2006), Eső et al. (2011) on flexible (variable) retirement (Appendix G), Simonovits (2007) about voting on pensions (Sect. 12.3), Simonovits (2011) on the functioning of the second pillar (Sect. 13.4), Garay et al. (2012) on the neoclassical model of the dynamics of tax evasion with tax morale, Méder et al. (2012) on an agent-based version of the former (both related to Sect. 2.3), Simonovits (2013) on the dependence of the socially optimal tax rate on the tax morale (Sect. 2.3); Simonovits (2015a) on the contribution cap (Chapter 7); Simonovits (2015b) on paternalism against myopia (Sect. 3.2) and Simonovits (2015c) on longevity risk (Appendix G) Czeglédi et al. (2017) on fragmented labor careers (Sect. 9.4). Király and Simonovits (2018) used agent-based modeling of learning to save in a voluntary pension system. Other chapters (in older versions) are also available as working papers.

By its modular structure, the book can be read in a number of ways. Those who are only interested in taxation, must read Chapters 2 and 10 and Sects. 12.2 and 15.2. Others, who want to obtain an introduction into pensions, must read at least Chapters 3 and 4 and Sect. 12.3. Another group of Readers with a special interest in advanced pension models, may start with Chapters 5, 7 and 8. The peculiar phenomenon of jumping the gap is discussed in Sect. 3.2, Chapter 11 and especially Appendix I. The basic moral of the whole book can be summarized as follows: a good economist chooses the appropriate model to the appropriate problem.

It is true that in the literature, there are a number of models, typically much more sophisticated than our minimal models. Even in a static model, the problem of time-inconsistency in private savings (e.g., Laibson 1997 and Diamond and Kőszegi 2003) can be studied. Even remaining within the neoclassical framework, a lot if not all the complications presented above can be put together in a single supermodel. (In fact, there are related models, where the population and wage growth, public and private pensions and taxation are fully discussed.) I have refrained from this, because it would not answer all the relevant questions and due to its excessive complexity, it would not be helpful.

Furthermore, since the seminal book of Auerbach and Kotlikoff (1987), the static world has been replaced by truly dynamic overlapping cohort models in many cases. But let me hope that the simple (mostly) static models presented in this book may have contributed to a better understanding of inter- and intragenerational redistributions.

Table 1.18 displays the foregoing models and their key assumptions: the number of types, the presence of intergenerational redistribution, flexible labor supply and nonlinearity.

At the end, I warn the Reader of five serious omissions of the book and more generally, the literature. (i) I deliberately neglected the problem of those regions and strata, where the bulk of the population lacks access to paid work (Sen 1999). In this case, designing transfers need different models. (ii) I also neglected the in-kind transfers occurring in the family and the society (cf. Gál et al. 2014; Lee and Mason 2011; Leroux and Pestieau 2014). (iii) I have assumed away the impact of relative position on social welfare (for a fresh treatment, Tenhunen and Tuomala 2010.) (iv) For simplicity, I have also neglected the special cost of entering work (extensive margin) and the multi-rate personal income taxes (Diamond and Saez 2011). (v) Last but not least, in our artificial world there is no room for the heavy impact of unpredictability of government policies.

We also assume that the gross or total wage rates are independent of the transfer rates. True general equilibrium models also determine the wage rates (see Salanié 2011) as a function of transfer rates. Let us make only a simple remark: when personal income taxes were introduced in post-socialist countries (in Hungary, as early as in 1988), the previous net wages for every job were grossed-up to yield the same post-tax incomes as before.

Finally, we outline the basic idea of a number of our models, coming from the Stackelberg game of leader and follower. To borrow from Sect. 2.2, let the government (the leader) chooses a single tax rate θ and the worker (the follower) supplies workhours l per year. Their utility

Table 1.18 Models and assumptions

Model	Types	Intergen	Flex labor/ Evasion	Nonlinear
Introduction				
Taxation and labor (S2.2)	+	−	+	−
Tax morale (S2.3)	++	−	−	−
Myopia and pension (S3.2)	−	+	−	−
Risk and annuity (S3.3)	−	+	−	−
Tax + insurance (S3.4)	+	+	+	−
Two-type systems				
Proportional (S4.2)	+	+	−	−
Means-tested (S4.3)	+	+	−	+
Capped (S4.4)	+	+	−	+
Voluntary (S4.5)	+	+	−	+
Multi-type systems				
Contribution (C5)	++	+	−	−
Progressive system (C6)	++	+−	−+	+
Cap (C7)	++	+	−	+
Voluntary pension (C8)	++	+	−	+
Advanced models				
Flexible retirement (C9)	−+	−	+	−
Fertility (C10–11)	−+	+	−	−
Voting on taxes (S12.2)	++	−	+	+
Voting on pensions (S12.3)	++	+	+	−
Imperfect knowledge (S13.3)	×	+	−	−
Entry to second pillar (S13.4)	×	+	−	−
Variable retirement (S13.4)	×	+	−+	−
Heterogeneous longevity (C14)	++	+	−	−
Tax reduction (S15.3)	−	+	−	−
Overlapping generations (S15.4)	−	+	−	+

Remarks. 1. S2.3 = Section 3 of Chapter 2, C1 = Chapter 1, 2. Number of types: $- = 1, + = 2, ++ > 2, -+$ means 1 and 2 types, respectively. Intergen = intergenerational transfer, 3. Flex labor/evasion = flexible labor supply/tax evasion, 4. Nonlinear = cap or means-tested

functions V and U, respectively depend on these variables: $V(\theta, l)$ and $U(\theta, l)$. Knowing θ, the worker chooses l to maximize $U(\theta, l)$: $l(\theta)$. Anticipating this conditional choice, the government chooses θ to maximize $V(\theta, l(\theta))$: θ^*. The basic problem of these models is as follows: what is the welfare effect of transfer systems, i.e., the relation $V(\theta^*) > V(0)$

and what income distribution is achieved if there are more than one type of workers.

In the Introduction, we displayed some empirical background to the book. We also tried to spell out the specifics of our book. Finally, we outlined the content of the book. The remaining chapters will present the details.

References

Andersen, T. M., & Bhattacharya, J. (2011). On Myopia as Rationale for Social Security. *Economic Theory, 47,* 135–138.

Atkinson, B. A., & Bourguignon, F. (Eds.). (2006). *Handbook of Income Distribution.* Amsterdam: Elsevier.

Auerbach, A. J., & Kotlikoff, L. J. (1987). *Dynamic Fiscal Policy.* Cambridge: Cambridge University Press.

Augusztinovics, M., & Köllő, J. (2008). Pension Systems and Fragmented Labor Market Careers. In R. I. Gál, I. Iwasaki, & Zs. Széman (Eds.), *Assessing Intergenerational Equity* (pp. 154–170).

Augusztinovics, M., & Köllő, J. (2009). Decreased Employment and Pensions. The Case of Hungary. In R. Holzmann, L. MacKellar, & J. Repansek (Eds.), *Pension Reform in Southeastern Europe. Linking Labor and Financial Market Reform.* Washington, DC: World Bank.

Banyár, J. (2016). *Model Options for Mandatory Old-Age Annuities.* Gondolat: Budapest.

Barr, N., & Diamond, P. (2008). *Reforming Pensions: Principles and Policy Choices.* Oxford: Oxford University Press.

Boadway, R., & Keen, M. (2006). "Redistribution". In B. A. Atkinson, & F. Bourguignon (Eds.). 677–789.

Chetty, R. (2015). Behavioral Economics and Public Policy: A Pragmatic Approach. *American Economic Review, Papers and Proceedings, 105,* 1–33.

CIA. (2010). *World Fact Book.*

Cremer, H., & Pestieau, P. (2011). Myopia, Redistribution and Pensions. *European Economic Review, 55,* 165–175.

Czeglédi, T., Simonovits, A., Szabó, E., & Tir, M. (2017). What Has Been Wrong with the Retirement Rules in Hungary? *Acta Oeconomica, 67,* 359–387.

Diamond, P., & Kőszegi, B. (2003). Quasi-hyperbolic Discounting and Retirement. *Journal of Public Economics, 87,* 1839–1872.

Diamond, P. A., & Saez, E. (2011). The Case for a Progressive Tax: From Basic Research to Policy Prescriptions. *Journal of Economic Perspectives, 23*(4), 165–190.

Eső, P., Simonovits, A., & Tóth, J. (2011). Designing Benefit Rules for Flexible Retirement: Welfare and Redistribution. *Acta Oeconomica, 61*, 3–32.

Feldstein, M. S. (1985). The Level of Social Security Benefits. *Quarterly Journal of Economics, 100*, 302–320.

Feldstein, M. S. (1987). Should Social Security Be Means-Tested? *Journal of Political Economy, 95*, 468–484.

Garay, B., Simonovits, A., & Tóth, J. (2012). Local Interaction in Tax Evasion. *Economic Letters, 111*, 412–415.

Gál, R. I., Szabó, E., & Vargha, L. (2014). The Age-Profile of Invisible Transfers: The True Size of Asymmetry in Inter-age Reallocation. *Journal of the Economics of Ageing, 5*, 98–104.

Geanakoplos, J., Mitchell, O. S., & Zeldes, S. P. (1998). Social Security Money's Worth (NBER WP 6722). Cambridge. *MA; appeared: Mitchell. Meyers and Young (Eds.), 1999*, 137–157.

van Groezen, B., Leers, Th., & Meijdam, L. (2003). Social Security and Endogenous Fertility: Pensions and Child Benefits as Siamese Twins. *Journal of Public Economics, 87*, 233–251.

Király, B., & Simonovits, A. (2018). Learning to Save in a Voluntary Pension System: Toward an Agent-Based Model. *Journal of Economic Interaction and Coordination*, 1–25.

Kleven, H. J. (2014). How Can Scandinavians Tax so Much? *Journal of Economic Perspectives, 28*(4), 77–98.

Kőszegi, B. (2014). Behavioral Contract Theory. *Journal of Economic Literature, 52*, 1075–1118.

Laibson, D. (1997). Golden Eggs and Hyperbolic Discounting. *Quarterly Journal of Economics, 112*, 443–477.

Laps, J. (2015). *Essays on Demography-Driven Inequality and the Long-Run Welfare Consequences of Government Intervention.* Dissertation, Heidelberg University.

Lee, R., & Mason, A. (Eds.). (2011). *Population Aging and the Generational Economy: The Global Perspective.* Cheltenham: Edward Elgar.

Leroux, M.-L., & Pestieau, P. (2014). Social Security and Family Support. *Canadian Journal of Economics, 14*, 115–149.

Mankiw, N. G., Weinzierl, M. C., & Yagan, D. (2009). Optimal Taxation in Theory and Practice. *Journal of Economic Perspectives, 23*(4), 147–174.

Méder, Zs, Simonovits, A., & Vincze, J. (2012). Tax Morale and Tax Evasion: Social Preferences and Bounded Rationality. *Economic Analysis and Policy, 42*, 171–188.

Mirrlees, J. A. (1971). An Exploration in the Theory of Optimum Income Taxation. *Review of Economic Studies, 38*, 175–208.

Mirrlees, J. A., Adam, S., Besley, T., Blundell, R., Bond, S., Choten, R., et al. (Eds.). (2010). *Dimensions of Tax Design*. Oxford: Oxford University Press.

Mirrlees, J. A., Adam, S., Besley, T., Blundell, R., Bond, S., Choten, R., et al. (Eds.). (2011). *Tax by Design*. Oxford: Oxford University Press.

Mitchell, O. S., Meyers, R. J., & Young, H. (Eds.). (1999). *Prospects for Social Security Reform*. Pension Research Council: University of Pennsylvania Press.

Northon, M. I., & Ariely, D. (2011). Building a Better America-One Wealth Quintile at a Time. *Perspectives of Psychological Science, 6*, 9–12.

OECD. (1985). *Social Expenditure 1960–1990*. Paris: Problems of Growth and Control.

OECD. (2011). *Glance at Pensions*. Paris.

OECD. (2015). *Glance at Pensions*. Paris.

Paulus, A., Figari, F., & Sutherland, H. (2009). The Effects of Taxes and Benefits on Income Distribution. In T. Ward, O. Lelkes, H. Sutherland, & I. Gy. Tóth (Eds.), *Social Inclusion and Income Distribution in the European Union* (pp. 153–175). Budapest: Tárki.

Rabin, M. (1998). Psychology and Economics. *Journal of Economic Literature, 36*, 11–46.

Razin, A., Sadka, E., & Swagel, P. (2002). The Aging Population and the Size of the Welfare State. *Journal of Political Economy, 110*, 900–918.

Rodrik, D. (2015). *Economics Rules: Rights and Wrongs of the Dismal Science*. New York: W. W. Norton.

Rubinstein, A. (2017). Comments on Economic Models, Economics and Economists: Remark on Economics Rules by Dani Rodrik. *Journal of Economic Literature, 55*(1), 163–172.

Salanié, B. (2011). *The Economics of Taxation* (2nd ed.). Cambridge, MA: MIT Press.

Samuelson, P. A. (1937). A Note on Measurement. *Review of Economic Studies, 4*, 156–161.

Samuelson, P. A. (1958). An Exact Consumption-Loan Model of Interest with or Without the Social Contrivance of Money. *Journal of Political Economy, 66*, 467–482.

Samuelson, P. A. (1975). Optimum Social Security in a Life-Cycle Growth Model. *International Economic Review, 16*, 539–544.

Scheve, K., & Stasavage, D. (2016). *Taxing the Rich: A History of Fiscal Fairness in the United States and Europe*. New York: Russell Saga Foundation.

Sen, A. (1999). *Development as Freedom*. Oxford: Oxford University Press.

Simonovits, A. (2003). *Modeling Pension Systems*. Basingstoke: Palgrave Macmillan.

Simonovits, A. (2006). Optimal Design of Old-Age Pension Rule with Flexible Retirement: The Two-Type Case. *Journal of Economics, 89*, 197–222.

Simonovits, A. (2007). Can Population Aging Imply a Smaller Welfare State? European. *Journal of Political Economy, 23*, 534–541.

Simonovits, A. (2011). The Mandatory Private Pension Pillar: An Obituary. *International Social Security Review, 64*(3), 81–98.

Simonovits, A. (2013). Does Higher Tax Morale Imply a Higher Optimal Labor Income Tax Rate? *Danube (Law and Economics), 5*, 97–114.

Simonovits, A. (2015a). Socially Optimal Contribution Rate and Cap in a Proportional Pension System. *Portuguese Economic Journal, 14*, 45–63.

Simonovits, A. (2015b). Paternalism in Pension Systems. In B. Hámori & M. Rosta (Eds.), *Fecundating Thoughts: Studies in Honor of Eighty-Fifth Birthday of János Kornai* (pp. 151–160). Cambridge: Cambridge Scholar Publishers.

Simonovits, A. (2015c). Benet-Retirement Age Schedules in Public Pension Systems. *Czech Economic and Financial Review, 65*, 362–376.

Stiglitz, J. E. (2000). *Economics of Public Sector* (3rd ed.). New York: W. W. Norton.

Tenhunen, S., & Tuomala, M. (2010). On Optimal Lifetime Redistribution Policy. *Journal of Public Economic Theory, 12*, 171–198.

Varian, H. R. (1980). Redistributive Taxation as Social Insurance. *Journal of Public Economics, 14*, 49–68.

World Bank. (1994). *Averting Old-age Crisis*. Washington, DC: World Bank.

2
Introductory Tax Models

2.1 Introduction

Between 1930 and 1980 the ratio of government tax and social security revenues to the GDP had risen sharply and has remained at a high level since the 1980s in the developed world (cf. Table 1.15). It is a commonplace that rising labor income (and other) tax rates may diminish labor supply and increase tax evasion, therefore, labor supply and tax evasion (compared to the GDP) may have been decreasing and increasing, respectively.

This chapter introduces the Reader into the world of tax models, confining attention to intragenerational redistribution. In the first model (Sect. 2.2), we analyze the case of flexible labor supply for linear income taxation (started by Sheshinski 1972). (Note that the much more sophisticated nonlinear income taxation under asymmetric information was initiated by Mirrlees 1971.) There are at least two types of workers, differing in productivities. Their labor supply is flexible and a flat basic income is financed from a proportional tax system which diminishes inequalities. Total redistribution is destructive but depending on the strength of labor disutility, a well-chosen tax rate can eliminate the worst inequalities.

A. Simonovits, *Simple Models of Income Redistribution*,
https://doi.org/10.1007/978-3-319-72502-4_2

The second model (Sect. 2.3) takes the opposite extreme position. Already Allingham and Sandmo (1972) analyzed income tax evasion, neglecting the flexibility of labor supply and emphasizing the role of random auditing and fining the caught cheaters. In a sequel to that paper, Sandmo (1981) extended the research on tax evasion into the direction of social welfare maximization with flexible labor supply and raised a weaker form of the basic result of Sect. 2.3 (p. 279): "a natural question to ask is whether ... the marginal tax rate in some sense ought to be lower than otherwise have been because of the presence of tax evasion."[1] This conjecture is proved. Appendix A (to be found at the end of the book) considers a very special model, where the socially optimal progressive income tax is probably linear.

2.2 Intragenerational Redistribution with Flexible Labor Supply

As a starter, we cite Prescott (2004) explaining why Europeans have been working much less than Americans from the 1980s. Measuring labor supply as hours worked per person aged 15–64 per week, he argued that in the seventies, Germans worked slightly more than the Americans, while they paid moderately higher taxes than the Americans. In the nineties, Germans worked much less than the Americans, and paid much higher taxes but the German unification may somewhat distort the picture. (Great Britain lies between Germany and the United States.) As Prescott himself admitted, other factors, like the share of consumption-to-output are also important explanatory factors, but he was convinced that the higher the tax rate, the lower the labor supply. Other authors (e.g., Blanchard 2004; Alesina and Angeletos 2005) gave a more nuanced view but we skip them (Table 2.1).

We replace Prescott's model with a simpler one: we confine our attention to the linear personal income tax and neglect any other tax or pension

[1] Later on (p. 282), he gave alternative sufficient conditions, namely either "regular income is now a less reliable indicator of economic welfare" or "the numerical value of the compensated supply derivative in the regular market is increased" but did not commit himself to their validity. (For a good survey on tax evasion, see Andreoni et al. 1998; Sandmo 2012, 20–21; Slemrod and Gillitzer 2014.)

Table 2.1 Actual and predicted labor supply and tax rates

Period	Country	Actual	Predicted	Tax rate	Consumption per output
		Labor supply[a]			
1993–1996	Germany	19.3	19.5	0.59	0.74
	Great Britain	22.8	22.8	0.52	0.77
	United States	25.9	24.6	0.40	0.81
1970–1974	Germany (W)	24.6	24.6	0.52	0.66
	Great Britain	25.9	24.0	0.45	0.77
	United States	23.5	26.4	0.40	0.74

[a]Hours/week
Source. Prescott (2004, p. 7, Table 2)

contribution. Let w be the *total wage* (or full compensation) *rate* of a certain worker, T be his annual (or life) time limit, l be his corresponding labor supply, $0 < l < T$, then wl is his earning. Let θ be the personal income tax rate (representing all other taxes as well, including pension and health contributions), $0 \leq \theta \leq 1$ and γ be the basic income.[2] The worker's consumption is equal to

$$c = \gamma + (1 - \theta)wl. \tag{2.1}$$

We make a short detour: for a minute, let θ_c be the value-added tax rate, then the consumption function changes into

$$(1 + \theta_c)c = \gamma + (1 - \theta)wl.$$

Dividing both sides by $1 + \theta_c$, the consumption is given by

$$c = \frac{\gamma}{1 + \theta_c} + \frac{1 - \theta}{1 + \theta_c}wl. \tag{2.1$'$}$$

[2]Note that in several countries, a family consisting of a wife and a husband, has a reduced joint basic income, 1.5γ rather than 2γ.

Then, the net basic income $\tilde{\gamma}$ is lower than the nominal one and the composite personal income tax rate $\tilde{\theta}$ is higher than θ:

$$\tilde{\gamma} = \frac{\gamma}{1+\theta_c} \text{ and } \tilde{\theta} = 1 - \frac{1-\theta}{1+\theta_c} = \frac{\theta+\theta_c}{1+\theta_c} > \theta$$

while $c = \tilde{\gamma} + (1-\tilde{\theta})wl$.

Table 1.7 contains some data on the structure of taxes and its impacts in Sweden, Germany and the United States.

We turn to the determination of the optimal labor supply. Though Aguiar and Hurst (2005) emphasized the importance of nonseparability of consumption and labor supply in the utility, we copy the simplest utility function from Doerrenberg et al. (2012)[3]:

$$U(w,c,l) = 2c - wl^2. \tag{2.2}$$

Substituting (2.1) into (2.2), we arrive to the *reduced* utility function with parameter w and variable l:

$$U[w,l] = 2\gamma + 2(1-\theta)wl - wl^2. \tag{2.3}$$

The worker takes the value of the basic income as given. Due to the strict concavity of $U[w,\cdot]$, the optimal labor supply is determined as the root of the marginal utility—labor supply function:

$$0 = U_l'[w,l] = 2(1-\theta)w - 2wl. \tag{2.4}$$

We have arrived to

Lemma 2.1. *For any given tax rate θ, the optimal labor supply and the corresponding utility function are respectively equal to*

$$l(\theta) = 1-\theta \quad \text{and} \quad U[w,l(\theta)] = 2\gamma + w(1-\theta)^2. \tag{2.5}$$

[3]By doubling the consumption in the utility function, the occurrence of fractions is minimized.

Ceteris paribus, the optimal labor supply in (2.5) is independent of the wage rate and of the basic income and is a decreasing function of the tax rate.

Having determined the individual optima, we turn to the macro relations. Denoting expectation over the wage rate distribution by **E**, and choosing an appropriate unit of measurement, the average wage rate can be taken unity: $\mathbf{E}(w) = 1$. Then the per-worker tax revenue is given by

$$\gamma = \theta\mathbf{E}(wl(\theta)) = \theta(1-\theta) \tag{2.6}$$

and the maximal tax revenue is achieved at $\theta^* = 1/2$.

To determine the socially optimal linear tax system, we shall use the simplest social welfare function, namely the Rawlsian one which is the minimum of the individual utility functions:

$$V(\theta) = \min_w U[w, l(\theta)].$$

Denoting the lowest wage rate by $w_\mathrm{m} \in (0, 1)$; according to (2.5), $V(\theta) = U[w_\mathrm{m}, l(\theta)]$. Substituting (2.6) into (2.5) gives the social welfare as a function of the tax rate:

$$V(\theta) = 2\theta(1-\theta) + w_\mathrm{m}(1-\theta)^2. \tag{2.7}$$

Since the socially optimal tax rate satisfies the necessary first-order condition: $0 = V'(\theta) = 2(1-\theta) - 2\theta - 2w_\mathrm{m}(1-\theta) = 2 - 2w_\mathrm{m} - 2\theta$ $(2 - w_\mathrm{m})$, and $V'(\cdot)$ changes sign from + into – at θ^*, we have

Theorem 2.1. *The Rawlsian optimal tax rate is equal to*

$$\theta^* = \frac{1-w_\mathrm{m}}{2-w_\mathrm{m}} < \frac{1}{2}, \quad \text{where } 0 < w_\mathrm{m} < 1. \tag{2.8}$$

It is not enough to determine the social optimum, we have to evaluate the efficiency gain having an optimal tax system with respect to having a suboptimal one or no tax system. Since the numerical value of V has no direct meaning, we define the *relative efficiency* (also called *compensating variation*) ε of θ^* with respect to $\theta = 0$ as follows: multiplying the earnings by a positive scalar ε such that the social welfare of the no tax system $V[\varepsilon, 0]$ is the same as the social welfare of the optimal tax with the original wages $V[1, \theta^*]$. Denoting the dependence of the welfare on the (average) wage ε, we have the following formal definition for efficiency:

$$V[\varepsilon, 0] = V[1, \theta^*]. \tag{2.9}$$

By simple calculations, (2.7)–(2.8) yield

$$V[\varepsilon, 0] = \varepsilon w_{\mathrm{m}} \quad \text{and} \quad V[1, \theta^*] = \frac{1}{2 - w_{\mathrm{m}}}. \tag{2.10}$$

By (2.9)–(2.10), the relative efficiency is equal to

$$\varepsilon = \frac{1}{w_{\mathrm{m}}(2 - w_{\mathrm{m}})} > 1.$$

This is as expected: the lower the minimal wage rate (in terms of the average wage rate), the higher the relative efficiency of the optimal tax system to the no tax. Numerical example: if $w_{\mathrm{m}} = 1/2$, then $\varepsilon = 4$.

We have paid a high price for getting the explicit formula (2.8): (i) we had to rely on the Rawlsian social welfare function, because the utilitarian social welfare function $\mathbf{E}U^*$ would yield zero optimal tax rate; (ii) total redistribution ($\theta = 1$) would imply zero labor supply ($l(\theta) = 0$) overshadowing the importance of the size of the elasticity of labor supply; (iii) in the two-period model of the next chapter, the linear consumption utility would make perfect substitution between the young- and old-age consumption, undermining the pension problem. As a way out, from Chapter 3, we shall always consider the appropriate variant of the Cobb–Douglas utility functions of the form

$$U(c, d) = \log c + \delta \log d, \tag{3.2}$$

where c and d are young- and old-age consumption, respectively and δ is the discount factor. (The original Cobb–Douglas-utility function is multiplicative, but its logarithmic version—displayed here—is additive.) Adding productive firms, the interest rate and the wage rate become endogenous and the phasing-out of social security could also be modeled.

2.3 Income Redistribution with Tax Morale

In this section, we replace flexible labor supply with tax evasion. Replacing punishment with tax morale, we repeat Allingham and Sandmo (1972)'s analysis. Tax morale refers to the propensity to pay taxes or captures "the readiness with which individuals leave the official economy and enter the illegitimate (untaxed) hidden economy" (Frey and Weck-Hannemann 1984), for a recent survey, see Luttmer and Singhal (2014). We shall obtain similar results as with flexible labor supply.

To relate our highly theoretical observation to the real world, we only sketch the empirical background. Table 2.2 describes various combinations of tax morale (lower and higher) and tax shares (low, medium, high), the latter defined as the ratio of tax (and pension) revenues to the GDP.[4] The tax morale can be approximated by the corruption index (10 minus the traditional one). We tentatively interpret Table 2.2 as showing that a medium tax share may be *socially optimal* for a country with lower tax morale (e.g., the Czechia versus Slovakia or Hungary with an approximately common corruption index value of 5), while a high tax share may be optimal for a country with higher tax morale (like Sweden versus United States or Germany with corruption index values below 2.5). If we knew three countries with very low tax morale with low, medium and high tax shares, denoted by L, M, H, respectively, then the welfare order would be $L > M > H$.

Following Doerrenberg et al. (2012), we replace the quadratic labor disutility of Sect. 2.2 with a quadratic morale disutility.

There are $I(>1)$ types in the population, indexed as $i = 1, \ldots, I$. Labor supply is uniformly equal to unity. Type i's pretax *wage* (independently of the tax system) is $w_i > 0$. To achieve income redistribution, the government operates a linear tax with a *flat (marginal) tax rate* θ,

[4] The tax share in indexation—somewhat unreliable but still characteristic—refers to the precrisis era and contains many things directly *not* related to our problem (budget deficits, interest payments, different public pension systems, etc.).

Table 2.2 Tax shares, tax morale and ranking by social welfare

Tax share	Low cc. 30%		Medium cc. 40%		High cc. 50%
Lower morale	Slovakia	$<$	Czechia	$>$	Hungary
Higher morale	United States	$<$	Germany	$<$	Sweden

$0 \le \theta \le 1$ and pays every worker a *basic income* $\gamma \ge 0$. Type i *hides* $e_i \ge 0$ from his earning, i.e., he evades tax θe_i, therefore his *declared (or taxable) earning* is $y_i = w_i - e_i$ and his *net tax* is equal to $\theta y_i - \gamma = \theta(w_i - e_i) - \gamma$. Consequently, his *consumption* is given by

$$c_i = \gamma + (1 - \theta)w_i + \theta e_i. \tag{2.11}$$

Note that for any positive basic income $\gamma > 0$, even the flat-rate tax is progressive in the sense that the (average) net tax rate $(\theta y_i - \gamma)/y_i$ is increasing in the declared earning y_i. (Although they are very important, really non-linear tax—income schedules (see, e.g., Diamond and Saez 2011) are only discussed in Appendix A and Sect. 6.2; otherwise are beyond the scope of this book!)

At this point, we present the section's main concept, the *exogenous tax morale* η. It is a parameter, represented by a real positive number. Due to the linearity of consumption utility, we still have to truncate the traditional pure social welfare function. We shall rely on linear—quadratic utility functions and obtain an explicit formula for the optimal tax evasion. In addition to a usual linear *consumption utility* $2c_i$ but replacing the quadratic *labor disutility* function $-w_i l_i^2$ (2.2) by a quadratic *morale disutility* function of tax evasion $-\eta w_i [e_i/w_i]^2$, ($\eta > 0$ being the coefficient of tax morale, for short, the tax morale).[5] In sum, type i's utility function is

$$U_i(c_i, e_i) = 2c_i - \eta w_i^{-1} e_i^2. \tag{2.12}$$

[5]We shall see that factor w_i equalizes the optimal share of undeclared earning to the inverse tax morale. Note that unlike Simonovits (2013), we do *not* imitate Yitzaki (1974), who made the penalty to be proportional to the evaded tax rather than the undeclared earning.

Inserting (2.11) into (2.12), we receive the *reduced* utility function

$$U_i[e_i] = 2\gamma + 2(1-\theta)w_i + 2\theta e_i - \eta w_i^{-1} e_i^2. \tag{2.13}$$

Taking γ constant, and equating $U'_{i,e_i}[e_i] = 2\theta - 2\eta w_i^{-1} e_i$ to zero, we obtain

Lemma 2.2. *For any tax rate θ, the individually optimal undeclared income is*

$$e_i(\theta) = \eta^{-1}\theta w_i. \tag{2.14}$$

Remark. Note the simple meaning of this rule: the optimal undeclared earning $e_i(\theta)$ is equal to wage w_i times the tax rate θ divided by the tax morale η. To ensure $e_i < w_i$ for any $\theta \in (0, 1)$, we require $\eta \geq 1$.

Later on we shall make further assumptions on the range of values of η. Note that the optimal reported earning $y_i(\theta) = w_i - e_i(\theta) = (1-\eta^{-1}\theta)w_i$ is an increasing function of the tax morale and a decreasing function of the tax rate.

Turning from individual to aggregate behavior, note that the basic income is equal to the average tax revenue:

$$\gamma = \theta \sum_{i=1}^{I} f_i y_i(\theta).$$

Without loss of generality, we assume that the weight of type i in the population is uniform, i.e., $f_i = 1/I$. We shall need the average wage, to be normalized to unity:

$$W = \frac{1}{I}\sum_{i=1}^{I} w_i = 1.$$

Now the budget constraint yields the balanced basic income:

$$\gamma = \theta(1-\eta^{-1}\theta) = \theta - \eta^{-1}\theta^2. \tag{2.15}$$

Before continuing with the maximization of social welfare, we discuss here the traditional view.

The Traditional Model

The government of a traditional economist takes the tax revenue γ in (2.15) as given and looks for a balanced tax rate θ. As a preparation, first we determine the maximal γ: a simple calculation shows that it is achieved at $\bar{\theta} = \eta/2$. We must distinguish between two cases: either $\bar{\theta} \le 1$ (feasible) and $\bar{\theta} > 1$ (infeasible), i.e., either $\eta \le 2$ or $\eta > 2$. In both cases we prove the traditional view.

Theorem 2.2. *(a) If the tax morale is weak:* $1 < \eta \le 2$*, then the basic income* γ *is feasible if and only if*

$$0 < \gamma < \bar{\gamma}_a = \frac{\eta}{4}. \tag{2.16a}$$

(b) If the tax morale is strong: $\eta > 2$*, then the basic income* γ *is feasible if and only if*

$$0 < \gamma < \bar{\gamma}_b = 1 - \frac{1}{\eta}. \tag{2.16b}$$

(c) In both cases, the balanced tax rate is given by

$$\theta_\gamma[\eta] = \frac{1 - \sqrt{1 - 4\eta^{-1}\gamma}}{2}\eta$$

and is a decreasing function of the tax morale.

Remarks. 1. For any weak tax morale, there is another balanced tax rate but it may be larger than 1, namely if $\bar{\gamma}_b < \gamma$. Note that $\bar{\gamma}_a \ge \bar{\gamma}_b$, because $(\eta - 2)^2 \ge 0$.

2. If $\eta \to \infty$ (white economy), then $\gamma(\theta) \approx \theta$, i.e., $\theta_\gamma[\infty] = \gamma$ for $0 < \gamma \le 1$.

Table 2.3 illustrates the balanced tax rate for varying tax morale and $\gamma = 0.1$. As the tax morale rises from 1 to 4, the balanced tax rate drops from 0.276 to 0.211. In the limit, $\theta_\infty = \gamma = 0.1$.

Table 2.3 Tax morale and balanced tax rate

Tax morale, η	1	2	3	4	...	∞
Balanced tax rate, $\theta_\gamma[\eta]$	0.276	0.225	0.215	0.211	...	0.1

Social Welfare Maximization

We move now to social welfare maximization. But instead of the rather special Rawlsian function, we shall use now a more general truncated social welfare function (cf. Ravaillon 1997). To find the socially optimal tax rate and the corresponding basic income, it is worth expressing the optimally reduced utilities as *indirect* utility functions:

$$U_i(\theta) = U_i[e_i(\theta)] = [2(1-\theta) + \eta^{-1}\theta^2]w_i + 2\theta(1-\eta^{-1}\theta). \quad (2.17)$$

We shall follow Diamond and Saez (2011) and replace the utilitarian welfare function by a truncated one. (We cannot use a *purely utilitarian* social welfare function, because the individual utility is a linear (rather than strictly concave) function of the individual consumption—making any income redistribution not only useless but counterproductive.) Generalizing the Rawlsian approach, we shall introduce *truncated* utilitarian social welfare functions, defined as the average of the J lowest utilities, J being the cutoff index, $J < I$. Note that in the present model, these indirect utilities are increasing linear functions of the individual wages (2.17). If we index the latter as $w_1 < w_2 < \cdots < w_{I-1} < w_I$, then $U_1(\theta) < U_2(\theta) < \cdots < U_{I-1}(\theta) < U_I(\theta)$. Hence the definition of the J-truncated social welfare function is simple[6]:

$$V_J(\theta) = \frac{1}{J}\sum_{i=1}^{J} U_i(\theta), \qquad J = 1, 2, \ldots, I. \quad (2.18)$$

The higher the cutoff index J, the more indifferent the social planner to the type-specific utility differences. We display the two limit cases.

[6]For practical reasons, the untruncated V_I is also included.

The purely utilitarian case:

$$V_I = \frac{1}{I}\sum_{i=1}^{I} U_i(\theta).$$

The Rawlsian case:

$$V_1 = U_1(\theta).$$

Note that the social welfare functions $V_1, \ldots, V_{I-1}$ fail to depend on all the utilities but they are simple and approximate the much more complex CRRA (cf. Appendix B) social welfare functions well, therefore, we can safely rely on them.

Before announcing our main theorem, as a counterpart to V_J, we shall define the average wage of the J lowest types (for short, J-minimum average wage):

$$W_J = \frac{1}{J}\sum_{i=1}^{J} w_i, \quad j = 1, 2, \ldots, I. \tag{2.19}$$

Because w_is are increasing, so do W_Js: $w_1 = W_1 < W_2 < \cdots < W_{I-1} < W_I = W = 1$.

Here is our major result.

Theorem 2.3. *Let us choose a cutoff index $J < I$. Then for the J-truncated social welfare function (2.18), the J-optimal tax rate is equal to*

$$\theta_J^* = \frac{1 - W_J}{2 - W_J}\eta > 0; \tag{2.20}$$

provided the tax morale is lower than the J-critical one:

$$1 < \eta < \eta_J = \frac{2 - W_J}{1 - W_J}. \tag{2.21}$$

(b) The optimal tax rate–tax morale function $\theta_J^*(\eta)$ is increasing.

Remark. For a fixed tax morale η and an inclusion index J, the higher the W_J, i.e., the lower the wage inequality, the lower the optimal tax rate.

Proof. (a) Substituting (2.17) into (2.18), simple calculations yield

$$V_J(\theta) = [2(1-\theta) + \eta^{-1}\theta^2]W_J + 2[\theta - \eta^{-1}\theta^2]. \tag{2.22}$$

To obtain the J-optimal tax rate, take the partial derivative of V_J with respect to θ and set it to zero:

$$0 = V_J'(\theta) = [-2 + 2\eta^{-1}\theta]W_J + 2[1 - 2\eta^{-1}\theta].$$

This yields θ_J^* in (2.20). The condition (2.21) is just equivalent to $\theta_J^* < 1$.
(b) Obvious from (2.20) and $\theta_J < 1$.

Remark. If we gave up the uniformity of the tax morale, then the ordering of the indirect utilities became cumbersome, etc.

The following arbitrary numerical calculation illustrates the result: $J = 3$, $\eta = 1$. Column 1 of Table 2.4 displays five wage types, yielding $\theta_3^* = 0.286$ and $\gamma_3^* = 0.204$. Column 2 reports the corresponding optimal undeclared wage. The tax system requires type i pay a net transfer paid $t_i^* = \theta^*(w_i - e_I^*) - \gamma^*$, this rises from -0.122 to 0.204 (column 3). The consumption $c_i^* = w_i - t_i^*$, rises from 0.522 to 1.796 (column 4).

We turn now to the dependence of the optimal tax rate on the cutoff index J, measuring the extent of exclusion of the richer groups from the domain of the social welfare function. Intuitively, we expect that the lower

Table 2.4 Redistribution for 5-types

Wage, w_i	Undeclared wage, e_i^*	Net transfer paid, t_i^*	Consumption, c_i^*
0.4	0.114	–0.122	0.522
0.6	0.171	–0.082	0.682
0.8	0.229	–0.041	0.841
1.2	0.343	0.041	1.159
2.0	0.571	0.204	1.796

Table 2.5 The impact of cutoff index and tax morale

Cutoff, J	Tax morale, η	Optimal tax rate, θ_J^*	Basic income, γ
1	1.5	0.563	0.352
	2.0	0.750	0.469
3	1.5	0.429	0.306
	2.0	0.571	0.408

the cutoff index, i.e., the more progressive the social welfare function, the higher the optimal tax rate. Indeed, this is the case.

Theorem 2.4. *Let K be a nonnegative integer such that the tax morale η lies between η_K and η_{K+1} (2.21). Then the socially optimal positive tax rates are decreasing in the cutoff index $J: \theta_1^* > \theta_2^* > \cdots > \theta_K^* > \theta_{K+1}^* = \cdots = \theta_I^* = 0$.*

Table 2.5 shows how strongly does the optimal tax rate depend on the tax morale and the progressivity for two cutoff indices (1 and 3) and two values of tax morale (1.5 and 2).

Remark. 1. Note that in this specification, the white economy (where $\eta = \infty$) is *not* the limit of grey economies, which ends here at $\eta = 2$ or $\eta_J > 2$.

2. Theorem 2.4 sheds some light on a paradox: though the tax morale is roughly the same in Sweden and the United States, and the wage inequality is definitely lower in the former than the latter, the US tax rate is much lower instead of being higher than its Swedish counterpart. The reason is simple, at least in our framework: the inclusion index is much higher in the United States than in Sweden.

While the present model only discussed *exogenous* tax morale, Garay et al. (2012) and Méder et al. (2012) investigated the *dynamics* of the tax evasion process with *endogenous* tax morale in a classical and an agent-based model, respectively. Here, the individual endogenous (final) tax morale is a result of an individual exogenous morale and the experience with public transfers.

Introducing *elasticity of taxable income* Feldstein (1999) synthesized flexible labor supply and tax evasion into a unified framework (see also

Chetty 2009). Note that Kleven et al. (2011) demonstrated that only the entrepreneurs have really wide room for cheating, the employees' tax is paid by their employers.

2.4 Conclusions

We have discussed two elementary tax models, where labor disutility and less than perfect tax morale obviously limited the size of income redistribution. In our linear schedule, the optimal tax rate also depends on the chosen social welfare function: the closer the criterion to the utilitarian function, the lower the optimal tax rate. (Appendix A considers nonlinear tax—reported income schedules.) The existence of pensions and child benefits makes the issue more complicated.

References

Alesina, A., & Angeletos, G. M. (2005). Fairness and Redistribution. *American Economic Review, 95*, 960–980.

Allingham, M., & Sandmo, A. (1972). Income Tax Evasion: A Theoretical Analysis. *Journal of Public Economics, 1*, 323–338.

Andreoni, J., Erard, B., & Feinstein, J. (1998). *Tax Compliance. Journal of Economic Literature, 36*, 818–860.

Blanchard, O. (2004). The Economic Future of Europe. *Journal of Economic Perspectives, 18*(4), 3–26.

Chetty, R. (2009). Is Taxable Income Elasticity Sufficient to Calculate Deadweight Loss? The Implications of Evasion and Avoidance. *American Economic Journal: Economic Policy, 1*(1), 31–52.

Diamond, P. A., & Saez, E. (2011). The Case for a Progressive Tax: From Basic Research to Policy Prescriptions. *Journal of Economic Perspectives, 23*(4), 165–190.

Doerrenberg, P., Duncan, D., Fuest, C., & Peichl, A. (2012). *Nice Guys Finish Last: Are People with Higher Tax Morale Taxed More Heavily?* (IUA Discussion Paper 6275).

Feldstein, M. (1999). Tax Avoidance and the Deadweight Loss of the Income Tax. *Review of Economics and Statistics, 81*, 674–680, full text: NBER Working Paper 5055, 1996.

Frey, B. S., & Weck-Hannemann, H. (1984). The Hidden Economy as an 'Unobserved' Variable. *European Economic Review, 26*, 33–53.

Garay, B., Simonovits, A., & Tóth, J. (2012). Local Interaction in Tax Evasion. *Economic Letters, 111*, 412–415.

Kleven, H. J., Knudsen, M. B., Kreiner, C. T., Pedersen, S., & Saez, E. (2011). Unwilling or Unable to Cheat? Evidence from a Randomized Tax Audit Experiment. *Econometrica, 79*, 651–692.

Luttmer, E. F. P., & Singhal, M. (2014). *Tax Morale. Journal of Economic Perspectives, 28*(4), 149–168.

Méder, Z., Simonovits, A., & Vincze, J. (2012). Tax Morale and Tax Evasion: Social Preferences and Bounded Rationality. *Economic Analysis and Policy, 42*, 171–188.

Mirrlees, J. A. (1971). An Exploration in the Theory of Optimum Income Taxation. *Review of Economic Studies, 38*, 175–208.

Prescott, E. C. (2004). Why Do Americans Work so Much More Than Europeans. *Federal Reserve Bank of Minneapolis, Quarterly Review, 28*(1), 2–13.

Ravaillon, M. (1997). Measuring Social Welfare with or Without Poverty Lines. *American Economic Review Paper and Proceedings, 84*, 359–364.

Sandmo, A. (1981). Income Tax Evasion. *Journal of Public Economics, 16*, 265–288.

Sandmo, A. (2012). An Evasive Topic: Theorizing About the Hidden Economy. *International Tax and Public Finance, 19*, 5–24.

Sheshinski, E. (1972). Optimal Linear Income Tax. *Review of Economic Studies, 39*, 297–302.

Simonovits, A. (2013). Does Higher Tax Morale Imply a Higher Optimal Labor Income Tax Rate? *Danube (Law and Economics), 5*, 97–114.

Slemrod, J., & Gilltzer, Ch. (2014). Insights from a Tax-Systems Perspectives. *CESifo Economic Studies, 60*, 1–31.

Yitzaki, S. (1974). Income Tax Evasion: A Theoretical Analysis. *Journal of Public Economics, 3*, 201–202.

3

Introductory Pension Models

3.1 Introduction

Modern pension systems appeared around 1900 in different forms: In Germany, it was started as a proportional (earnings-related) system, while in Great Britain it served poverty relief. With the New Deal, a pay-as-you-go pension system was introduced in the United States in 1935, which has been followed all over the world after 1945. We will discuss the differences between these and other pension systems along the book, here we only introduce the basic models.

Three models serve as introduction to pension modeling, dealing with intergenerational transfers with labor supply independent of the pension system. In the first one (Sect. 3.2), there is a myopic representative agent. It is shown that there is a critical interest factor at which the optimal private saving without pensions is equivalent to the optimal public pension without private saving. If the interest factor is lower than the critical one, then the public pension is superior to the private saving.

In the second model (Sect. 3.3), we introduce longevity risk into the first one. While the public pension is paid as a life annuity, there is no private life annuity. Then for sufficiently strong risk and sufficiently

A. Simonovits, *Simple Models of Income Redistribution*,
https://doi.org/10.1007/978-3-319-72502-4_3

low-interest rate, public pension is socially superior even for totally far-sighted workers.

Following Varian (1980), the third introductory pension model (Sect. 3.4) studies the impact of a stochastic disturbance on the socially optimal pension insurance. It turns out that as the size of the disturbance grows, the socially optimal tax increases and the saving decreases.

Later in the book, we shall consider multi-type systems, with various modifications. For example, Sect. 6.3 will take up the interaction of flexible labor supply and pension. Concerning interaction between evading contributions and pensions, we refer to Simonovits (2009) and Leroux et al. (2015).

Appendix B explains the significance of restricting CRRA utility functions to Cobb–Douglas ones. Appendix C outlines three numerical methods of finding the roots of nonlinear scalar equations. Appendix D discusses how Feldstein (1985) undervalued the optimal Social Security. (Appendices are to be found at the end of the book.)

3.2 Myopia and Mandatory Pension

One of the basic ideas of pension economics is that mandatory pensions are needed because the workers are myopic and they would not privately save enough for their old-age.

Following Feldstein (1985, Sects. I and II), in this model (see Simonovits 2015), the whole society is represented by a single individual, living for two periods. For simplicity, in the bulk of the book, the economy and the population are assumed to be stationary (for an exception, see Chapters 4, 9 and 10, and Sect. 12.3). Let c and d be the worker's young- and old-age consumption, respectively. He only works in the first period, his pretax earning is 1 and he saves s. In the second period, he enjoys the fruits of his savings, ρs, where $\rho \geq 1$ is the interest factor = 1 + interest rate.[1] (Note the impressive simplification stemming from working with interest factor

[1]Another simplification, which we cannot eliminate is that we neglect the basic fact that every year, the accumulated saving is increased by the annual interest. Rather, we assume that the capitalization takes place at the middle of the working period and its decumulation is concentrated at the middle of the retirement period. The error of this approximation is discussed in Appendix E.

rather than interest rate in our discrete time framework.) Counterfactually, here we follow the usual approach and identify the lengths of the working and of the retirement periods but later on we shall replace it with a realistic assumption, making the latter the share of the former.

In addition, the government charges a pension contribution rate τ for workers, yielding a pension τ at old-age. In our mixed system, a worker's consumption is equal to net wage less private saving, and the pensioner's consumption is equal to public pension plus private saving plus interests[2]:

$$c = 1 - \tau - s \quad \text{and} \quad d = \tau + \rho s. \tag{3.1}$$

The individual has a Cobb–Douglas lifetime utility function

$$U(c, d) = \log c + \delta \log d, \tag{3.2}$$

where δ is the discount factor, $0 \leq \delta \leq 1$. (It is quite widespread but superfluous to work with the time preference rate ι with relation $\delta = 1/(1+\iota)$.) Inserting (3.1) into (3.2), the reduced utility function is equal to

$$U[s] = \log(1 - \tau - s) + \delta \log(\tau + \rho s). \tag{3.3}$$

Taking the derivative of (3.3) and equate it to zero yields the optimality condition and the optimal saving (intention), respectively:

$$U'[s] = -\frac{1}{1-\tau-s} + \frac{\delta}{\rho^{-1}\tau + s} = 0,$$
$$\text{i.e.,} \quad \tilde{s}(\tau) = \frac{\delta - \tau(\delta + \rho^{-1})}{1+\delta}, \tag{3.4}$$

where $\tilde{s}$ refers to the saving *intention*.

[2]Since in the whole book (except for Sect. 3.3), private savings are used up like indexed life annuities, they can be conceived as private pensions. Cap on subsidized contributions will only be introduced in Chapter 8.

Denoting the *separator* contribution rate by τ_ρ at which the saving intention is just zero [cf. (3.5)], i.e.,

$$\tau_\rho = \frac{\delta}{\delta + \rho^{-1}}, \tag{3.5}$$

we have the following classification: for $0 \le \tau < \tau_\rho$, the saving intention is positive (*slack* credit constraint); for $\tau_\rho < \tau < 1$, the saving intention is negative (*tight* credit constraint). Because of the existence of credit constraint, negative saving intention becomes zero savings, while positive intention is preserved: $s = \max(\tilde{s}, 0) = \tilde{s}_+$.

We have the following result.

Lemma 3.1. *For given contribution rate τ, the optimal consumption pair of the two regimes are respectively*

$$c_{\mathrm{S}}(\tau) = \frac{1 - (1 - \rho^{-1})\tau}{1 + \delta} \quad \text{and} \quad d_{\mathrm{S}}(\tau) = \delta\rho c_{\mathrm{S}}(\tau) \quad \text{if} \quad 0 \le \tau < \tau_\rho \tag{3.6 – S}$$

and

$$c_{\mathrm{T}}(\tau) = 1 - \tau \quad \text{and} \quad d_{\mathrm{T}}(\tau) = \tau \ \text{ if } \ \tau_\rho \le \tau < 1. \tag{3.6 – T}$$

To avoid uninteresting cases (see below), we assume that $\delta\rho < 1$, implying $\tau_\rho < 1/2$.

To evaluate the social welfare of a system with contribution rate τ, we shall use the *paternalistic* social welfare function (hinted by Samuelson 1975b)

$$V(\tau) = \log c(\tau) + \log d(\tau). \tag{3.7}$$

To find its maximum, we will separate the two cases depicted in (3.6).

Both $c_{\mathrm{S}}(\tau)$ and $d_{\mathrm{S}}(\tau)$ are decreasing functions in $0 < \tau < \tau_\rho$ (crowding-out effect), therefore, the corresponding maximum is achieved at $\tau = 0$, and its value is

$$V(0) = \log c_{\mathrm{S}}(0) + \log d_{\mathrm{S}}(0).$$

In the second interval, $c_{\mathrm{T}}(\tau)$ is decreasing but $d_{\mathrm{T}}(\tau)$ is increasing, therefore to find the optimum, we need to take the derivative of $V(\tau)$:

$$V'(\tau) = -\frac{1}{1-\tau} + \frac{1}{\tau}. \tag{3.8}$$

V' is positive in the interval $[\tau_\rho, 1/2)$ and it is negative in the interval $(1/2,1)$ thus V reaches its maximum at $\bar{\tau} = 1/2$. (Note that without the assumption $\delta\rho < 1$, inequality $\tau_\rho \geq \bar{\tau}$ would hold, i.e., there would be no room for a socially advantageous pension system!) The corresponding social welfare is equal to

$$V(1/2) = \log c_{\mathrm{T}}(1/2) + \log d_{\mathrm{T}}(1/2).$$

We shall call τ_ρ the socially *worst* contribution rate.

Compare the two pairs of consumptions:

$$c_{\mathrm{S}}(0) = \frac{1}{1+\delta} \quad \text{and} \quad d_{\mathrm{S}}(0) = \frac{\delta\rho}{1+\delta}, \tag{3.9 – S}$$

while

$$c_{\mathrm{T}}(1/2) = \frac{1}{2} = d_{\mathrm{T}}(1/2). \tag{3.9 – T}$$

To obtain $c_{\mathrm{S}}(0) > c_{\mathrm{T}}(1/2)$ (due to myopia) and $d_{\mathrm{S}}(0) < d_{\mathrm{T}}(1/2)$ (due to coercion) we assume a little more than before ($\delta\rho < 1$), namely

$$\rho < \frac{1+\delta}{2\delta} \quad \text{or equivalently} \quad \delta < \frac{1}{2\rho - 1}.$$

We are interested in the case when the socially optimal pension system is superior to the pure private system: $V(1/2) > V(0)$. Inserting the corresponding formulas into this inequality results in

$$-2\log 2 > -2\log(1+\delta) + \log\delta + \log\rho.$$

It is easy to see that for any discount factor $\delta < 1$, there exists a critical interest factor $\rho_\delta > 1$, for which the two welfares are equal to each other:

$$-2\log 2 = -2\log(1+\delta) + \log\delta + \log\rho_\delta,$$
$$\text{i.e.,}\quad \rho_\delta = \frac{(1+\delta)^2}{4\delta}. \tag{3.10}$$

Probably it is more realistic to invert the causation: The quadratic equation $\delta^2 - 2(2\rho - 1)\delta + 1 = 0$ results in

$$\delta_\rho = 2\rho - 1 - 2\sqrt{\rho^2 - \rho}. \tag{3.10*}$$

For $0 < \delta < \delta_\rho (< 1)$, there exists a *neutral* contribution rate $\tau_o \in (\tau_\rho, \bar{\tau})$ for which the transfer system provides the same social welfare as the private system does: $V(\tau_o) = V(0)$.

We have arrived to a phenomenon already mentioned in the Introduction: choosing the contribution rate, the government has to jump the gap of low welfare to improve the system.

Theorem 3.1. *For any given interest factor* $\rho > 1$, *for any subcritical factor* δ $(0 < \delta < \delta_\rho(< 1))$, *there exists an interval* $(0, \tau_o)$ *(with* $\tau_o < \bar{\tau}$*) of contribution rates for which the public pension system delivers lower welfare than the private system does; and another interval* $(\tau_o, \bar{\tau})$, *where the public pension system delivers higher welfare than the private system does.*

Notwithstanding all deficiencies of the model, Table 3.1 demonstrates numerically how the critical value of the interest factor depends on the discount factor. Considering 30-year-long life-stages, our illustration applies only *annual* factors, derived from

$$\delta[1] = \delta^{1/30} \quad \text{and} \quad \rho[1] = \rho^{1/30}.$$

For example, in the second line of Table 3.1, the annual interest rate of 2% defines an annual critical discount rate of cc. 5%, and the ratio of old- to young-age consumption is equal to 0.37. But increasing the interest rate to 10%, the critical discount rate drops to cc. 13%.

We continue the illustration of Theorem 3.1 in Table 3.2. To evaluate the welfare properties of the optimal public pension system, we define

Table 3.1 Autonomy and paternalism, interest and discount factors

Annual factor		Consumption without transfer	
Interest, $\rho[1]$	Critical discount, $\delta_{\rho[1]}[1]$	Young-age, $c(0)$	Old-age, $d(0)$
1.00	1.000	0.500	0.500
1.02	0.947	0.835	0.300
1.04	0.924	0.916	0.273
1.06	0.904	0.954	0.262
1.08	0.886	0.975	0.257
1.10	0.869	0.985	0.254

Table 3.2 The impact of interest factor on the two systems

Annual interest factor, $\rho[1]$	Worst	Neutral	Public system's relative efficiency, ε
	Contribution rate		
	τ_ρ	τ_o	
1.01	0.054	0.056	2.180
1.02	0.071	0.077	1.881
1.03	0.093	0.106	1.625
1.04	0.121	0.149	1.406
1.05	0.155	0.215	1.218
1.06	0.196	0.339	1.056

Remark. Annual discount factor: $\delta[1] = 0.9$

the relative efficiency as a scalar ε, by which multiplying the wage, and correspondingly the consumption pair of the private system, the two social welfare values are equal. By simple calculation,

$$V(0) + 2\log\varepsilon = V(\bar{\tau}), \quad \text{i.e.,} \quad \varepsilon = \exp[(V(\bar{\tau}) - V(0))/2].$$

Let $\delta[1] = 0.9$ and run $\rho[1]$ between 1 and $\rho_{\delta[1]}[1] = 1.06$. Table 3.2 shows that the socially worst contribution rate τ_ρ is slowly rising from 0 to 0.196, while the neutral contribution rate τ_o is steeply rising from 0.056 to 0.339. The relative efficiency of the public system drops from 2.18 to 1.056.

3.3 Longevity Risk and Public Lifetime Annuity

In the whole book, we shall generally neglect longevity risk but in this section, we model it in the simplest form: either at the start or at the end of the retirement period (of unitary length), the worker dies with probability $1-p$ and p, respectively, $0 < p < 1$. We shall refer to p as the survival probability. While the pension benefit is a lifetime annuity, the private saving is not (Davidoff et al. 2003). Since every worker pays contribution τ but draws benefit only with probability p, through insurance each lucky survivor receives benefit $p^{-1}\tau$. Therefore, the consumption equations are now

$$c = 1 - \tau - s \quad \text{and} \quad d = p^{-1}\tau + \rho s. \tag{3.1'}$$

We assume that the unintended bequest has no utility and the worker is fully farsighted, therefore, the expected lifetime utility function is equal to

$$U(c, d) = \log c + p \log d. \tag{3.2'}$$

Inserting (3.1′) into (3.2′) yields the reduced utility function

$$U[s] = \log(1 - \tau - s) + p \log(p^{-1}\tau + \rho s). \tag{3.3'}$$

To determine the optimal saving intention, we take the derivative and equalize it to zero:

$$0 = U'[s] = \frac{-1}{1 - \tau - s} + p\frac{\rho}{p^{-1}\tau + \rho s}, \tag{3.4a'}$$

hence

$$\tilde{s}(\tau) = \frac{p\rho(1-\tau) - \tau}{\rho(1+p)} = \frac{p(1-\tau) - p^{-1}\rho^{-1}\tau}{1+p}. \tag{3.4b'}$$

The credit constraint is slack if and only if the contribution rate is low enough:

$$0 \le \tau \le \tau_\rho = \frac{p}{p + p^{-1}\rho - 1}. \tag{3.5'}$$

Substituting (3.4*b*′) into (3.1′) yields

Lemma 3.2. *For low contribution rates* $0 \le \tau < \tau_\rho$, *the optimal S-consumption pair are equal to*

$$c_S(\tau) = \frac{1 - \lambda\tau}{1 + p} \quad \text{and} \quad d_S(\tau) = p\rho c_S(\tau), \quad \lambda = 1 - p^{-1}\rho^{-1} \tag{3.6' - S}$$

and for high contribution rates $\tau_\rho \le \tau \le 1$, *the optimal T-consumption pair are*

$$c_T(\tau) = 1 - \tau \quad \text{and} \quad d_T(\tau) = p^{-1}\tau. \tag{3.6' - T}$$

Turning to welfare maximization, note that now the worker does not discount the future consumption, therefore, the social welfare function is equal to the expected lifetime utility function. By (3.6′), $U_S[\tau]$ changes together with either consumption. We distinguish three cases: (i) $p\rho > 1$, i.e., $\lambda > 0$, $c_S(\tau)$ and $d_S(\tau)$ are decreasing, (ii) $p\rho = 1$, i.e., $\lambda = 0$, $c_S(\tau)$ and $d_S(\tau)$ are constant and (iii) $p\rho < 1$, i.e., $\lambda < 0$, $c_S(\tau)$ and $d_S(\tau)$ are increasing.

Like in (3.8), $U_T[\tau]$ increases in $\tau_\rho \le \tau < \tau_T^* = p/(1 + p)$, and decreases in $\tau_T^* \le \tau \le 1$. It is easy to see that $\tau_T^* > \tau_\rho$ (nonempty interval) if and only if (iii) holds.

The S- and T-optima are as follows:

$$c_S(0) = \frac{1}{1 + p}, \quad d_S(0) = \frac{p\rho}{1 + p} \tag{3.10' - S}$$

and

$$c_T(\tau_T^*) = \frac{1}{1 + p} = d_T(\tau_T^*)) \tag{3.10' - T}$$

Comparing $(3.10' - S)$ and $(3.10' - T)$, we have now $c_S(0) = c_T(\tau^*)$ and $d_S(0) < d_T(\tau^*)$ if and only if (iii) holds.

Theorem 3.2. *Suppose the representative worker is farsighted. (a) For a supercritical survival probability* $(1/\rho < p < 1)$*, the optimal contribution rate is zero.*

(b) For the critical survival probability $(p = 1/\rho < 1)$*, the optimal contribution rate is indeterminate in the interval* $[0, \tau_\rho]$.

(c) For a subcritical survival probability $(0 < p < 1/\rho < 1)$*, the optimal contribution rate is maximal:* τ^*_T.

3.4 Social Insurance of Old-Age Income

Section 3.3 already studied the interaction of public pensions and longevity risk. This section considers another social insurance problem frequently neglected: how to insure people against bad luck without undermining work and saving incentives. Here, we slightly reformulate a simple but apt pension insurance model by Varian (1980). Consider a collective of *ex ante* identical workers, who earn $w > 0$ when young and each of them saves s for his old-age. There is no real interest, thus a typical old-aged person could consume s but an idiosyncratic random variable X hits everybody, independently of each other, where $\mathbf{E}X = 0$. We assume that X takes only two values, $\pm\zeta$, where $0 \le \zeta \le 0.5$ with equal probability of 50–50%.

For simplicity, the government runs an old-age insurance system, ensuring an old-age income d dependent on the corresponding observed gross old-age income $s + X$. This function is assumed to be linear: $d = \gamma + \beta(s + X)$, where β denotes the accrual rate. The stochastic errors cancel each other, therefore the expected old-age net income (as well as consumption) is equal to $\mathbf{E}d = \gamma + \beta s$.

Finally, the age-specific consumption pair are

$$c = w - s \quad \text{and} \quad d = \gamma + \beta(s + X). \tag{3.11}$$

To concentrate on the insurance rather than myopia, we assume that any worker maximizes his expected undiscounted lifetime utility function

$$U(c, d) = u(c) + \mathbf{E}u(d), \tag{3.12}$$

where $u(\cdot)$ is the per-period utility function. To obtain analytical results, we assume a linear-quadratic form:

$$u(y) = wy - \frac{y^2}{2}. \tag{3.13}$$

(Note that $u'(y) = w - y > 0$ in the interval $0 < y < w$.)

The government totally redistributes savings among the pensioners. The balance condition is

$$s = \gamma + \beta s. \tag{3.14}$$

First, we determine the individually optimal saving for any given transfer system.

Lemma 3.3 *(Varian 1980). Given γ and β, the individually optimal saving is equal to*

$$s(\beta) = \frac{\beta w}{1+\beta} \tag{3.15}$$

and the consumption pair are equal to

$$c(\beta) = \frac{w}{1+\beta} \quad \text{and} \quad d(\beta) = \frac{\beta w}{1+\beta} + \beta X. \tag{3.16}$$

Remarks. 1. It is surprising that the individual optimal saving is independent of the value of the basic pension γ.

2. The lower the β, the smaller the impact of the random disturbance but also the lower is the saving rate. The inevitable contradiction between self-control and insurance appears here.

Proof. Substituting the consumption pairs (3.11) into $u(\cdot)$, and then into $U(c, d)$ (3.12) yields

$$U[s] = u(w - s) + \mathbf{E}u(\gamma + \beta(s + X)),$$

or using the parametric form (3.13),

$$\begin{aligned} U[s] = \; & w(w - s) - 0.5(w - s)^2 + \mathbf{E}([\gamma + \beta(s + X)]w) \\ & -0.5\mathbf{E}(\gamma + \beta(s + X))^2. \end{aligned}$$

Using the expected value and the variance of the binary random variable before taking the derivative of $U[s]$:

$$\begin{aligned} U'[s] = \; & -w + (w - s) + \beta w - 0.5[(\gamma + \beta(s + \zeta))\beta \\ & +(\gamma + \beta(s - \zeta))\beta] = 0. \end{aligned}$$

With simplification,

$$U'[s] = -s + \beta w - (\gamma + \beta s)\beta = 0.$$

Substituting the balance condition (3.14) into the last equation yields (3.15)–(3.16). ■

Example 3.1. If there is no transfer system, then $\gamma = 0$ and $\beta = 1$, i.e., $s(1) = w/2$. Otherwise, if $0 < \beta < 1$ and $\gamma > 0$, then $c(\beta) > w/2$ and $\mathbf{E}d(\beta) < w/2$.

Turning to the utilitarian social welfare maximization, we obtain the parameter values of the socially optimal transfer system.

Theorem 3.3 *(Varian 1980). There is a unique solution to*

$$\frac{1 - \beta}{(1 + \beta)^3} = \beta\zeta^2 \tag{3.17}$$

and this accrual rate maximizes the social welfare $V(\beta) = \mathbf{E}U[s(\beta)]$.

Proof. (a) Substituting (3.15)–(3.16) into the social welfare function:

$$
\begin{aligned}
V(\beta) &= \frac{w}{1+\beta} - 0.5\frac{1}{(1+\beta)^2} + \frac{\beta w}{1+\beta} \\
&\quad -0.25\left(\frac{\beta}{1+\beta} + \beta\zeta\right)^2 - 0.25\left(\frac{\beta}{1+\beta} - \beta\zeta\right)^2 \\
&= w - 0.5\frac{1+\beta^2}{(1+\beta)^2} - 0.5\beta^2\zeta^2. \qquad (3.18)
\end{aligned}
$$

Take the derivative of V and equate it to zero:

$$V'(\beta) = \frac{1-\beta}{(1+\beta)^3} - \beta\zeta^2 = 0.$$

This is (3.17).

(b) To show the existence and the uniqueness of the root of (3.17), we shall analyze the behavior of function $V'(\beta)$: $V'(0) = 1$, $V'(1) = -\zeta^2$ and $V'(\cdot)$ is a continuous decreasing function, therefore, there exists a unique root β^*. ■

To evaluate the efficiency of the insurance with respect to the no-insurance ($\beta = 1$), note that

$$V(1) = w - 0.5\frac{1+1}{(1+1)^2} - 0.5\zeta^2 = w - 0.25 - 0.5\zeta^2.$$

Denoting efficiency by ε, we look for such a number for which

$$V[\varepsilon, 1] = V[1, \beta^*],$$

i.e.,

$$\varepsilon = 1.25 - 0.5\frac{1+\beta^{*2}}{(1+\beta^*)^2} + 0.5(1-\beta^{*2})\zeta^2. \qquad (3.19)$$

Finally, we illustrate numerically Varian's findings in Table 3.3, running the shock ζ from 0 to 0.5. Note that one has to use a numerical algorithm

Table 3.3 Disturbance and insurance

Size of disturbance, ζ	Net-of-tax rate, β^*	Saving, s^*	Relative efficiency, ε
0.0	1.000	0.500	1.000
0.1	0.933	0.483	1.000
0.2	0.810	0.447	1.004
0.3	0.694	0.410	1.015
0.4	0.603	0.376	1.036
0.5	0.528	0.346	1.066

Remark. Cf. Varian (1980, Table 1, p. 57). $w = 1$. Note that the original table sometimes contained slightly different numbers, due to round-off

for finding the root of the nonlinear equation (3.17). It is of some interest that the most common method, namely the Newton–Raphson algorithm (Appendix C(ii)) cannot be applied because the underlying function has multiple roots. We rather use the slower but sturdier *chord method* (Appendix C(iii)). Note that as the size of the disturbance grows from 0 to 0.5, the optimal net wage decreases from 1 to 0.528, while the optimal saving drops from 0.5 to 0.35. The relative efficiency of the transfer to the no-transfer start rising very slowly but then accelerates; from 1 to 1.066.

Note that Varian (1980) also considered general utility functions $u(\cdot)$, general random disturbance X and nonlinear net-of-tax functions $d(s + X)$.

3.5 Conclusions

We have discussed three elementary pension models. The first one justified the mandatory public pension system as a reaction of the paternalistic government to the myopia of the representative worker. The second model extended the analysis to the longevity risk, where unlike the public pension, the private saving does not buy life annuity. The third model discussed the problem of how a public scheme can diminish the risk of private pensions. In the further chapters, we shall concentrate on the myopia but add wage heterogeneity as well.

References

Davidoff, T., Brown, J. R., & Diamond, P. A. (2003). Annuities and Individual Welfare. *American Economic Review, 103*, 1573–1590.

Feldstein, M. S. (1985). The Level of Social Security Benefits. *Quarterly Journal of Economics, 100*, 302–320.

Leroux, M.-L., Maldonaldo, D., & Pestieau, P. (2015). *Compliance* (p. 2015055). CORE Discussion Paper: Informality and Contributive Pensions.

Simonovits, A. (2009). *Underreported Earning and Age-Specific Income Redistribution in Post-Socialist Economies*. IE-HAS Discussion Papers 27.

Simonovits, A. (2015). Paternalism in Pension Systems. In B. Hámori & M. Rosta (Eds.), *Fecundating Thoughts: Studies in Honor of Eighty-Fifth Birthday of János Kornai* (pp. 151–160). Cambridge: Cambridge Scholar.

Varian, H. R. (1980). Redistributive Taxation as Social Insurance. *Journal of Public Economics, 14*, 49–68.

4
Four Pension Models with Two Types

4.1 Introduction

In this chapter, we expand the basic pension model already presented in Sect. 3.2. We generalize that model by replacing homogeneous workers by heterogeneous ones differing in wages and discount factors. To increase the realism of the pension models, we replace the common unrealistic assumption of the two-generation models that the lengths of the working and of the retirement periods are equal (Simonovits 2000). Here it costs almost nothing to multiply the utility of the old-age consumption by a positive scalar, representing the relative length of the old-age period to the young-age period (cf. Simonovits 2007 in Sect. 12.3). The same transformation should be applied to the lifetime budget constraint, defining the equality of lifetime expenditures and incomes. (Note that the random longevity in Sect. 3.3 above already foreshadowed this generalization.)

For simplicity, here we only consider two types, the lower-earner totally discounts the future, while the higher earner does not discounts it at all. In addition to heterogeneity, beyond the proportional system, we shall discuss three alternative pension systems: means-tested, capped and voluntary systems, respectively. We delay the outline of the practical background to

A. Simonovits, *Simple Models of Income Redistribution*,
https://doi.org/10.1007/978-3-319-72502-4_4

Chapters 5–8, where we generalize the foregoing four models to multi-type models one-by-one.

The structure of this chapter is as follows. Continuing Appendix D's analysis, Sects. 4.2 and 4.3 revisit Feldstein's (1985) and (1987) proportional and means-tested models with two types, respectively. Section 4.4 replaces means-testing with a cap on the pension contribution base. Section 4.5 introduces voluntary pension with contributions matching Section 4.6 concludes.

4.2 Proportional (Earnings-Related) Pension

At this point, we introduce a central parameter of the book, already mentioned in the Introduction: the *length ratio*, defined as the ratio of the lengths of retirement period to that of the working period, to be denoted by μ. Note that the usual simplification of $\mu = 1$ rather distorts the quantitative relations. (There are quite few two-generation models which scaled-down the old-age, and among them at least one, namely Borck (2007) did this in an inconsistent way. Note also that in Sect. 3.3, the survival probability is also equal to the expected length of the retirement period: $p = \mu$.)

We have fixed labor supply, heterogeneous wages and population growth factor ν, productivity growth factor g, calculated for a period of 30 years. There are only two types: type L earns w_L and totally discounts the future, while type H earns $w_H > w_L$ and does not discount at all. (More realistic description will be given in Chapter 5 with $0 \leq \delta_L < \delta_H \leq 1$ and the spanned interval is filled with a continuum of workers.) Their frequencies are denoted by $f_L > 0$ and $f_H > 0$ respectively, where $f_L + f_H = 1$. To simplify the calculations, we assume that the average wage is unity: $f_L w_L + f_H w_H = 1$, i.e., $w_L < 1 < w_H$. In this section, we shall consider proportional (earnings-related) pensions.

Note that in a proportional pension system, the benefit function is given by $b_i = \mu^{-1} \tau \nu g w_i$. This only differs from (D.1) in taking into account that the retirement period's length is equal to μ times the work period's length. Then, we should also multiply the benefits by μ^{-1}.

Hence the type-dependent consumption functions are as follows:

$$c_i = (1-\tau)w_i - s_i \quad \text{and} \quad d_i = \mu^{-1}(\nu g w_i \tau + \rho s_i), \qquad i = L, H. \tag{4.1}$$

The lifetime utility functions are

$$U(c_i, d_i) = \log c_i + \mu\delta_i \log d_i, \qquad i = L, H, \tag{4.2}$$

where $\delta_L = 0$ and $\delta_H = 1$. Having chosen extreme discount factors, the individually optimal savings, are respectively, equal to

$$\begin{aligned} s_L(\tau) &= 0, \quad s_H(\tau) = \frac{\mu\rho(1-\tau) - \nu g\tau}{\rho(1+\mu)} w_H \\ &= \frac{\mu(1-\tau) - R^{-1}\tau}{1+\mu} w_H, \end{aligned} \tag{4.3}$$

where $R = \rho/(\nu g)$ denotes the *relative* interest factor. We shall assume *dynamic efficiency*: $R > 1$. To exclude $s_H(\tau) < 0$, we assume

$$0 \le \tau \le \tau_R = \frac{1}{1+\mu^{-1}R^{-1}}.$$

Substituting (4.3) into (4.1) yields the following lemma:

Lemma 4.1. *For a given contribution rate τ, the optimal consumption pairs are equal to*

$$c_L(\tau) = (1-\tau)w_L, \qquad d_L(\tau) = \mu^{-1}\tau g \nu w_L \tag{4.4L}$$

and

$$c_H(\tau) = \frac{1-\lambda\tau}{1+\mu} w_H, \qquad d_H(\tau) = \rho c_H(\tau), \quad (\lambda = 1 - R^{-1}). \tag{4.4H}$$

To calculate the social welfare function, we drop the constant terms (with respect to the contribution rate) because they drop out at calculating the first-order necessary optimality conditions:

$$\tilde{V}(\tau) = f_L[\log(1-\tau) + \mu \log \tau] + f_H(1+\mu)\log(1-\lambda\tau) \quad (4.5)$$

implying

$$\tilde{V}'(\tau) = -\frac{f_L}{1-\tau} + \frac{f_L\mu}{\tau} - \frac{f_H(1+\mu)\lambda}{1-\lambda\tau} = 0, \quad 0 \le \tau \le \tau_R. \quad (4.6)$$

We have obtained

Theorem 4.1. *The socially optimal contribution rate of the proportional system* (τ_{P}^*) *is equal to the lower root of the quadratic equation*

$$A\tau^2 - B\tau + C = 0 \quad (4.7a)$$

with coefficients

$$A = (1+\mu)\lambda, \quad B = (1+\mu)f_L + \mu f_L\lambda + (1+\mu)f_H\lambda \quad \text{and} \quad C = \mu f_L. \quad (4.7b)$$

Remarks. 1. Note that for $f_H = 0$, after some calculations we obtain the maximal contribution rate which maximizes the respective social welfare function:

$$\bar{\tau} = \frac{1}{1+\mu^{-1}}. \quad (4.8)$$

Recall that for $\mu = 1$, $\bar{\tau} = 1/2$, as it appears after (3.8). Note that $\bar{\tau} < \tau_R$, i.e., $s_H(\tau) > 0$ in the interval $[0, \bar{\tau}]$.

2. Returning to $0 < f_H < 1$ and considering $V'(0+0) = \infty$ and $V'(1-0) = -\infty$, there exists at least one root in (0, 1). It can be shown that the root is less than the maximal contribution rate. Turning to the numerical illustrations, let $\mu = 1/2$, $\nu = 1.01^{30}$, $g = 1.02^{30}$,

Table 4.1 Socially optimal solutions, proportional system

Annual interest factor, $\rho[1]$	Optimal contribution rate, τ_P^*	Myopic		Farsighted	
		Worker	Pensioner	Worker	Pensioner
		Consumption			
		c_L^*	d_L^*	c_H^*	d_H^*
1.04	0.305	0.348	0.745	1.233	3.998
1.06	0.267	0.367	0.652	1.129	6.483
1.08	0.247	0.377	0.602	1.084	10.909
1.10	0.236	0.382	0.576	1.063	18.543

etc. With the hindsight of the international financial and economic crisis, we do not confine the discussion to the exceptionally high interest rate, annually 11.4% (sometimes 8%) used in Feldstein. Rather, we display a series of annual interest rates, starting with 4% and ending with 10%. We fix $f_L = 2/3$ and $f_H = 1/3$ and the lower wage is $w_L = 0.5$, the higher wage is $w_H = 2$.

For moderate annual interest factors, the socially optimal proportional contribution rate is close to the maximal, and the old-age–young-age consumption-ratio is sensible ($c_i^* = c_i(\tau^*)$, etc.). Note the absurdity of the results for the farsighted when the annual interest rate is high enough: for 10%, the old-age consumption is 17.4 times as high as the young-age consumption, while the secular growth multiplier is equal to only 2.44. Unlike in other chapters, here we cannot calculate the relative efficiency with respect to the no-pension system because the latter is infeasible with $\delta_L = 0$ (Table 4.1).

4.3 Means-Tested Pension System

We continue Sect. 4.2 with the modification that in the means-tested system, type H does not receive any public pension. Notwithstanding our criticism of Feldstein's (1987) quantitative results, his qualitative results survive: the means-tested pension is more efficient than the proportional pension. Since only share f_L of the population receive pension at all, therefore the consumption equations (4.1) change into

$$c_L = (1-\tau)w_L, \qquad d_L = \mu^{-1} f_L^{-1} \nu g \tau w_L \tag{4.9L}$$

and

$$c_H = (1-\tau)w_H - s_H, \qquad d_H = \mu^{-1} \rho s_H. \tag{4.9H}$$

The lifetime utility function of type H becomes

$$U_H[s_H] = \log((1-\tau)w_H - s_H) + \mu \log(\mu^{-1} \rho s_H). \tag{4.10}$$

Taking the derivative of $U_H[\cdot]$ with respect to s_H and solving for zero, equation

$$\frac{-1}{(1-\tau)w_H - s_H} + \frac{\mu}{s_H} = 0$$

yields the optimal saving $s_H(\tau)$ and with substitutions, consumptions $c_H(\tau)$ and $d_H(\tau)$.

We have arrived to

Lemma 4.2. *Regardless of the values of the triplet* (ν, g, ρ), *for any contribution rate* τ, *the H-type's optimal decisions with means-testing are*

$$s_H(\tau) = \frac{1-\tau}{1+\mu^{-1}} w_H, \quad c_H(\tau) = \frac{1-\tau}{1+\mu} w_H$$
$$\text{and} \quad d_H(\tau) = \rho c_H(\tau). \tag{4.11}$$

Feldstein (1987) discussed a possible anomaly: by voluntary saving a part of its income, type H may end up with a lower utility than type L. In fact, Feldstein identified the two wages: $w_H = w_L = 1$. Then the anomaly arises if

$$\log c_H(\tau) + \mu \log d_H(\tau) < \log c_L(\tau) + \mu \log d_L(\tau).$$

With substitution:

$$(1+\mu)[\log(1-\tau) \ -\log(1+\mu)] + \mu \log \rho < \log(1-\tau) \\ + \mu \log(\nu^{-1} f_L^{-1} \nu g \tau),$$

i.e., the incentive compatibility condition is the opposite:

$$\mu[\log(1-\tau) \ -\log \tau] \geq (1+\mu)\log(1+\mu) + \mu \log(\nu^{-1} f_L^{-1} R^{-1}), \\ R = \rho/(\nu g).$$

Continuing with welfare maximization, we return to wage heterogeneity. Taking into account (4.11), the simplified social welfare function now is as follows:

$$\tilde{V}(\tau) = f_L[\log(1-\tau) + \mu \log \tau] + f_H(1+\mu)\log(1-\tau). \quad (4.12)$$

Taking the derivative of $\tilde{V}$ with respect to τ and equating it to zero:

$$\tilde{V}'(\tau) = -\frac{f_L}{1-\tau} + \frac{\mu f_L}{\tau} - \frac{f_H(1+\mu)}{1-\tau} = 0. \quad (4.13)$$

Solving for the socially optimal contribution rate yields

Theorem 4.2. *The socially optimal contribution rate of the means-tested pension system is equal to*

$$\tau_{\mathrm{M}}^* = \frac{f_L}{1+\mu^{-1}} = f_L \bar{\tau}. \quad (4.14)$$

Remark. Note that for the means-tested pension system, the socially optimal contribution rate is simply equal to the share of myopes *times* the maximal contribution rate (4.8).

It is not easy to show analytically that $\tau_{\mathrm{M}}^* < \tau_{\mathrm{P}}^*$ holds, at least assuming the incentive compatibility conditions. We shall also see from our numerical illustrations that the optimal means-tested system remains welfare superior to the optimal proportional one.

Table 4.2 Socially optimal solutions, means-tested system

Annual interest factor, $\rho[1]$	Optimal contri-bution rate, τ_M^*	Myopic		Farsighted		Relative efficiency, ε
		Worker	Pensioner	Worker	Pensioner	
		Consumption				
		c_L^*	d_L^*	c_H^*	d_H^*	
1.04	0.300	0.350	1.099	1.234	4.004	1.094
1.06				1.103	6.337	1.092
1.08				1.030	10.368	1.088
1.10				0.989	17.263	1.084

To give a feeling of the efficiency gain obtained from replacing the proportional with the means-tested system, we use again the relative efficiency indicator. Here is its formula:

$$V_M(1, \tau_M^*) = V_P(\varepsilon, \tau_P^*) = V_P(1, \tau_P^*) + (1+\mu)\log\varepsilon,$$
$$\varepsilon = \exp\frac{V_M(1, \tau_M^*) - V_P(1, \tau_P^*)}{1+\mu}.$$

In the foregoing interval, $\varepsilon \approx 1.09$, i.e., to obtain the same social welfare in the proportional system as in the means-tested one, the wages should be raised in the former by about 9% (Table 4.2).

4.4 Cap on the Pension Contribution Base

Another method to relieve the higher-paid and more farsighted workers from the burden of the mandatory pension system is to impose a *cap* on the pension contribution base. (For details, see Chapter 7.) Let $\bar{w}$ be the *cap*, a real number between the low and the high wages: $w_L \le \bar{w} \le w_H$. In a capped system, type H's pension contribution is equal to $\tau\bar{w}$ rather than τw_H. It is worth introducing the cap-high wage-ratio $\psi = \bar{w}/w_H$, yielding the capped contribution $\tau\psi w_H$ as if it were paid without subject to the cap. Therefore, the equations of Sect. 4.2 remain valid if τw_H is replaced by $\tau\psi w_H$ in the respective places. It is easy to see that the social optimum arises when $\bar{w} = w_L$, i.e., $\psi^* = w_L/w_H = 1/\omega$.

First, we formulate

Lemma 4.3. *For any contribution rate* $\tau < \bar{\tau}$ *and cap-ratio* ψ, *the optimal H-consumption pair are equal to*

$$c_H(\tau) = \frac{1-\lambda\psi\tau}{1+\mu} w_H \quad \text{and} \quad d_H(\tau) = \rho c_H(\tau). \tag{4.15}$$

Then (4.5) is replaced by

$$\tilde{V}(\tau,\psi) = f_L[\log(1-\tau) + \mu\log\tau] + f_H(1+\mu)\log(1-\lambda\psi\tau). \tag{4.16}$$

Taking $\tilde{V}$'s partial derivative with respect to τ, and equating it to zero:

$$\tilde{V}'_\tau(\tau,\psi) = -\frac{f_L}{1-\tau} + \frac{f_L\mu}{\tau} - \frac{f_H(1+\mu)\lambda\psi}{1-\lambda\psi\tau} = 0. \tag{4.17}$$

Theorem 4.3. *The socially optimal cap is equal to the lower wage:* $\bar{w}^* = w_L$ *and the contribution rate of the capped system* (τ_C^*) *is equal to the lower root of the quadratic equation*

$$\bar{A}\tau^2 - \bar{B}\tau + \bar{C} = 0 \tag{4.18}$$

with coefficients

$$\bar{A} = (1+\mu)\lambda/\omega, \quad \bar{B} = (1+\mu)f_L + \mu f_L\lambda/\omega + (1+\mu)f_H\lambda/\omega$$
$$\text{and } \bar{C} = \mu f_L. \tag{4.19}$$

Remark. Though $\tau_C^* > \tau_P^*$, the effective contribution rate is lower: $\tau_C^*\bar{w}/w_H < \tau_P^*$.

Table 4.3 Socially optimal solutions, capped system

Annual interest factor, $\rho[1]$	Optimal contribution rate, τ_C^*	Myopic		Farsighted		Relative efficiency, ε
		Worker	Pensioner	Worker	Pensioner	
		Consumption				
		c_L^*	d_L^*	c_H^*	d_H^*	
1.04	0.326	0.337	0.797	1.306	4.237	1.021
1.06	0.317	0.341	0.774	1.273	7.309	1.048
1.08	0.312	0.344	0.761	1.255	12.625	1.062
1.10	0.309	0.346	0.754	1.245	21.721	1.070

Remark. $\bar{w} = w_L = 0.5$

We put numbers into our third model, too. As expected, the new socially optimal rate is also a decreasing function of the interest factor. At the same time, the introduction of the cap increases the socially optimal contribution rate with respect to the proportional system. For example, for the modest annual interest factor $\rho[1] = 1.04$, the contribution rate τ_P^* rises from 0.305 to $\tau_C^* = 0.326$. Even at the fabulous annual interest factor 1.1, the socially optimal contribution rate rises from 0.236 to 0.309. The relative extra efficiency is rising from 2.1% (at $\rho[1] = 1.04$) to 7% (at $\rho[1] = 1.1$) but remains below those of the corresponding means-tested system (Table 4.3).

4.5 Voluntary Pensions

We will devote the whole Chapter 8 to voluntary pensions. Here, we only create a model as a prelude to the general, infinite-type models. There are two types as before, L and H, and there is a cap $\bar{z}$ on voluntary saving z which is matched by a factor $\alpha > 0$. Though modelers frequently overlook the cost of such a matching, called tax expenditure; we introduce a proportional earmarked tax with tax rate θ. Due to $\delta_L = 0$, only type H has a voluntary contribution z_H. The balance condition is simply $\theta = \alpha f_H z_H$.

To avoid unnecessary complications, we assume that the cap is high enough that all H's savings enjoy matching: $z_H < \bar{z}$. Introducing the net-of-tax-cum-contribution rate $\hat{t} = 1 - \tau - \theta$, the consumption equations (4.1) become

$$c_L = \hat{t} w_L \quad \text{and} \quad d_L = \mu^{-1} \nu g w_L \tau, \tag{4.20L}$$

$$c_H = \hat{t} w_H - z_H \quad \text{and} \quad d_H = \mu^{-1}[\nu g w_H \tau + \rho z_H (1+\alpha)]. \tag{4.20H}$$

(4.3) becomes

$$z_H = \frac{\mu(1+\alpha)\hat{t} - R^{-1}\tau}{(1+\alpha)(1+\mu)} w_H. \tag{4.21}$$

We can substitute $\theta = \alpha f_H z_H$ into $\hat{t}$ and (4.21) yields an explicit formula for z_H:

$$z_H(\tau, \alpha) = \frac{\mu(1+\alpha)(1-\tau) - R^{-1}\tau}{(1+\alpha)[1+\mu+\mu\alpha f_H w_H]} w_H$$
$$\text{for } 0 \le \tau \le \frac{\mu(1+\alpha)}{\mu(1+\alpha) + R^{-1}}. \tag{4.22}$$

It is obvious that z_H is a decreasing function of τ.

Substituting (4.22) into $\theta = \alpha f_H z_H$ and then into (4.20H) yields an explicit but overly complex formula for c_H and d_H. What we can say here is the following: in that extreme situation ($\delta_L = 0$), the introduction of the voluntary pension only robes the low-earner by the high-earner.

To maximize the social welfare function, we consider

$$\tilde{V}(\tau, \alpha) = f_L[\log((1 - \tau - \theta(\alpha))w_L) + \log(\mu^{-1}\nu g \tau w_L)] + f_H$$
$$[1 + \mu(1+\alpha)\rho] \log([1 - \tau - \theta(\alpha)]w_H - z_H(\tau, \theta(\alpha))].$$

Here we fix a single interest factor $\rho[1] = 1.04$. Because the impact of the contribution rate is hardly noticeable, we fix $\tau = \tau_P$ and display the behavior of the relative efficiency in terms of the socially optimal proportional system as a function of the matching rate. Italicized first row represents the characteristics of no-matching. It diminishes by 3–8% for half and full matching, respectively (Table 4.4).

Table 4.4 The impact of matching rates

Matching rate, α	Myopic worker consumption, c_L^*	Farsighted			Relative efficiency, ε
		Worker		Pensioner	
		Saving	Consumption		
		z_H^*	c_H^*	d_H^*	
0.0	*0.348*	*0.157*	*1.233*	*3.998*	*1.000*
0.5	0.327	0.241	1.068	5.197	0.971
1.0	0.301	0.279	0.925	5.998	0.920

Remark. $\rho[1] = 1.04$, $\tau = 0.305$, $d_L^* = 0.745$

4.6 Conclusions

Having discussed the four simplest, two-type pension models, we extend three of them in the next four chapters by introducing continuous wage distributions (the fourth model is an outlier). Moreover, we add some factual information on these pension systems. But before moving on, Appendix E analyzes the approximation error in calculating with concentrated savings and dissavings and Appendix F considers the impact of heterogeneity of life spans and earnings.

References

Borck, R. (2007). On the Choice of Public Pensions When Income and Life Expectancy Are Correlated. *Journal of Public Economic Theory, 9*, 711–725.

Feldstein, M. S. (1985). The Level of Social Security Benefits. *Quarterly Journal of Economics, 100*, 302–320.

Feldstein, M. S. (1987). Should Social Security Be Means-Tested? *Journal of Political Economy, 95*, 468–484.

Simonovits, A. (2000). Parables and Realism in Overlapping Cohorts Models. In A. Simonovits & A. Maskin (Eds.), *Planning, Shortage and Transformation, Essays in Honor of J. Kornai* (pp. 95–107). Cambridge, MA: MIT Press.

5

Proportional (Earnings-Related) Pension System

5.1 Introduction

Since the publication of World Bank (1994), the debate on privatization and prefunding of the unfunded public pension systems has focused attention on the socially optimal choice of the *contribution rates* to the arising two pillars and of the *degree of redistribution* achieved in the public pillar. In terms of gross wage, the public contribution rate varies across time and space dramatically: while the US social security contribution rate is as low as 12.4%, the Hungarian rate was as high as 34% until 2017.

Such differences are due to differences in the breakdown to the employer's and the employee's rates, the dependency rates (the ratios of pensioners' number to the workers'), the replacement rates (the ratios of average benefits to average wages) and the share of the private pillar in the total pension system. Similar differences exist among the degrees of redistribution in the public pillars (cf. Disney 2004): in the Netherlands and Great Britain, the public pensions are flat or flat-rate, respectively; in Germany and most other European continental countries, the benefits are proportional to lifetime contributions or wages (Table 1.10). In between, there are progressive systems with various degrees of redistribution: strong

A. Simonovits, *Simple Models of Income Redistribution*,
https://doi.org/10.1007/978-3-319-72502-4_5

in the United States and weak in Hungary. Note the interaction between the degree of redistribution and the contribution rate: the more progressive the system, statistically the lower the contribution rate.

Using Feldstein's elementary framework, in Chapters 3 and 4, we have already outlined the problem in a one- or two-type system. Retaining the elementary framework, Cremer et al. (2008) generalized Feldstein's model to wage heterogeneity with flexible labor supply and linear benefit–wage function. Since the benefit is a sum of a positive flat part and a proportional one, it is progressive. Concerning myopia, the foregoing authors assumed a population consisting of complete myopes and complete farsighted in given proportions; moreover, the discount factors are independent of the wages. Furthermore, Cremer et al. put the efficiency of private and of public savings equal. In their socially optimal linear pension system, the level of benefits and the link between wage and benefits are typically increasing with the share of myopes. (Cremer and Pestieau 2011 surveyed a large part of the literature!)

In the present and later chapters (see Simonovits 2015), we reconsider the problem of socially optimal contribution (and replacement) rate(s). Retaining the wage heterogeneity of Cremer et al. and Chapter 4, we add a special form of discount factor heterogeneity. While in footnote 6 on p. 308, Feldstein (1985) dismissed the importance of "the distribution of degrees of myopia," we shall demonstrate that the distribution of the discount factors *is* important. For the sake of simplicity, in this chapter, we confine our analysis to proportional (defined contribution, contributive) pension systems, where the flat part is zero. Such systems have much stronger incentives to supply labor and to report the true earnings than the progressive ones have, therefore, these problems can be neglected in a first approximation. We have retained the assumption of superiority of private over public pensions, as a tool to model the efficiency problems with the public system.

We shall make the following idealizations: (a) the higher the wage, the higher the discount factor (i.e., the more farsighted the worker) and (b) any dollar saved privately rather than in a public pension system raises the old-age consumption. *Then a well-chosen pension contribution rate ensures sufficient mandatory savings for the low-earning shortsighted but leaves sufficient room for the more efficient voluntary savings for the high-earning farsighted.*

We are aware that our idealizations are only approximately valid. (a) In addition to the pairs described above, in reality, there are low-paid workers who are farsighted and there are high-paid workers who are shortsighted, too. (Becker and Mulligan 1997 provided a rich theory on the endogenous determination of time preferences but see also Hausehofer and Fehr 2014.) Nevertheless, the correlation between discount factors and wages appears to be strongly positive, therefore, the atypical combinations can be neglected in a first approximation (Strotz 1956). (b) In fact, the voluntary (private) saving may also be less rather than more efficient than the mandatory (public) one, see Barr and Diamond (2008, Chapter 6). We only use idealization (b) to allow for certain incentive problems—e.g., flexible labor supply—occurring in the mandatory public pension system.

Correspondingly, we consider a very simple model, where workers only differ by their wages and discount factors but have the same given ages when they start working, retire or die, respectively. (Chapter 9 will study flexible retirement age as well.) Using a *paternalistic* utilitarian social welfare function, where individual discounting is eliminated, a socially optimal pension system successfully combines the dual task. To prepare the ground for the analysis of the capped (Chapter 7) and of the voluntary systems (Chapter 8), we use a continuous-type model. When making numerical illustrations, we shall work with a Pareto distribution because it is analytically very convenient and approximates the distribution of high wages quite well (cf. Diamond and Saez 2011).

Reiterating the results of Sect. 4.2, we show again that in a heterogeneous framework, Feldstein's result does not hold in general: even though the bulk of the workers is far from being completely myopic but encounters realistically low enough interest rates, the *socially optimal net replacement rate is high, close to 1* and even in wider domain, stays far from 0.

We warn again that the use of two-period models (especially numerical ones) is problematic, their main justification is their simplicity. By now there are many realistic, numerically calibrated models characterizing the optimal pension systems, unfortunately with widely diverging messages. For example, including endogenous wages and interest rates, detailed age structure etc. but assuming away any myopia, Auerbach and Kotlikoff

(1987) proved the optimality of no public pension system at all. Introducing wage heterogeneity and other features, Imrohoroğlu et al. (1995) obtained optimal gross replacement rates in the interval 30–60% without relying on myopia! Unlike our static model, these models can consider the dynamic problem of carving out a private pillar from a public one (e.g., Fehr 2000; Diamond and Orszag 2004 vs. Feldstein 2005).

The structure of the remaining part of the chapter is as follows: Sect. 5.2 presents and discusses the model, while Sect. 5.3 displays numerical illustrations.

5.2 Model

We consider a very simple pension model with stationary economy and population (the inclusion of the growth rates of real wages and population would only quantitatively change the results, see Chapter 4). Here, workers only differ in lifetime wages and discount factors. Starting with the (total) wage, it is assumed that $w \in [w_{\mathrm{m}}, w_{\mathrm{M}}]$, where $0 < w_{\mathrm{m}} < w_{\mathrm{M}}$. Workers with wage w pay contributions τw, where $\tau \in [0, 1)$ is the *contribution rate* to the mandatory unfunded pension system.

By assumption, every pension benefit is proportional to the total wage: $b = \beta w$, $\beta \geq 0$ is the *gross replacement rate,* while $\beta_n = \beta/(1 - \tau)$ is the *net replacement rate.* Everybody works for a unit period, and everybody spends a shorter (or equal) period in retirement with a common length μ, $0 < \mu \leq 1$. Hence, the pension balance is simply $\mu\beta = \tau$ or $\mu\beta_n = \tau/(1 - \tau)$. (One worker contributes τw to μ pensioners having benefit βw.) From now on we shall consider the choice of contribution and of gross replacement rates as equivalent. Since the two periods' lengths are different, we use *intensities,* i.e., quantities per a unit period even if it is not always mentioned.

In addition to paying pension contributions, workers can also save privately for old-age: $s \geq 0$. Denoting the compound interest factor by $\rho > 1$, the intensity of the decumulated saving is approximately $\mu^{-1}\rho s$.

Individual Optima

We can now describe the young-and the old-age consumption (intensities):

$$c = (1 - \tau)w - s \quad \text{and} \quad d = \mu^{-1}(\tau w + \rho s). \tag{5.1}$$

To determine the individually optimal savings, we introduce the lifetime discounted utility function:

$$U(c, d) = u(c) + \delta\mu u(d), \tag{5.2}$$

where $u(\cdot)$ is the increasing per-period utility (felicity) function. As is usual, in addition to smoothness and concavity, we also assume $u'(0+) = \infty$ and $u'(\infty) = 0$. Furthermore, the *discount factor* δ represents the degree of farsightedness: the higher the δ, the more farsighted the worker.

Inserting the consumption functions (5.1) into the utility function (5.2) yields the *reduced discounted lifetime utility function*

$$U[s] = u((1 - \tau)w - s) + \delta\mu u(\mu^{-1}(\tau w + \rho s)). \tag{5.3}$$

Taking the derivative of $U[s]$ and equalizing it to zero provides for the *individually optimal saving intention*:

$$U'[\tilde{s}] = -u'((1 - \tau)w - \tilde{s}) + \delta\rho u'(\mu^{-1}(\tau w + \rho\tilde{s})) = 0. \tag{5.4}$$

Excluding negative saving (5.4) determines the *optimal saving function*

$$s(\tau, w, \delta) = \begin{cases} \tilde{s}(\tau, w, \delta) & \text{if } \tilde{s}(\tau, w, \delta) \geq 0; \\ 0, & \text{if } \tilde{s}(\tau, w, \delta) < 0. \end{cases}$$

Optimal consumption pairs are denoted as $c(\tau, w, \delta)$ and $d(\tau, w, \delta)$.

Social Optimum

We continue with studying the impact of the pension contribution rate on the social welfare and determine its socially optimal value.

To have a one-dimensional distribution over wages and discount factors, we assume plausibly that the discount factor is an increasing function of the wage: $\delta = \delta(w)$ being defined on $[w_{\mathrm{m}}, w_{\mathrm{M}}]$. (Sometimes, as a further simplification, we shall consider wage-invariant discount factors as well!) We shall introduce the following abbreviation: $s[\tau, w] = s(\tau, w, \delta(w))$. Hence for a given contribution rate τ, the *critical wage* w_τ is defined as the highest wage for which saving is zero: $s[\tau, w_\tau] = 0$.

We introduce the wage distribution function to be denoted by F, the density function $f = F'$ and the corresponding expectations by **E**. We need the *paternalistic*, undiscounted indirect utility function:

$$U^*[\tau, w] = u(c(\tau, w, \delta(w)) + \mu u(d(\tau, w, \delta(w)). \tag{5.5}$$

By choosing the contribution rate τ, the government maximizes the utilitarian social welfare function, i.e., the expected value of the paternalistic indirect utilities:

$$V(\tau) = \mathbf{E}U^*[\tau, w]. \tag{5.6}$$

Theorems 5.1 and 5.2 will show that if every worker is either completely myopic or farsighted, then the socially optimal contribution rate is equal to maximum or zero, respectively. The former is the case, where nobody saves, therefore, the government equalizes the consumption intensity of the young and of the old:

$$(1 - \tau)w = \mu^{-1}\tau w, \quad \text{i.e.,} \quad \bar{\tau} = \frac{1}{1 + \mu^{-1}}, \tag{5.7}$$

and $\bar{\tau}$ will be called *maximal* contribution rate.

Theorem 5.1. *If everybody is totally myope: $\delta \equiv 0$, then the social welfare is an increasing function of the contribution rate in $[0, \bar{\tau})$ and a decreasing function in $(\bar{\tau}, 1)$, having the optimum at $\bar{\tau}$.*

Remark. This was proved for the Cobb–Douglas utility function and $\mu = 1$ in a related model by Feldstein (1985, Sect. I) and Theorem 3.1. Note also that $\bar{\tau}$ is an increasing function of the length ratio μ. This will be relevant in Sect. 12.3: the older the population, the higher is the maximal contribution rate.

Proof. Taking the derivative of $V(\tau) = \mathbf{E}[u((1-\tau)w) + \mu u(\mu^{-1}\tau w)]$, (5.5)–(5.6) results in

$$V'(\tau) = \mathbf{E}\{w[-u'((1-\tau)w) + u'(\mu^{-1}\tau w)]\}$$

which is positive for $\tau < \bar{\tau}$ and negative for $\tau > \bar{\tau}$, hence the optimum is reached at $\bar{\tau}$. ■

From now on we assume that the contribution rate is less than or equal to the maximum:

$$0 < \tau \leq \bar{\tau}.$$

A formula above directly proves.

Theorem 5.2. *If everybody is sufficiently farsighted:* $\delta \equiv \rho^{-1}$*, then the social welfare is a decreasing function of the contribution rate in* $[0, 1)$*, therefore the social optimum is no-pension at all.*

To have myopes and not so myopes, from now on we also assume that $\delta(w_{\rm m})\rho < 1 < \delta(w_{\rm M})\rho$. It is easy to prove that in interval $w_{\rm m} \leq w < w(\tau)$, $U^*[\tau, w]$ is increasing with τ, while in interval $w(\tau) < w \leq w_{\rm M}$, $U^*[\tau, w]$ is decreasing. Unfortunately, the usual approach (determining the stationary points of $V(\tau)$) is not helpful because in a wide domain of the parameter space, there is more than one stationary point (see the jump the welfare gap in Sect. 3.2). Note that this complication made (Samuelson 1975) to select a minimum rather than a maximum (cf. Deardorf 1976). Therefore, we have to be satisfied with modest analytical results as is

Theorem 5.3. *The maximal pension (with a contribution rate* $\bar{\tau}$*) is welfare superior to the no-pension if and only if*

$$(1+\mu)\mathbf{E}u(w/(1+\mu^{-1})) > \mathbf{E}u(w - s[0, w]) + \mu\mathbf{E}u(\mu^{-1}\rho s[0, w]), \tag{5.8}$$

where

$$u'(w - s[0, w]) = \delta\rho u'(\mu^{-1}\rho s[0, w])$$

uniquely determines $s[0, w]$.

Cobb–Douglas Utility Function

To sharpen our results above and prepare the numerical calculations, we specialize our utility function to Cobb–Douglas-utility function (cf. Feldstein 1985 and Chapters 3 and 4). Let $u(x) = \log x$. Then our formulas (5.4) and (5.1) simplify respectively

$$\tilde{s}[\tau, w] = \frac{\delta(w)\rho(1-\tau) - \mu^{-1}\tau}{[\delta(w) + \mu^{-1}]\rho} w,$$

$$c(\tau, w, \delta(w)) = \frac{1 - (1 - \rho^{-1})\tau}{1 + \mu\delta(w)} w, \; w > w_\tau.$$

Hence the critical wage w_τ is a root to $\delta(w) = \tau/[\mu\rho(1-\tau)]$.

For this special case, everything is very simple. Most noteworthy, Theorem 5.3 can be generalized as follows. For a moment forget about the dependence of the discount factor on wage and introduce the critical discount factor δ_ρ for which the paternalistic utility function's two end values are equal to each other:

$$\log c(0, w, \delta_\rho) + \mu \log d(0, w, \delta_\rho) = \log c(\bar{\tau}, w) + \mu \log d(\bar{\tau}, w).$$

Because the optimal consumptions are proportional to wages, the critical discount factor δ_ρ is independent of the wage:

$$\log c(0, 1, \delta_\rho) + \mu \log d(0, 1, \delta_\rho) = \log c(\bar{\tau}, 1) + \mu \log d(\bar{\tau}, 1).$$

Returning to wage-dependent discount factors, now Theorem 5.1 is transformed into

Theorem 5.1*. *Assume that the workers have Cobb–Douglas utility functions with wage-dependent discount factors* $\delta(w)$.

(a) *If everybody is sufficiently myopic (subcritical):* $\delta(w_{\mathrm{M}}) < \delta_\rho$, *then the social welfare is an increasing function of the contribution rate in* $[0, \bar{\tau})$ *and decreasing in* $(\bar{\tau}, 1)$, *having the optimum at* $\bar{\tau}: \tau_{\mathrm{P}}^* = \bar{\tau}$.
(b) *If everybody is sufficiently farsighted (supercritical):* $\delta(w_{\mathrm{m}}) > \delta_\rho$, *then the social welfare is a decreasing function of the contribution rate in* $[0, 1)$, *therefore the social optimum is no-pension at all:* $\tau_{\mathrm{P}}^* = \bar{\tau}$.
(c) *Otherwise,* $0 \leq \tau_{\mathrm{P}}^* \leq \bar{\tau}$.

Remark. The economic content of Theorem 5.1* (a) is as follows: if every worker's discount factor is low enough, then the maximal pension is superior to the no-pension.

Still confining our attention on the wage-invariant discount factor for a moment, we calculate the critical discount factor δ_ρ, which equalizes the welfare provided by the optimal no-pension with that of the optimal pension. To do so, we have to generalize (3.10):

$$-(1+\mu)\log(1+\delta_\rho\mu) + \mu\log\delta_\rho + \mu\log\rho = -(1+\mu)\log(1+\mu).$$

With transformation:

$$\frac{\delta_\rho^\mu \rho^\mu}{(1+\delta_\rho\mu)^{1+\mu}} = \frac{1}{(1+\mu)^{1+\mu}}.$$

Unlike (3.10), this equation cannot generally be solved explicitly for δ_ρ. Even if specification $\mu = 1/2$ yields a cubic equation, practically its solution also needs numerical methods.

We also specify our Theorem 5.3 as follows:

Theorem 5.3*. *With Cobb–Douglas utility functions, the maximal pension (with a contribution rate* $\bar{\tau}$*) is welfare superior to the no-pension if and only if*

$$(1+\mu)\log(1+\mu^{-1}) \\ < (1+\mu)\mathbf{E}\log(1+\mu\delta(w)) - \mu\log\rho - \mu\mathbf{E}\log(\delta(w)). \quad (5.9)$$

Proof. Indeed, inserting

$$c(0, w, \delta(w)) = \frac{w}{1 + \mu\delta(w)} \quad \text{and}$$
$$d(0, w, \delta(w)) = \delta(w)\rho c(0, w, \delta(w))$$

into (5.8) yields (5.9). ■

Pareto Distribution

To sharpen our results and prepare for numerical illustrations, we assume that wages follow the *Pareto distribution* with a density function

$$f(w) = \sigma w_{\mathrm{m}}^{\sigma} w^{-1-\sigma} \quad \text{for} \quad w \geq w_{\mathrm{m}} > 0,$$

where $\sigma > 1$ is the exponent of the distribution and w_{m} is the minimum wage. It is easy to give an explicit formula for the distribution function:

$$F(w) = \int_{w_{\mathrm{m}}}^{w} f(\omega)\, d\omega = 1 - w_{\mathrm{m}}^{\sigma} w^{-\sigma} \quad \text{for} \quad w \geq w_{\mathrm{m}} > 0. \tag{5.10}$$

Hence $F(w_{\mathrm{m}}) = 0$ and $F(\infty) = 1$; furthermore, its expectation can explicitly be calculated:

$$\mathbf{E}w = \int_{w_{\mathrm{m}}}^{\infty} w f(w)\, dw = \frac{\sigma w_{\mathrm{m}}}{\sigma - 1}.$$

Since we normalized the expected wage as unity, the minimum wage is a simple function of index σ:

$$w_{\mathrm{m}} = \frac{\sigma - 1}{\sigma}.$$

In practice, $\sigma \approx 2$, i.e., $w_{\mathrm{m}} \approx 1/2$. We also display the second moment of the Pareto distribution:

$$\mathbf{E}w^2 = \frac{\sigma w_{\mathrm{m}}^2}{\sigma - 2} = \frac{(\sigma - 1)^2}{\sigma(\sigma - 2)} \quad \text{for} \quad \sigma > 2 \quad \text{and}$$

$$\mathbf{E}w^2 = \infty \quad \text{otherwise.}$$

For our unbounded distribution, let w_{N} be the maximal value at which the wage distribution is cut in the numerical illustrations and we represent all the wages above w_{N} by a cleverly chosen w_{K}. By definition,

$$1 = \int_{w_{\mathrm{m}}}^{w_{\mathrm{N}}} wf(w)\,dw + [1 - F(w_{\mathrm{N}})]w_{\mathrm{K}}. \tag{5.11}$$

The expected censored wage (given in the integral in (5.11)) is equal to

$$\mathbf{E}\min(w, w_{\mathrm{N}}) = 1 - \frac{w_{\mathrm{m}}^{\sigma} w_{\mathrm{N}}^{-\sigma+1}}{\sigma - 1}, \tag{5.12}$$

hence (5.10), (5.11) and (5.12) yield

$$w_{\mathrm{K}} = \frac{\sigma}{\sigma - 1} w_{\mathrm{N}}.$$

For example, for $\sigma = 2$, the representative highest wage is double of the "maximum": $w_{\mathrm{K}} = 2w_{\mathrm{N}}$.

5.3 Numerical Illustrations

We shall assume that wages are distributed along a Pareto-2 distribution. To give a flavor of the behavior of this distribution, Table 5.1 displays selected values of the distribution function and anticipating the topic of Chapter 7, namely the cap, the share of covered earnings. The median wage is about 0.71. Note how fast the probability of earning below w

converges to 1 as the relative value of w (in terms of the average wage) goes to 4, and how slowly the share of the lower-earnings does so. For example, 1.6% of all the earners still have 12.5% of the total earnings (last row).

Recall that in our model, the discount factor is an increasing function of the wage: $\delta = \delta(w)$. To map an infinite interval into a finite one, we assume the simple relation

$$\delta(w) = \delta_M - (\delta_M - \delta_m)e^{\eta(w_m - w)}, \tag{5.13}$$

where $\eta > 0$ measures the sensitivity of the discount factor to the wage. Note that for any finite w_N, $\delta(w_N) < \delta_M$, but for high enough w_N/w_m, the difference is small. We shall work with $\delta_m = 0$, $\delta_M = 1$. For this special choice, $\eta = -\delta'(w)/[1 - \delta(w)]$ is a kind of a discount factor–wage elasticity.

We shall divide the interval $[w_m, w_N]$ into $n = 200$ subintervals such a way that the division points w_i form a geometrical sequence: and at integration, the representative points are the geometrical means of the subsequent points: $w_{i+1} = qw_i$ and $z_i = \sqrt{w_i w_{i+1}}$. The mass of the remaining infinite part is $1 - F(w_N) = 0.0001$ (with $w_N = 50$) and the earning $w_K = 100$ represents the average highest wage.

In the remainder, we shall investigate the sensitivity of the social optimum to the parameter values, namely to the wage elasticity of the discount factor and to the interest factor.

Table 5.1 Pareto probabilities and covered earnings for varying caps

Earning cap, $\bar{w}$	Probability, $F(\bar{w})$	Share of lower-earnings, $F(\bar{w})\mathbf{E}(w \mid w < \bar{w})$
0.707	0.500	0.250
1.0	0.750	0.500
1.5	0.889	0.667
2.0	0.938	0.750
2.5	0.960	0.800
3.0	0.972	0.833
4.0	0.984	0.875

Remark. $\sigma = 2$

Table 5.2 Critical discount factor as a function of interest factor

Annual interest factor, $\rho[1]$	1.020	1.040	1.060	1.080
Annual critical discount factor, $\delta_{\rho[1]}[1]$	0.952	0.928	0.909	0.891

Unlike others (e.g., Feldstein 1985, 1987; Cremer et al. 2011) we have distinguished the lengths of the working and of the retirement periods. (On the other hand, from now on we will confine attention to a stationary population and economy!) Assuming 40-year working and 20-year retirement periods, the length ratio is 1/2 rather than 1. By this way, we receive more realistic numbers. For example, even in our stationary economy and population, the socially optimal contribution rate $\bar{\tau} = 1/(1 + \mu^{-1})$ in (5.7) drops from 1/2 to 1/3 as we replace $\mu = 1$ by 0.5. If we took into account that the socially optimal discount factor is less than 1 (e.g., labor disutility, reduced family size, etc., as postulated by Cremer et al. 2008), then we could reduce the contribution rate further, even to 1/4.

It is worth discussing at least one curve $V(\tau)$ more carefully: for example, for $\eta = 0.6$, the social welfare function decreases in the tiny interval $\tau \in [0, 0.02]$, increases in the interval $\tau \in [0.02, 0.14]$, then have a plateau and then again decreases to $\tau \geq 0.19$. Note that $V(0.05) = V(0.29) = V(0)$, i.e., there are two stationary points: the lower for minimal, the higher for maximal social welfare.

We start with the tabulation of the critical discount factor as a function of the interest factor in Table 5.2. Recall that for workers with subcritical discount factors, the maximal contribution rate is optimal; while for workers with supercritical discount factors, the zero contribution rate is optimal (cf. Theorem 5.1*). It is qualitatively obvious that the lower the interest factor, the higher the critical discount factor. Table 5.2 gives the quantitative answer. For example, for the modest annual interest factor of 1.02, the critical annual discount factor is quite high: 0.952, while for the super high annual interest factor of 1.08, the critical annual discount factor is quite low: 0.891.

Next, we discuss the sensitivity of our results to the distribution of myopia, more precisely, to the elasticity of the discount factor to the wage. Fixing the interest factor at $\rho[1] = 1.04$ we vary η from 0.1 to 0.7.

Table 5.3 The socially optimal contribution and replacement rates, changing elasticity

Wage elasticity of discount factor, η	Contribution rate, τ_P	Optimal		Relative efficiency, $\varepsilon_{P\|0}$
		Net replacement rate, β_n	Expected saving, $\mathrm{E}s_P$	
0.1	0.330	0.985	0.007	1.738
0.2	0.324	0.959	0.015	1.417
0.3	0.312	0.907	0.024	1.269
0.4	0.299	0.853	0.033	1.181
0.5	0.282	0.786	0.042	1.122
0.6	0.263	0.714	0.053	1.080
0.7	0.235	0.614	0.066	1.049

Remark. $\rho[1] = 1.04$

Table 5.4 The socially optimal contribution and replacement rates, changing interest factor

Annual interest factor, $\rho[1]$	Contribution rate, τ_P	Optimal		Relative efficiency, $\varepsilon_{P\|0}$
		Net replacement rate, β_n	Expected saving, $\mathrm{E}s_P$	
1.02	0.332	0.994	0.007	1.716
1.03	0.329	0.981	0.011	1.558
1.04	0.324	0.959	0.017	1.417
1.05	0.312	0.907	0.023	1.293
1.06	0.291	0.821	0.030	1.186
1.07	0.261	0.706	0.039	1.098
1.08	0.198	0.494	0.051	1.030

Remark. $\eta = 0.2$

Table 5.3 shows how slowly drop the socially optimal contribution and the replacement rates from the maximum to zero. Even for $\eta = 0.7$, $\tau_P = 0.235$ and $\beta_n = 0.614$. Since workers of zero discount factor have a mass zero, we are able to calculate the efficiency of the system with respect to the no-pension.

In Table 5.4, we discuss the sensitivity of the outcomes to the interest factor. As the annual interest factor $\rho[1]$ rises from 1.02 to 1.08, the socially optimal contribution rate slowly drops from 0.33 to 0.20 and the corresponding net replacement rate sinks from 0.99 to 0.49. The efficiency of the socially optimal pension system with respect to the no-pension drops from 1.72 to 1.03.

5.4 Conclusions

In Chapter 5, we studied of proportional pension systems with continuum of workers, whose discount factor was an increasing function of the wage. Using Pareto wage distribution, we could numerically illustrate the dependence of the socially optimal contribution rate on the elasticity of the discount factor and the interest factor.

References

Auerbach, A. J., & Kotlikoff, L. J. (1987). *Dynamic Fiscal Policy*. Cambridge: Cambridge University Press.

Barr, N., & Diamond, P. (2008). *Reforming Pensions: Principles and Policy Choices.* Oxford: Oxford University Press.

Becker, G., & Mulligan, C. B. (1997). On the Optimal Determination of Time Preferences. *Quarterly Journal of Economics, 112*, 729–758.

Cremer, H., & Pestieau, P. (2011). Myopia, Redistribution and Pensions. *European Economic Review, 55*, 165–175.

Cremer, H., De Donder, P., Maldonado, D., & Pestieau, P. (2008). Designing a Linear Pension Scheme with Forced Savings and Wage Heterogeneity. *International Tax and Public Finance, 15*, 547–562.

Deardorf, A. W. (1976). The Optimum Growth Rate for Population: Comment. *International Economic Review, 17*, 510–514.

Diamond, P. A., & Orszag, P. (2004). *Saving Social Security: A Balanced Approach.* Washington, DC: Brookings Institution.

Diamond, P. A., & Saez, E. (2011). The Case for a Progressive Tax: from Basic Research to Policy Prescriptions. *Journal of Economic Perspectives, 23*(4), 165–190.

Disney, R. (2004). Are Contributions to Public Pension Programmes a Tax on Employment? *Economic Policy, 39*, 267–311.

Fehr, H. (2000). Pension Reform During the Demographic Transition. *Scandinavian Journal of Economics, 102*, 419–443.

Feldstein, M. S. (1985). The Optimal Level of Social Security Benefits. *Quarterly Journal of Economics, 100*, 302–320.

Feldstein, M. S. (1987). Should Social Security be Means-Tested? *Journal of Political Economy, 95*, 468–484.

Feldstein, M. (2005). Structural Reform of Social Security. *Journal of Economic Perspectives, 19*(1), 33–55.

Hausehofer, J., & Fehr, E. (2014). Psychology of Poverty. *Science, 344*(6186), 862–867.

Imrohoroğlu, A., Imrohoroğlu, S., & Joines, D. H. (1995). A Life Cycle Model of Social Security. *Economic Theory, 6*, 83–114.

Samuelson, P. A. (1975). The Optimum Growth Rate for Population. *International Economic Review, 16*, 531–538.

Simonovits, A. (2015). Socially Optimal Contribution Rate and Cap in a Proportional Pension System. *Portuguese Economic Journal, 14*, 45–63.

Strotz, R. H. (1956). Myopia and Inconsistency of Dynamic Utility Maximization. *Review of Economic Studies, 23*, 165–180.

World Bank. (1994). *Averting Old-Age Crisis.* Washington, DC: World Bank.

6

Progressive Transfer Systems

6.1 Introduction

Mandatory pension systems have a number of functions. To name only two of the most important functions: these systems (i) force myopic workers to save for their old-age and (ii) alleviate old-age poverty of the low-earners. Evidently, contributions to a mandatory system diminish voluntary savings of life-cycler workers and influence the labor supply of myopic and life-cycler workers. A socially optimal pension system has to harmonize these features carefully. In this chapter, we return to studying various progressive transfer systems. (Note that while Chapters 5, 7 and 8 generalize Sects. 4.2, 4.4 and 4.5, respectively, this chapter does not fit into this line with respect to Sect. 4.3.) In Sect. 6.2, we present two alternatives to the doubly proportional income tax and pension system, namely progressive tax *cum* proportional pension and proportional income tax *cum* progressive pension. In Sect. 6.3, we reconsider the socially optimal means-tested (Sect. 4.3) and pension credit systems (see also Simonovits 2012).

A. Simonovits, *Simple Models of Income Redistribution*,
https://doi.org/10.1007/978-3-319-72502-4_6

6.2 Progressive Taxation or Progressive Pensions

In this section, we shall discuss three simple models. Our starting point is the current Hungarian system: proportional taxation and pension. The problem with this combination is that it pays too low pension to those who earn at the minimum and too high pension to those at the maximum. As an alternative, we analyze progressive taxation combined with proportional pensions (like Germany) and finally proportional taxation combined with progressive pensions (suggested for Hungary).

In all the three models, we replace our customary total wage w by the more widespread but economically questionable gross wage $\mathbf{w}$, running between $0 < \mathbf{w}_{\mathrm{m}} < \mathbf{w}_{\mathrm{M}}$; v stands for net wage, which is equal to the gross wage less the personal income tax less the employee's pension contribution. (The total wage cost is equal to the net wage plus the employer's contribution.)

Proportional Taxation and Pension

In the doubly proportional system, there is a single contribution rate τ and a single tax rate θ.
The net wage is simply

$$v = (1 - \tau - \theta)\mathbf{w}, \quad \text{where} \quad \mathbf{w}_{\mathrm{m}} \le \mathbf{w} \le \mathbf{w}_{\mathrm{M}} \tag{6.1}$$

and the pension benefit is given by

$$b = \beta v, \quad \text{where} \quad \beta > 0. \tag{6.2}$$

In a proportional system, all the calculations are independent of the distribution of the gross wages. Anticipating nonproportional systems, we introduce $I > 1$ types of workers with gross wage $\mathbf{w}_i$ and frequency $f_i > 0$, normalized by

$$\sum_{i=1}^{I} f_i = 1 \quad \text{and} \quad \sum_{i=1}^{I} f_i \mathbf{w}_i = 1. \tag{6.3}$$

In our numerical illustration, the number of types is $I = 7$, with step-size and bend points

$$h = \frac{\mathbf{w}_M - \mathbf{w}_m}{I - 1} \quad \text{and} \quad \mathbf{w}_i = \mathbf{w}_1 + (i-1)h, \quad \text{for} \quad i = 2, \ldots, 7. \tag{6.4}$$

Let the minimal and the maximal (covered) gross wages be $\mathbf{w}_m = 0.5$ and $\mathbf{w}_M = 2$, respectively.

We choose the current Hungarian income tax rate $\theta = 0.15$ and the worker's social insurance contribution rate 0.17. (If the dependency rate is $\mu = 0.6$, then the employer's pension rate is $\tilde{\tau} = 0.226$, and the total wage is $w = (1+\tilde{\tau})\mathbf{w}$.) Table 6.1 displays gross and net wages, frequencies plus the corresponding benefits (6.1)–(6.2). Note that the minimal benefit is equal to 0.272, too low. It is easy to check that both normalizations in (6.4) hold. The main pitfall of this combination is that the low-paid receive too low benefits.

Progressive Taxation with Proportional Pensions

Like in several other countries, progressive personal income taxation and proportional pensions characterized the Hungarian transfer system until 2012, at least in its steady-state outlook. In the simplest form, this could be modeled as follows.

Table 6.1 Gross and net wages, benefits: Proportional taxes, proportional benefits

Gross wage, $\mathbf{w}_i$	Frequency, f_i	Net wage, v_i	Benefit, b_i
0.50	0.25	0.34	0.272
0.75	0.20	0.51	0.408
1.00	0.20	0.68	0.544
1.25	0.15	0.85	0.680
1.50	0.10	1.02	0.816
1.75	0.05	1.19	0.952
2.00	0.05	1.36	1.088

Table 6.2 Gross and net wages, benefits: Progressive taxes, proportional benefits

Gross wage, $\mathbf{w}_i$	Net wage, v_i	Benefit, b_i
0.50	0.365	0.292
0.75	0.547	0.438
1.00	0.690	0.552
1.25	0.833	0.666
1.50	0.975	0.780
1.75	1.118	0.894
2.00	1.260	1.008

*R*emark. Frequencies are taken from Table 6.1

There are now two tax rates: $0 \leq \theta_1 < \theta_2 < 1$. Then the net wage–gross wage schedule has two branches:

$$v = \begin{cases} (1 - \tau - \theta_1)\mathbf{w} & \text{if } \mathbf{w}_\mathrm{m} \leq \mathbf{w} \leq \mathbf{w}_\mathrm{o}; \\ v_\mathrm{o} + (1 - \tau - \theta_2)(\mathbf{w} - \mathbf{w}_\mathrm{o}) & \text{if } \mathbf{w}_\mathrm{o} \leq \mathbf{w} \leq \mathbf{w}_\mathrm{M}, \end{cases} \tag{6.5}$$

where $v_\mathrm{o} = (1 - \tau - \theta_1)\mathbf{w}_\mathrm{o}$. Furthermore, $b = \beta v$.

To obtain comparable numbers in the two systems, in Table 6.2 we assume that the total tax and total pension remain invariant. With $\mathbf{w}_\mathrm{o} = 0.75$, this is compatible for example, with $\theta_1 = 0.1$ and $\theta_2 = 0.26$. Then the lowest benefit rises and the highest benefit declines with respect to Table 6.1.

Proportional Taxation with Progressive Pensions

Finally, we discuss a proportional tax system and a progressive pension system. There are now single tax and contribution rates; and a progressive reduction coefficient $\chi < 1$, active above the critical net wage v_1. Then (6.1) is replaced by

Net wage

$$v = (1 - \tau - \theta)\mathbf{w}, \tag{6.6}$$

Table 6.3 Gross and net wages, benefits: Proportional taxes, progressive benefits

Gross wage, $\mathbf{w}_i$	Net wage, v_i	Benefit, b_i	Replacement rate, $b_i/\mathbf{w}_i$
0.50	0.34	0.282	0.829
0.75	0.51	0.423	0.829
1.00	0.68	0.564	0.829
1.25	0.85	0.676	0.796
1.50	1.02	0.789	0.774
1.75	1.19	0.902	0.758
2.00	1.36	1.015	0.746

Remark. Frequencies are taken from Table 6.1

Table 6.4 Gross replacement rates with three rules

Tax	Benefit	Gross wage		
		Minimal, $b_m/\mathbf{w}_m$	Average, $b_4/\mathbf{w}_4$	High, $b_M/\mathbf{w}_M$
Proportional	Proportional	0.544	0.544	0.544
Progressive	Proportional	0.594	0.552	0.504
Proportional	Progressive	0.564	0.564	0.507

but now—contrary to (6.2)—the benefit function has two branches:

$$b = \begin{cases} \beta v & \text{if } v \le v_1; \\ \beta[v_1 + \chi(v - v_1)] & \text{if } v > v_1. \end{cases} \tag{6.7}$$

Again $\theta = 0.15$ but with $\chi = 0.8$ and $v_1 = 1 - \tau - \theta$, $\beta = 0.829$. According to (6.5), the lowest benefit lies between the two variants, replacement rate b/v is declining from 0.829 to 0.746 as the gross wage rises from 0.5 to 2 (Table 6.3).

Finally, we construct Table 6.4 to display the gross replacement rates, reflecting the yield of a unit contribution for three wages and three systems. In both progressive systems, $b_m/\mathbf{w}_m$ is higher and $b_M/\mathbf{w}_M$ is lower than in the proportional system.

Note that in the United States, there are three rather than two progressive benefit coefficients, but they relate to gross rather than net wage and $\beta = 1$. The bend points are $\mathbf{w}_o^1$ and $\mathbf{w}_o^2$. Using $\chi_1 = 0.9$, $\chi_2 = 0.32$ and

$\chi_3 = 0.15$, in the highest interval, the benefit function is given by

$$b = \chi_1 \mathbf{w}_o^1 + \chi_2(\mathbf{w}_o^2 - \mathbf{w}_o^1) + \chi_3(\mathbf{w} - \mathbf{w}_o^2).$$

Numeric monthly values in 2017 were as follows: $\mathbf{w}_o^1 = \$885$ and $\mathbf{w}_o^2 = \$5336$, while the cap is $\bar{w} = \$10{,}600$.

6.3 Flat vs Means-Tested Pension and Pension Credit

A universal flat pension alleviates old-age poverty with modest mandatory contributions but requires complementary proportional (earnings-related) benefits to replace the income of the high-earner workers. A benefit proportional to lifetime contributions (contributive system) provides a generous relative pension for everybody but requires quite high mandatory contribution rate. If the benefit is the sum of the two pure benefits, then the resulting *flat-plus system* may correspond to both functions. Here, the lower-paid retain their incentives to work and save but the higher-paid may not. Another solution is *means-testing*. Here, the flat part is conditional and if the proportional benefit (in the income-tested variant) or the asset (in the asset-tested variant) is lower than the critical value, then the benefit is topped up to the minimum. In such a system, the high-earners retain the strong incentives to work and save, but the low-earners may have quite weak incentives to do so. To extend old-age income redistribution to young-age, a progressive personal income tax is introduced into the model.

All these systems have a common generalization: *pension credit* or tapering (e.g., Clark and Emmerson 2003). For a low proportional benefit (due to low earnings), only a fraction of it is added (i.e., credited) to the flat one, until the total benefit falls short of the proportional benefit, then this latter gives the total benefit. If the taper rate is either 0 or 1, then we have either a flat-plus or a means-tested system, respectively.

The issue of universal flat versus means-tested pensions was already discussed by Friedman and Cohen (1972): they suggested the replacement of the former by the latter, thus reducing the size of the welfare program.

In his pioneering work, Feldstein (1987) analyzed a two-type model with fully myope and life-cycler types (cf. Sect. 4.2). Cremer et al. (2008) generalized Feldstein (1987) by introducing flexible labor supply and wage heterogeneity.

Bütler et al. (2017) analyzed an important and interesting case, where our elementary approach breaks down. In Switzerland, a progressive public and a proportional private pillar coexist (both mandatory). In the first pillar annuitization is mandatory, while in the second, it is optional. Since a generous means-testing exist, low-income pensioners typically take out a lump-sum private benefit, while high-income people typically choose life annuity.

In a very sophisticated model, Sefton et al. (2008) considered the pension credit and demonstrated: this innovation raises the savings of the low-earner but reduces the others', only modestly improving the overall situation. Extending the steady-state comparisons to the complete process, Fehr et al. (2013) and Fehr and Uhde (2013) called into question these claims.

We shall combine and modify Feldstein's and Cremer et al.'s models in the following way: we assume flexible labor supply, wage heterogeneity, progressive income tax and implied earnings-related benefits, and compare proportional, means-tested, flat-plus and pension credit systems. Having a proportional pension component, we apply the means-testing and pension tapering to it rather than to the private savings.

At certain stages, analytical complications also compel us to apply numerical calculations. Our two-type result generalizes Feldstein's: means-testing may reduce the size of the optimal pension system and raise the social welfare.

We start with the core of the model and then derive closed-form solutions for conditional optimal decisions. The section closes with the outline of the macroeconomic and welfare economic framework.

The Core of the Model

The population is stationary and the individual earnings are stationary. Every young person works and every old person is retired. A worker is employed for a unit time period and a pensioner enjoys his retirement for another period of length μ, $0 < \mu \leq 1$. His total wage cost rate, for short, wage rate is a positive real w. We assume that his labor supply is a variable l, a real between 0 and T, therefore, his lifetime earning is equal to wl. Denoting the (pension) contribution rate by τ, his lifetime contribution is equal to $\tau wl > 0$ and his benefit is b to be defined below. The pension system is balanced, i.e., its revenues are equal to its expenditures.

We assume that in addition to his pension contribution, a worker pays a proportional personal income tax θw and receives a cash-back $\iota > 0$, resulting in a progressive income tax with a tax rate θ. The contribution cum tax rate is equal to $t = \tau + \theta$. In addition, the worker saves $s \geq 0$. Due to a private saving technology, as a pensioner, he will have capital ρs to dissave, where $\rho > 1$.

Obviously, the individual's young- and old-age consumption intensities are respectively

$$c = \hat{t}wl - s + \iota \quad \text{and} \quad d = b + \mu^{-1}\rho s. \tag{6.8}$$

We shall need the lifetime budget constraint, free from private saving:

$$c + \mu\rho^{-1}d = \hat{t}wl + \iota + \mu\rho^{-1}b. \tag{6.9}$$

First, we introduce the special systems of flat-plus and means-tested pensions: $b = \gamma + \beta wl$ and $b = \max[\gamma, \beta wl]$, respectively. Next, we define the generalized system, called *pension credit.* We assume that a given share of the proportional benefit βwl is deducted from the flat benefit γ until the residual drops to zero. Denoting the *taper rate* (or 1-pension credit rate) by χ, $0 \leq \chi \leq 1$, and using x_+ for the positive part of x: $x_+ = x$ if $x \geq 0$, $x_+ = 0$ otherwise, we have the formula

$$b(wl) = [\gamma - \chi\beta wl]_+ + \beta wl. \tag{6.10}$$

It is worth rewriting the formula as follows:

$$b(wl) = \max[\gamma + (1 - \chi)\beta wl, \ \beta wl].$$

In words: the benefit is equal to the maximum of two quantities: (i) the flat-plus the reduced proportional benefits and (ii) the proportional benefit.

To get rid of the notational complexities of branches, we shall introduce the simplifying notations in (6.10)

$$b(wl) = \tilde{\gamma} + \tilde{\beta} wl, \tag{6.11}$$

where

$$\tilde{\gamma} = \gamma \quad \text{and} \quad \tilde{\beta} = (1 - \chi)\beta \quad \text{if} \quad \gamma > \chi\beta wl : \quad \text{flat-plus}$$

and

$$\tilde{\gamma} = 0 \quad \text{and} \quad \tilde{\beta} = \beta \quad \text{if} \quad \gamma \le \chi\beta wl : \quad \text{proportional.}$$

Now the lifetime budget constraint (6.9) becomes

$$c + \mu\rho^{-1} d = \hat{\tau} wl + \iota + \mu\rho^{-1}(\tilde{\gamma} + \tilde{\beta} wl). \tag{6.12}$$

As was already mentioned in the introduction to this section, for $\chi = 0$, the benefit reduces to a flat-plus benefit, while for $\chi = 1$, the benefit rule reduces to means-testing.

Optimal Decisions

In this subsection, we shall determine the conditional optimal decisions. An individual's *subjective* lifetime utility function consists of two parts: (i) the worker's utility $u(c, l)$ and (ii) the pensioner's utility $\mu\delta u(d, 0)$, where δ is the discount factor, $0 \le \delta \le 1$ and μ stands for the length ratio. In formula,

$$U(c, l, d) = u(c, l) + \mu\delta u(d, 0). \tag{6.13a}$$

To simplify the calculations, we shall use Cobb–Douglas utility functions:

$$u(c, l) = \log c + \xi \log(T - l) \quad \text{and} \quad u(d, 0) = \log d + \xi \log T. \tag{6.13b}$$

At this point, we shall separate the slack and tight credit constraints: $s > 0$ and $s = 0$. We shall start with the former and continue with the latter.

Slack Credit Constraint

If a type has a slack credit constraint, then he decides on two variables, namely s and l. Insert the formulas for c and d (6.8) into (6.13a, 6.13b). Looking for the subjective optimum, take the partial derivatives of the reduced utility function

$$U[s, l] = \log(\hat{\tau} wl - s + \iota) + \xi \log(T - l)$$
$$+\mu\delta \log(\tilde{\gamma} + \tilde{\beta} wl + \mu^{-1} \rho s) \tag{6.14}$$

with respect to s and l and equate them to zero. Substituting c and d into the optimality conditions are

$$U'_s = \frac{-1}{c} + \frac{\delta\rho}{d} = 0 \tag{6.15}$$

and

$$U'_l = \frac{\hat{\tau} w}{c} - \frac{\xi}{T - l} + \frac{\mu\delta\tilde{\beta} w}{d} = 0. \tag{6.16}$$

$U'_s = 0$ implies $d = \delta\rho c$. Substituting it into $U'_l = 0$ and using the lifetime budget constraint (6.9) provides the optimal variables respectively. In details, introducing notation

$$\pi = \hat{\tau} + \mu\tilde{\beta}\rho^{-1}$$

(6.16) reduces to

$$\frac{\pi w}{c} = \frac{\xi}{T - l}. \tag{6.17}$$

Using $d = \delta\rho c$ (6.15) again and introducing notation $\tilde{\iota} = \iota + \mu\rho^{-1}\tilde{\gamma}$, (6.16) reduces to

$$(1 + \mu\delta)c = \pi wl + \tilde{\iota}. \tag{6.18}$$

Substituting the optimal labor supply l (6.17) into (6.18), c can also be eliminated:

$$l_{\mathrm{S}} = \frac{(1 + \mu\delta)\pi T - \xi\tilde{\iota}/w}{(1 + \mu\delta + \xi)\pi}.$$

Hence the S-optimal c and d obtain.

Tight Credit Constraints

In this case, the worker has only a single variable l to optimize under the constraint $d \geq \delta\rho c$. Taking the derivative of

$$U[0, l] = \log(\hat{\tau}wl + \iota) + \xi\log(T - l) + \mu\delta\log(\tilde{\gamma} + \tilde{\beta}wl)$$

with respect to l and equate it to zero yields

$$U_l' = \frac{\hat{\tau}w}{\hat{\tau}wl + \iota} - \frac{\xi}{T - l} + \frac{\mu\delta\tilde{\beta}w}{\tilde{\gamma} + \tilde{\beta}wl} = 0. \tag{6.19}$$

In general, we obtain a quadratic equation $Al^2 + Bl + C = 0$ for l^{T} (T is standing for tight) with coefficients

$$A = \hat{\tau}\tilde{\beta}w^2(1 + \mu\delta + \xi),$$

$$B = \hat{\tau}(1 + \xi)\tilde{\gamma}w + \xi\iota\tilde{\beta}w - \hat{\tau}(1 + \mu\delta)T\tilde{\beta}w^2 + \mu\delta\tilde{\beta}w\iota$$

and

$$C = \xi\iota\tilde{\gamma} - \mu\delta\tilde{\beta}w\iota T - \hat{\tau}w\tilde{\gamma}T.$$

Again, the lower root l_{T} lies in $(0, T)$ and this is the optimum.

For suitable parameter values, the optimal decisions are feasible: $s \geq 0$ and $0 < l < 1$. For given parameter values, one has to find out whether a given worker has a slack or a tight credit constraint.

Macroeconomy and Social Welfare Maximization

Having solved the individual optimization problems, we turn to the macro variables. Let $\mathbf{P}$ be the joint probability distribution of types and $\mathbf{E}$ be the corresponding expectation operator. The average total wage rate, the average labor supply, the average labor income and average benefit are respectively equal to

$$\mathbf{E}w, \qquad \mathbf{E}l, \qquad \mathbf{E}(wl), \qquad \mathbf{E}b. \tag{6.20}$$

We shall normalize the average total wage rate: $\mathbf{E}w = 1$, then the absolute constants ι and γ will be given in natural units.

The pension and the tax systems are separately balanced if

$$\tau\mathbf{E}(wl) = \mu\mathbf{E}b \quad \text{and} \quad \theta\mathbf{E}(wl) = \iota. \tag{6.21}$$

The existence of general equilibrium in this simple model is not easy to prove, especially because one type may have a slack credit constraint and another one may have a tight one. In numerical calculations, we always found the equilibrium.

Finally, we outline the government's welfare maximizing task. As a starting point, we define a *paternalistic* utility function for a typical individual as

$$U^*(c, l, d) = u(c, l) + \mu u(d, 0), \tag{6.22}$$

where the myopic discounting of $u(d, 0)$ is eliminated.

The utilitarian social welfare function is defined as the average of the paternalistic utilities, taken at the individually optimal decisions (i.e., (6.22)):

$$V(\gamma, \beta, t) = \mathbf{E}U^*(c(\gamma, \beta, t), l(\gamma, \beta, t), d(\gamma, \beta, t)).$$

The government looks for policy parameter values such that maximize the social welfare function. Since the numerical value of this function has no economic meaning, it is customary to compare two systems, say X and Y as follows. System Y has efficiency ε (a positive scalar) with respect to system X, if multiplying the wages uniformly by ε in X, then the two welfares become equal: $V_X(\varepsilon) = V_Y$.

Numerical Explorations

Since it is rather difficult to find analytic results, we explore our findings numerically. That way we obtain new quantitative results and illustrate our qualitative findings. We choose the following arbitrary parameter values: $T = 1.6$, $\rho = 1.3$ ($\rho[1] = 1.009$) and $\xi = 1.5$. We start the discussion with the representative worker and then move to the case of two types.

In the case of the representative worker, with $\delta = 0.7$ ($\delta[1] = 0.988$), the annual labor supply is $l^o = 0.758$, the socially optimal solution is $\tau^* = 1/3$, with tax rate $\theta^* = 0$, the consumption pair $c^* = d^* = 0.505$.

We turn to the case of two types, already studied in Chapter 4: $I = 2$ with low-earner: L and high-earner: H. Assume $w_L < 1 < w_H$. In conformity with reality, it is assumed that low-earners have a lower discount factor than the high-earners: $0 < \delta_L < \delta_H \leq 1$. We shall use the parameter values: $\delta_L = 0.5$ (annually: 0.977) and $\delta_H = 0.7$ (annually: 0.988); $f_L = 3/4$, and $w_L = 0.5$, $w_H = 2.5$. Tables 6.5 and 6.6 display the endogenous parameter values and the subjective optimal outcomes of the socially optimal pension credit system (row 1) and of the suboptimal means-tested system (row 2) and flat-plus one (row 3), separately.

Table 6.5 displays the optimal parameter values. Note that the optimal pension credit rate (approximately 0.75) is much closer to the means-tested value (1) than to the flat-plus (0). The former's efficiency is almost

Table 6.5 Parameters of the optimal systems: Two types

Type	Pension credit rate, χ	Accrual rate, β	Flat part, γ	Contribution rate, τ	Cashback, ι	Marginal income tax rate, θ	Relative efficiency, ε
Pension credit	0.75	0.22	0.25	0.250	0.14	0.245	1.000
Means-tested	1	0.15	0.25	0.219	0.13	0.224	0.952
Flat-plus	0	0.10	0.23	0.250	0.13	0.234	0.951

Table 6.6 Outcomes in optimal systems: Two types

Type	Low-earner			High-earner			
		Young	Old			Young	Old
	Labor, l_L^*	Consumption c_L^*	d_L^*	Labor, l_H^*	Saving, s_H^*	Consumption c_H^*	d_H^*
Pension credit	0.319	0.221	0.259	0.708	0.157	0.877	0.798
Means-tested	0.360	0.230	0.250	0.713	0.215	0.909	0.827
Flat-plus	0.360	0.223	0.248	0.675	0.146	0.856	0.779

equal to the optimal one, while the latter's is much lower: wages have to be uniformly increased by 5% in the flat-plus system to achieve the same social welfare as the pension credit. The socially optimal contribution rate oscillates: it is lowest for the means-tested system, but the efficiency is highest for the pension credit. Note the significant role of the personal income tax: $\theta^* \approx 0.23$ and $\iota^* \approx 0.13$.

Table 6.6 displays the individual outcomes: with the pension credit, the low-earner's labor supply is very low: $l_L^* = 0.32$, while that of the high-earner's is quite high: $l_H^* = 0.71$. With the means-tested system, the low-earner's labor supply is larger (0.36) than before, while the high-earner's labor supply is roughly the same (0.71). With the flat-plus system, the low-earner's labor supply remains (0.36), while the high-earner's labor supply is less (0.67). The consumption pairs vary similarly and even the low-paid's old-age consumption d_L is quite high with respect to the own share $w_L l_L/(1 + \mu)$, namely $0.25 \gg 0.5 \times 0.32/1.5 \approx 0.1$.

For other parameter values, the numbers vary, but we expect the ranking remains the same.

6.4 Conclusions

In this chapter, we analyzed progressive transfer systems. Section 6.2 compared various combinations of progressive taxation and of benefits without optimization. Section 6.3 returned to individual and social optimization and studied flat versus means-tested pensions and credit. Knowing that our results are very sensitive to the chosen functional forms, especially to that of labor disutility, we must accept these results with utmost care.

References

Bütler, M., Peijnenburg, K., & Staubli, S. (2017). How Much Do Means-Tested Benefits Reduce the Demand for Annuities. *Journal of Pension Economics and Finance, 16*, 419–449.

Clark, T., & Emmerson, C. (2003). Privatising Provision and Attacking Poverty? The Direction of UK Pension Policy Under New Labor. *Journal of Pension Economics and Finance, 2*(1), 67–89.

Cremer, H., De Donder, P., Maldonado, D., & Pestieau, P. (2008). Designing a Linear Pension Scheme with Forced Savings and Wage Heterogeneity. *International Tax and Public Finance, 15*, 547–562.

Fehr, H., & Uhde, J. (2013). On the Optimal Design of Pension Design. *Empirica, 40*, 457–482.

Fehr, H., Kallweit, M., & Kindermann, F. (2013). Should Pensions Be Progressive? *European Economic Review, 63*, 94–116.

Feldstein, M. S. (1987). Should Social Security Be Means-Tested? *Journal of Political Economy, 95*, 468–484.

Friedman, M., & Cohen, R. (1972). *Social Security: Universal or Selective*. Washington, DC: American Enterprise Institute.

Sefton, J., van de Ven, J., & Weale, M. (2008). Means Testing Retirement Benefits: Fostering Equity or Discourageing Saving? *Economic Journal, 118*, 556–590.

Simonovits, A. (2012): *Flat or Means-Tested Pensions? Pension Credit!* (IE-CERS-HAS Working Paper 21).

7

Cap on Contribution Base

7.1 Introduction

While the socially optimal replacement rate and its source, the contribution rate (cf. Chapter 5) has been widely studied, much less attention has been paid to the socially optimal choice of the *contribution (base) cap*, officially called the maximum for taxable earnings (see Simonovits 2015).[1] Such a cap (or ceiling) implies an upper limit on the mandatory pension contributions as well as on the future benefits. While the contribution rate and the degree of progressivity affect every individual, a well-designed cap only influences the higher-paid; nevertheless, the cap also deserves attention.

We give only two historical examples to illustrate poor design of the cap. (i) In the 1950s, in Great Britain the cap was fixed at the minimum wage (probably about half the average wage), degrading the usually

[1] For a summary statistics in terms of per capita GDP, see Table 1 in Valdés-Prieto and Schwarzhaupt (2011). The cap-to-gross wage-ratio is around 1.2 in Sweden and 1.8 in Germany, see OECD (2015, p. 129, Table 5.6). The usual statistics give the contribution rate as well as the cap's relative value with respect to the gross wage rather than to the total wage. Note that these rates depend on the economically meaningless break-up of contribution to employee's and employer's contributions.

A. Simonovits, *Simple Models of Income Redistribution*,
https://doi.org/10.1007/978-3-319-72502-4_7

earning-related contributions into flat ones. It was only realized much later that such a solution reduces excessively the flat-rate benefit and then was replaced by a much higher cap, making the rise of the benefit and the redistribution possible within the public system. (ii) In Hungary, the ratio of the cap to the average gross wage sank from 3.3 to 1.6 between 1992 and 1996 just to grow from 1.6 to 3.1 between 1997 and 2005. In 2013, the cap was removed.[2]

Like other experts, Barr and Diamond (2008, p. 63) mentioned two roles for the cap. (i) Under certain conditions, the cap acts as a hidden personal income tax. For example, in some countries, the cap only applies to the employee's contribution and the proportional (earnings-related) benefit, therefore, from an economic point of view the employer's contribution above the cap is a pure personal income tax.[3] Similarly, for progressive benefits, the cap limits the otherwise unbounded redistribution from the higher-paid to the lower-paid.[4] (ii) The government has no mandate to force high old-age consumption on high-earners and removing the cap would further increase the perverse redistribution from the poor to the rich caused by the strong correlation between lifetime earning and remaining life expectancy (Appendix F and Chapter 14).

To present a third role of the cap in the mandatory proportional public system, we recapitulate two widely accepted idealizations discussed in Sect. 5.2: (a) the higher the wage, the higher the discount factor and (b) any dollar saved privately rather than in a public pension system raises the old-age consumption. Then, the third role with a dual task can be formulated as follows: *the capped pension contribution ensures sufficient mandatory savings for the low-earning shortsighted but leaves sufficient room for the more efficient voluntary savings for the high-earning farsighted.* For practical reasons, it would be politically impossible to legislate different contribution rates for different types, therefore as a second-best solution,

---

[2]Note also that the cap on the contributions to the matched *voluntary* pension system is much lower and it interacts with the mandatory one; Chapter 8.

[3]In Hungary, the former contribution rate is 10% of the gross wage, while the latter oscillated around 24% until 2017. Until 2013, the uncapped contributions alone provided 6% of the total pension contributions and gave 10% of the *de facto* personal income tax.

[4]In the United States, the progressivity of the Social Security disappears above the cap, the latter being about 2.5 times the average wage recently.

the government may introduce a cap on the contributions.[5] For any fixed contribution rate, the cap reduces the *effective* contribution rate (i.e., the ratio of contribution to earning) of workers earning above the cap, making room for more private savings.[6]

Introducing the cap, the social welfare function has two rather than one independent variable: the contribution rate and the cap. To obtain sharper results than Theorem 4.3 did for the two-type model (namely the socially optimal cap is equal to the minimal wages), we use a continuous-type model framework introduced in Chapter 5. It is here that the advantage of having a continuous distribution shows up. We obtain an elementary theorem: imposing a cap equal to that wage, for which the capless saving intention disappears, is a Pareto-improvement over the capless system. We also formulate a conjecture and show by numerical calculations that *having a cap, the socially optimal replacement rate is higher than without a cap.*

Making numerical illustrations, we shall work again with the Pareto-2 distribution. Furthermore, for a sufficiently myopic population and moderate annual real interest rates, the socially optimal contribution rate is quite high and the socially optimal cap varies between 0.5 and 1.6 (in terms of the average wage, Tables 7.1 and 7.2). By pushing down the discount factor–wage curve or using alternative utility functions, the socially optimal cap can rise even higher.

Note, however, that as is usual, the utilitarian social welfare hardly changes with the cap in the relevant interval. There is a wide interval [0.75, 2], where—slightly raising the cap—the marginal gains of the lower-paid and shortsighted workers are approximately canceled by the marginal losses of the higher-paid and farsighted workers. But the cap is efficient: the government has to increase proportionally all wages by 1.1% in a capless system to have the same social welfare as in the optimal capped system with the original wages. For other parameter value vectors,

---

[5]One might object that in a number of countries, the self-employed have a significantly lower contribution rate than the employees have. Note, however, that this differentiation is connected more to the difficulty of auditing the former rather than the weaker rationality of the latter, see Chapter 3.

[6]Note also that in an imaginary world, where the discount factor is a decreasing rather than an increasing function of the wage, the cap should be replaced by a floor.

the *maximal efficiency gain* due to introducing the cap is about 0.3–4.5% with respect to the capless case.[7]

Already Valdés-Prieto and Schwarzhaupt (2011) analyzed the issue of the optimal coercion including the choice of cap. They considered a larger set of errors of judgments on remaining life span and future needs; furthermore, modeled various pension systems. They put the value of the optimal cap near the 80th percentile of the earning distribution.

Further research is needed to generalize the results for wider settings. We have already alluded to the lack of redistribution, of flexible labor supply and of the progressivity of the social welfare function in the present chapter. Deterministic and stochastic changes in the relative earnings position during one's lifetime may also be important. The dependence of type-specific life expectancy and private saving's efficiency on earning is also important in practice, and may call for progressive benefits.

Note that models of this type neglect real-life *dynamic* complications like growth, inflation and population aging. Therefore, we cannot evaluate proposals like Diamond and Orszag (2004, pp. 85–86) who would phase-in a 3% tax on incomes above the cap to reduce the long-term imbalance of the US Social Security and perverse redistribution.

The structure of the remainder is as follows. Section 7.2 presents the model, Sect. 7.3 displays numerical illustrations. Section 7.4 concludes.

7.2 Model

We return to the very simple pension model of Chapter 5, where workers only differ in wages and discount factors but their other characteristics do not vary with age. A type's important parameter is his total wage w. The average wage is normalized as $\mathbf{E}w = 1$. Workers pay contributions τw up to $\tau \bar{w}$, where $0 < \tau < 1$ is the *contribution rate* to the mandatory pension system and $\bar{w}$ is the *wage ceiling or cap.*

[7] To have an idea about these numbers, we cite two similar "German" numbers from the calibrated model of Fehr (2000, p. 436, Table 6): raising the retirement age from 60 to 62 years or reducing the replacement rate from 70 to 64% would increase the long-run welfare by 1 and 1.6%, respectively.

We shall introduce the *effective* contribution rate $\tilde{\tau}$, which is the ratio of the contribution to the wage. Distinguishing the below cap and above cap wages, we have

$$\tilde{\tau} = \begin{cases} \tau & \text{if } w \le \bar{w}; \\ \tau \bar{w}/w < \tau & \text{if } w > \bar{w}. \end{cases} \tag{7.1}$$

In a proportional system with a cap, the pension benefit is equal to the ratio of the contribution and the length ratio:

$$b = \mu^{-1} \tilde{\tau} w. \tag{7.2}$$

In addition to paying mandatory pension contributions, workers can also privately save for old-age: $s \ge 0$. The main advantage of having a cap is just to widen the scope for private saving. Denoting the compound interest factor by $\rho \ge 1$, the intensity of the decumulated saving is approximately $\mu^{-1} \rho s$.

We can now describe the young and the old-age consumption (intensities):

$$c = w - \tilde{\tau} w - s \quad \text{and} \quad d = \mu^{-1}(\tilde{\tau} w + \rho s). \tag{7.3}$$

We start with a general discounted lifetime utility function:

$$U(w, \delta, c, d) = u(c) + \mu \delta u(d), \tag{7.4}$$

where $u(\cdot)$ is an increasing and concave per-period utility (felicity) function, $u'(0) = \infty$, $u'(\infty) = 0$, and δ is the discount factor, $0 \le \delta \le 1$. Inserting (7.3) into (7.4), the optimum condition is $u'(c) = \delta \rho u'(d)$, the so-called Euler equation or having substituted (7.3)

$$u'(w - \tilde{\tau} w - \tilde{s}) = \delta \rho u'(\mu^{-1}(\tilde{\tau} w + \rho \tilde{s})). \tag{7.5}$$

This yields the optimal saving intention $\tilde{s}$. We have to distinguish two cases: either (i) nonnegative saving intention or (ii) negative saving intention. The saving intention materializes if it is positive or zero, and becomes zero otherwise: the actual saving is given by $s = \max(\tilde{s}, 0)$.

The function of the cap is as follows: lower-paid myopic workers can be locked into a pension system with a high contribution rate, but higher-paid farsighted workers pay a lower effective rate. At the same time, there is no reason to set the cap below the minimum wage, since in this case ($\bar{w} < w_{\rm m}$) by replacing the contribution rate τ by its multiple of $\bar{w}/w_{\rm m} < 1$, namely $\tau' = \tau\bar{w}/w_{\rm m} < \tau$, $(\tau, \bar{w})$ is equivalent to $(\tau', w_{\rm m})$. Therefore, we shall assume that the cap lies between the minimum and the maximum wages: $w_{\rm m} \le \bar{w} \le w_{\rm M}$.

Hence, the optimal consumption pair are

$$\begin{aligned} c(\tau, \bar{w}, w, \delta) &= w - \tilde{\tau} w - s(\tau, \bar{w}, w, \delta), \\ d(\tau, \bar{w}, w, \delta) &= \mu^{-1}[\tilde{\tau} w + \rho s(\tau, \bar{w}, w, \delta)]. \end{aligned} \tag{7.6}$$

As in Chapter 5 above, let the discount factor $\delta(w)$ be a monotone increasing function of the wage w in the interval $[w_{\rm m}, w_{\rm M}]$ with $0 < w_{\rm m} < w_{\rm M} \le \infty$ and be also continuous. Let the wage distribution have a positive density function f and a corresponding distribution function $F(w)$ with $F(w_{\rm m}) = 0$ and $F(w_{\rm M}) = 1$. Furthermore, $\delta_{\rm m} = \delta(w_{\rm m})$ and $\delta_{\rm M} = \delta(w_{\rm M})$, $0 \le \delta_{\rm m} < \delta_{\rm M} \le 1$. The social welfare function has now two rather than one variable:

$$V(\tau, \bar{w}) = \mathbf{E}U^*[\tau, \bar{w}, w] \to \max.$$

The optimum is achieved at $(\tau_{\rm C}, \bar{w}_{\rm C})$.

For a given contribution rate τ, we shall need the notion of *critical wage* w_τ (dependence on the cap $\bar{w}$ is suppressed), which makes the saving intention zero: $\tilde{s}(\tau, \bar{w}, w_\tau) = 0$. If there is no such a wage, i.e., for a high enough contribution rate, the saving intention is negative for any wage, then by definition, the critical wage is identified with the maximal wage, including ∞. For a given pair cap on the contribution base and wage, we can also speak of a critical contribution rate τ_w, defined by the implicit equation $\tilde{s}(\tau_w, \bar{w}, w) = 0$.

Note that depending on the value of the contribution rate, we have to choose between the two branches of the consumption functions:

$$c(\tau, \bar{w}, w) = \begin{cases} (1 - \tilde{\tau})w - s(\tau, \bar{w}, w) & \text{if } \tau < \tau_w; \\ (1 - \tilde{\tau})w & \text{if } \tau \geq \tau_w \end{cases} \tag{7.7}$$

and

$$d(\tau, \bar{w}, w) = \begin{cases} \mu^{-1}[\tilde{\tau}w + \rho s(\tau, \bar{w}, w)] & \text{if } \tau < \tau_w; \\ \mu^{-1}\tilde{\tau}w & \text{if } \tau \geq \tau_w \end{cases} \tag{7.8}$$

where $\tilde{\tau}$ is the effective contribution rate introduced above.

Building on the result of Chapter 5, we start with two elementary observations presented as a theorem and a conjecture. The following theorem states that introducing an appropriate cap, the social welfare can be raised with respect to the capless system.

Theorem 7.1. *Choosing the socially suboptimal contribution rate* τ_P *(the conditional optimum in the capless system), and introducing a cap equaling to the critical wage* w_{τ_P} *(where saving just disappears), the social welfare is increased:*

$$V(\tau_P, w_{\tau_P}) > V(\tau_P, w_M).$$

Proof. By definition, the introduction of this cap into the capless system, affects exactly those workers, who earn above the critical wage w_{τ_P}, and they would save from their newly found additional income more efficiently than in the mandatory public system. ■

Remark. Note that if the contribution rate were lower than the suboptimal value or the cap were lower than the critical wage, then the introduction of the corresponding cap would reduce the paternalistic welfare of those who earn close but below the critical wage. In both cases, complicated calculation would be needed to judge the welfare implications.

Next, we formulate a conjecture comparing the optimal contribution rates of the capless and the capped systems and providing an upper bound on the optimal cap.

Conjecture 7.1. *Assume that the suboptimal contribution rate in the capless system is lower than the maximum:* $0 < \tau_{\mathrm{P}} < \bar{\tau}$. *Then the socially optimal contribution rate* τ_{C} *in the capped system is higher than the suboptimum:* $\tau_{\mathrm{P}} < \tau_{\mathrm{C}} \leq \bar{\tau}$ *and the optimal cap* $\bar{w}_{\mathrm{C}}$ *is lower than the critical wage in the capless system:* $\bar{w}_{\mathrm{C}} < w_{\tau_{\mathrm{P}}}$.

The easiest way to visualize the conjecture is as follows: raise the cap continuously from w_{m} to w_{M} and determine the conditionally optimal contribution rate $\tau_{\bar{w}}$. One expects that the resulting function is decreasing and before reaching τ_{P} it goes though the unconditionally optimal τ_{C} at $\bar{w}_{\mathrm{C}}$.

In the simplest case, when there are only two types and both have a Cobb–Douglas utility function, Theorem 4.3 gave such a result: $\bar{w}_{\mathrm{C}} = w_{\mathrm{L}} < w_{\tau_{\mathrm{P}}}$. It can easily be generalized to arbitrary utility functions but its extension to multi-type models seems to be difficult.

It is not enough to determine the social optimum, we have to evaluate the efficiency gain of having a pension system $(\tau, \bar{w})$ with respect to having no cap. Since the numerical value of V has no direct meaning, we define the *relative efficiency* ε of $(\tau, \bar{w})$ with respect to $(\tau_{\mathrm{P}}, w_{\mathrm{M}})$ as follows: multiplying the earnings by a positive scalar ε such that the social welfare of the optimal capless system is the same as the social welfare of the optimal cap with the original wages. Denoting the dependence of the welfare on the (average) wage ε, we have the following definition for efficiency:

$$V[\varepsilon, \tau_{\mathrm{P}}, w_{\mathrm{M}}] = V[1, \tau, \bar{w}].$$

Due to the specific utility function, $(1 + \mu) \log \varepsilon$ can be separated in the LHS, i.e.,

$$V[1, \tau_{\mathrm{P}}, w_{\mathrm{M}}] + (1 + \mu) \log \varepsilon = V[1, \tau_{\mathrm{C}}, \bar{w}_{\mathrm{C}}],$$

i.e.,

$$\varepsilon_{\mathrm{C|P}} = \exp \frac{V[1, \tau_{\mathrm{C}}, \bar{w}_{\mathrm{C}}] - V[1, \tau_{\mathrm{P}}, w_{\mathrm{M}}]}{1 + \mu}.$$

7.3 Numerical Illustrations

Even though our framework is very elementary, our problem is quite involved, therefore, we turn to numerical illustrations, building on Sect. 5.3. We calculate the dependency of the relative efficiency with respect to no-pension on the cap in the interval $[0, w_{\rm M}]$ with the optimal contribution rate $\tau_{\rm C} = 0.33$; for $\rho[1] = 1.04$ and $\eta = 0.2$. (Note that in this example, where the contribution rate τ is given, we have to consider also caps below the minimum wage.) With the rise of the cap, the relative efficiency (in terms of no-pension) quickly rises above 1.41 at the minimum wage $w_{\rm m} = 0.5$, it reaches its maximum 1.433 at the average wage and then slowly decline to 1.417 at $\bar{w} = w_{\rm M} = \infty$.

By Conjecture 7.1, the introduction of the cap raises the optimal contribution rate with respect to the capless case. Comparing Tables 7.1 to 5.3, our conjecture is confirmed. When the share of myopes decreases, represented as η rising from 0.1 to 0.7, the socially optimal contribution stays close to the maximal one rather than dropping, while the socially optimal cap drops from 1.46 to 0.5. (For $\eta = 0.04$, not shown in Table 7.1, the socially optimal cap even rises to 3.6!) Calculating the relative efficiency of the capped system in terms of the corresponding mandatory pension system rather than in terms of no-pension, the indicator steeply rises.

Table 7.1 The socially optimal contribution rate and cap, changing elasticity

Wage elasticity of discount factor, η	Contribution rate, $\tau_{\rm C}$	Cap, $\bar{w}_{\rm C}$	Expected saving, ${\rm E}s_{\rm C}$	Relative efficiency, $\varepsilon_{\rm C\|P}$
0.1	0.333	1.46	0.028	1.004
0.2	0.333	0.92	0.048	1.011
0.3	0.333	0.70	0.065	1.020
0.4	0.333	0.61	0.079	1.026
0.5	0.335	0.55	0.090	1.032
0.6	0.330	0.51	0.100	1.036
0.7	0.321	0.50	0.109	1.039

Remark. $\rho[1] = 1.04$

Table 7.2 The socially optimal contribution rate and the cap, changing interest factor

Annual interest factor, $\rho[1]$	Contribution rate, τ_C	Cap, $\bar{w}_C$	Expected saving, $\mathbf{E}s_C$	Relative efficiency, $\varepsilon_{C\|P}$
1.02	0.333	1.720	0.033	1.002
1.03	0.333	1.190	0.041	1.005
1.04	0.333	0.920	0.048	1.011
1.05	0.333	0.720	0.055	1.021
1.06	0.332	0.590	0.060	1.032
1.07	0.330	0.510	0.064	1.043
1.08	0.300	0.500	0.067	1.049

Remark. $\eta = 0.2$

Finally, we check the impact of the interest factor ρ for a fixed elasticity of discounting, again $\eta = 0.2$. As the annual interest factor rises from 1.02 to 1.08 in Table 7.2, the socially optimal contribution rate drops slowly from 0.333 to 0.321. The decrease in the socially optimal cap starts immediately: from 1.72 to the minimum wage, namely 0.5. The relative efficiency of the capped system with respect to the corresponding mandatory pension steeply rises.

We have not yet commented the changes in saving as a result of imposing a cap (last columns of Tables 7.1 and 7.2 with respect to Tables 5.3 and 5.4). Typically, the socially optimal expected saving is higher than the suboptimal one: $\mathbf{E}s_C > \mathbf{E}s_P$.

7.4 Conclusions

In summary, by generalizing the model used in Chapter 5, we were able to demonstrate numerically that the introduction of a cap on the pension contribution base leaves more space to mandatory public pensions for low-earners. Some results (especially on the optimal contribution rate) are quite robust, while other results (notably on the socially optimal cap) are very sensitive to the key parameters of the model, namely to the discount factor–wage elasticity (η) and the interest factor (ρ).

References

Barr, N., & Diamond, P. (2008). *Reforming Pensions: Principles and Policy Choices.* Oxford: Oxford University Press.

Diamond, P. A., & Orszag, P. (2004). *Saving Social Security: A Balanced Approach.* Washington, DC: Brookings Institution.

Fehr, H. (2000). Pension Reform During the Demographic Transition. *Scandinavian Journal of Economics, 102*, 419–443.

OECD. (2015). *Glance at Pensions.* Paris.

Simonovits, A. (2015). Socially Optimal Contribution Rate and Cap in a Proportional Pension System. *Portuguese Economic Journal, 14*, 45–63.

Valdés-Prieto, S., & Schwarzhaupt, U. (2011). *Optimal Compulsion when Behavioural Biases Vary and the State Errs* (CESifo Working Paper 3316).

8

Voluntary Pension System

8.1 Introduction

In most developed countries, in addition to the mandatory (funded and/or unfunded, public or private) pension system, a voluntary pension system exists, based on tax and contribution subsidies.[1] The voluntary pension system is formed by individual *retirement accounts.* In the default case, these subsidized savings cannot be withdrawn until the owner retires. The proponents of such systems justify these subsidies as follows: a mandatory system does not and need not ensure high enough pensions, and the partially myopic (for short, myopic) workers have to be made interested in raising their old-age incomes through a voluntary system. The opponents are afraid that these subsidies are poorly targeted, mostly subsidize the high-earning savers, while worsening the burden of the others (low-earning myopes) by increasing the *tax expenditures.* Up to now these tax expenditures have generally been relatively low, thus they may be neglected, but under a possible contraction of the mandatory system (like is planned in Germany recently) they may become much higher and

[1]OECD (2005), Hinz et al. (2013) provide useful overviews.

A. Simonovits, *Simple Models of Income Redistribution*,
https://doi.org/10.1007/978-3-319-72502-4_8

then cannot be neglected. Baily and Kirkegaard (2009, p. 10) emphasized that "[t]he value of the tax breaks given to pensioners is very high in the US ... 1% of the GDP."

In this chapter, we will discuss the issue in a joint generalization of Sect. 4.5 (two-types with matched saving (cf. Simonovits 2011)) and Chapter 5 (continuous types without matched saving) but still do not investigate explicit redistribution in either pillar. Since there are no other taxes in the model, we will write earmarked taxes rather than tax expenditures, as if a special tax financed the subsidies.

Our model is a faithful description of the Hungarian system, where both pillars are basically proportional (earnings-related). In contrast, in the United States, the mandatory system is progressive and the voluntary is proportional.[2] Germany represents another combination, where the public system is proportional but the voluntary is progressive.[3]

More complex theoretical models were used by Imrohoroğlu et al. (1995), Fehr et al. (2008), Fehr and Habermann (2010). The latter pointed out the uncertainty of earning paths and longevity, and quantified the reduced quality of insurance following the setting up a voluntary pension pillar (cf. Sect. 3.3 without matching). Admitting the virtues of these complex models, we still hope that our toy model has its own advantage of being simple but illuminating.

The papers mentioned above followed an orthodox approach, because they heavily rely on time-consistency: as there is no new information or lack of will-power, the workers do not change their saving behavior with the passage of time. The present chapter also belongs to this group, it only deviates from orthodoxy by eliminating subjective discounting in the social welfare function.[4]

---

[2]Among the large number of US studies, we single out the following ones: Poterba et al. (1996) estimated that the introduction of tax-favored retirement accounts significantly increased total savings, while Engen et al. (1996) found the opposite. Trying at a synthesis, Hubbard and Skinner (1996) guessed that both trends are present but the positive trend outweighs the negative. Note that all the three studies identify savings and social welfare; further, they concentrate on the former rather than on the latter.

[3]Börsch-Supan et al. (2008), Pfarr and Schneider (2013).

[4]Thaler and Benartzi (2004, p. S164) invented a new program based on behavioral economics: "people commit in advance to allocate a portion of their future salary increases toward retirement savings." Heterodox models (e.g., Laibson 1997; Diamond and Kőszegi 2003; Findley and Caliendo 2009) employed hyperbolic discounting when explaining and evaluating the voluntary pension

Using behavioral economics, Choi et al. (2004) also found a quite unorthodox behavior: if the default option is changed, and the new employees are automatically enrolled into a pension fund, from which they can opt-out, then a much higher share will stay in the voluntary pillar than in the original default. Being partial equilibrium models, however, the latter models neglect the tax burden of such schemes, a central issue of this chapter.

The structure of the remainder of the present chapter is as follows: Sect. 8.2 presents the model and Sect. 8.3 displays the numerical illustrations. Section 8.4 concludes.

8.2 Model

In this section, we outline the model. First, we determine the optimal voluntary contributions and savings chosen by the individual workers, then we analyze the macrorelations and the welfare provided by various mandatory and voluntary systems.

Maximizing Individual Utility

We shall make the following extreme, nevertheless meaningful assumptions. The population and the economy are stationary. Every young-aged individual works and every old-aged individual is retired. Every worker is employed for a unit time period and every pensioner enjoys his retirement for a period of length μ, $0 < \mu < 1$. (In practice, the more one earns, the longer he lives on average (cf. Appendix F); and the retirement age depends on the pension system, but we neglect these relations.) We assume that a worker with wage w pays a positive mandatory contribution τw, where $\tau > 0$ is the mandatory contribution rate. (Contrary to Chapter 7, for simplicity, we neglect the cap on the mandatory contributions.)

pillar. To give a simple example: a worker plans to pay monthly voluntary contributions of 100 dollars during 480 months to get additional pension benefit of 200 dollars during 240 months. But he immediately realizes that if he skips the first month voluntary contribution, then his monthly benefit is only reduced by 46 cents, therefore he may safely skip the first month. But what happens if he goes on in the second, third etc. month? Homburg (2006) considered the problem of rational prodigals, and assuming endogenous labor supply, he argued for wage taxes and saving subsidies rather than mandatory pension as a second-best solution.

We assume that some types prefer additional old-age benefits over the mandatory ones, therefore they pay a *voluntary contribution* z over the mandatory contribution, where $z \in [0, \bar{z}]$, and $\bar{z} \geq 0$ is the *cap* on voluntary contribution. The government matches the voluntary contribution z according to $a = \alpha z$ but only up to $\alpha \bar{z}$.[5]

The pension paid as a life annuity consists of two terms: the earnings-related mandatory benefit $b = \mu^{-1}\tau w$ and the voluntary pension $\mu^{-1}\rho(1+\alpha)z$.[6]

Finally, there may exist types for whom even the maximal voluntary contribution $\bar{z}$ and the corresponding maximal subsidy $\bar{a} = \alpha \bar{z}$ are insufficient. These types can *traditionally save* an additional sum, denoted by $s \geq 0$. We assume that the efficiency of this traditional saving is the same as that of the mandatory pillar, i.e., the corresponding life annuity from private saving is $\mu^{-1}\rho[(1+\alpha)z + s]$.[7] In addition, the worker with wage w pays an *earmarked tax* θw into the budget, financing the subsidization of the voluntary pensions, where $\theta \geq 0$ is the earmarked tax rate.

The (intensities of) the young- and old-age consumption are, respectively, equal to

$$c = \hat{t}w - z - s \quad \text{and} \quad d = \mu^{-1}\{\tau w + \rho[z(1+\alpha) + s]\}, \tag{8.1}$$

where $\hat{t} = 1 - \tau - \theta$ stands for the net-of-tax-cum-contribution rate. Both c and d are positive.

We turn to the individual optimization. As in Chapters 5 and 7, we assume that the discount factor–wage function $\delta(w)$ is increasing, and $0 \leq \delta(w_{\mathrm{m}}) < \delta(w_{\mathrm{M}}) \leq 1$.

---

[5]This form is economically equivalent to the credit rebate. (Indeed, if the government immediately returns $a = \alpha z$ from the extended voluntary contribution z, then this is equivalent to a related system, where the voluntary contribution is only $z - a$ but the government adds *matching* a to the account. Saez (2009) analyzed the practical impact of this apparent difference.)

[6]As a matter of fact, voluntary pensions are seldom paid as life annuities, but this fact is irrelevant here, because we do not discuss the path and risk of consumption in the retirement period (cf. Sect. 3.3).

[7]Note that in our model, even the traditional savings are used up as if they were life annuities.

The *subjective* lifetime utility function of type w consists of two terms: (i) the utility $u(\cdot)$ of worker's consumption c and (ii) the utility $\mu\delta(w)u(d)$ of the pensioner's consumption d. In sum:

$$U(w, c, d) = u(c) + \mu\delta u(d). \tag{8.2}$$

The individual determines the voluntary contribution $z(w)$ and the traditional saving $s(w)$ by maximizing his lifetime utility $U(w, c, d)$ under the lifetime budget constraint. Again, we assume that each worker takes the earmarked tax rate as given, i.e., does not consider the indirect impact of his or others' choices. Substituting the consumption equations (8.1) into U [(8.2)], provides the reduced subjective utility:

$$U[w, z, s] = u(\hat{\tau} w - z - s) + \mu\delta(w)u(\mu^{-1}\{\tau w + \rho[(1+\alpha)z + s]\}). \tag{8.3}$$

The worker determines his *optimal* voluntary contribution $z(w)$ and traditional saving $s(w)$ by taking the partial derivatives with respect to decisions z and s. We have to take into account the possibility of corner solutions.

Lemma 8.1. *The different domains' nontrivial optimality conditions are as follows.*
Zero voluntary contribution, zero saving; $z = 0, s = 0$*:*

$$U'_z[w, 0, 0] = -u'(c) + \delta(w)\rho u'(d)(1+\alpha) \le 0. \tag{8.4A}$$

Positive voluntary contribution below cap, zero saving; $0 < z < \bar{z}, s = 0$*:*

$$U'_z[w, z, 0] = -u'(c) + \delta(w)\rho u'(d)(1+\alpha) = 0. \tag{8.4B}$$

Maximal voluntary contribution, zero saving; $z = \bar{z}, s = 0$*:*

$$U'_s[w, \bar{z}, 0] = -u'(c) + \delta(w)\rho u'(d) \le 0. \tag{8.4C}$$

Maximal voluntary contribution, positive saving; $z = \bar{z}, s > 0$*:*

$$U'_s[w, \bar{z}, s] = -u'(c) + \delta(w)\rho u'(d) = 0. \tag{8.4D}$$

Remarks. 1. The obvious conditions $U_s'[w, 0, 0] \leq 0$, $U_s'[w, z, 0] \leq 0$, $U_z'[w, \bar{z}, 0] \geq 0$ and $U_z'[w, \bar{z}, s] \geq 0$ are omitted in (8.4*A*)–(8.4*D*), respectively.

2. The classification is endogenous, and depending on the parameter values, certain domains can be empty.

Macro Framework

As in Chapters 5 and 7, the workers have a single independent characteristic: wage w. We assume that the probability distribution is given by F and its expectation by $\mathbf{E}w = 1$.

The transfer system has uniform mandatory contribution rate τ and earmarked tax rate θ, where every worker's mandatory contribution finances his own future pensions $(\mu^{-1}\tau w)$, while the earmarked taxes finance the subsidies on average. In formula:

$$\theta = \alpha \mathbf{E}z(w). \tag{8.5}$$

We also need the total savings, i.e., the aggregate voluntary savings (m), including the matching plus the aggregate traditional savings:

$$\mathbf{E}m = (1 + \alpha)\mathbf{E}z(w) + \mathbf{E}s(w). \tag{8.6}$$

A benevolent government determines the control vector $(\tau, \theta, \alpha, \bar{z})$ as to maximize an appropriately defined social welfare function subject to (8.5). First of all, the government removes discounting, and replaces subjective with *paternalistic* utility functions:

$$U^*(w, c, d) = u(c(w)) + \mu u(d(w)). \tag{8.7}$$

The utilitarian social welfare function is the average of the *undiscounted* individual objective utility functions, taken at the subjective optima:

$$V(\tau, \theta, \alpha, \bar{z}) = \mathbf{E}U^*(w, c(w), d(w)). \tag{8.8}$$

We shall use again a Cobb–Douglas (or logarithmic) utility function: $u(x) = \log x$.

To delineate the four possible domains, we shall introduce the separator wages w_A, w_B and w_C. It is obvious that $w_B \le w_C$ but to avoid complications we also assume that $w_A < w_B$ holds, then the savers in $[w_A, w_B]$ do not reach the cap.

Then Lemma 8.1 simplifies to

Lemma 8.2. *For the Cobb–Douglas-utility function and any given control vector* $(\tau, \theta, \alpha, \bar{z})$, *the regions are separated by wages* w_A, w_B *and* w_C *as follows:*

$$\delta(w_A) = \frac{\tau}{\mu(1+\alpha)\hat{t}}, \qquad \delta(w_B) = \frac{\tau w_B \rho^{-1} + (1+\alpha)\bar{z}}{(\hat{t} w_B - \bar{z})(1+\alpha)\mu},$$
$$\delta(w_C) = \frac{\tau w_C \rho^{-1} + (1+\alpha)\bar{z}}{(\hat{t} w_C - \bar{z})\mu}.$$

Zero voluntary contribution, zero saving, $w_m \le w < w_A$*:*

$$z(w) = 0, \qquad s(w) = 0. \tag{8.9A}$$

Positive voluntary contribution, zero saving, $w_A \le w < w_B$*:*

$$z(w) = \frac{\delta(w)(1+\alpha)\hat{t} - \mu^{-1}\rho^{-1}\tau}{(1+\alpha)[\mu^{-1} + \delta(w)]} w \in [0, \bar{z}), \qquad s(w) = 0. \tag{8.9B}$$

Maximal voluntary contribution, zero saving, $w_B \le w \le w_C$*:*

$$z(w) = \bar{z}, \qquad s(w) = 0. \tag{8.9C}$$

Maximal voluntary contribution, positive saving, $w_C < w \le w_M$*:*

$$z(w) = \bar{z}, \qquad s(w) = \frac{\delta(w)(\hat{t}w - \bar{z}) - \mu^{-1}[\tau w \rho^{-1} + (1+\alpha)\bar{z}]}{\mu^{-1} + \delta(w)}, \tag{8.9D}$$

Proof. We first discuss cases B and D with *variable* voluntary contribution or saving, respectively, and then the remaining cases A and C are trivial.

(B) Inserting equations $d = \mu^{-1}\tau w + \mu^{-1}\rho(1+\alpha)z$ and $c = \hat{t}w - z$ [(8.1)] into $d = \delta(w)\rho(1+\alpha)c$ [(8.4B)], yields

$$\mu^{-1}\tau w + \mu^{-1}\rho(1+\alpha)z = \delta(w)\rho(1+\alpha)(\hat{t}w - z).$$

Solving for z yields the optimal voluntary contribution (8.9B). Checking for $0 \le z \le \bar{z}$, defines domain B with two separator wages w_A and w_B, respectively.

(D) Inserting equations $d = \mu^{-1}\{\tau w + \rho[(1+\alpha)\bar{z} + s]\}$ and $c = \hat{t}w - \bar{z} - s$ into equation $d = \delta(w)\rho c$ (8.4D) yields

$$\mu^{-1}\{\tau w + \rho[(1+\alpha)\bar{z} + s]\} = \delta(w)\rho(\hat{t}w - \bar{z} - s).$$

Solving for s, yields the optimal saving (8.9D). Checking for $s > 0$, defines domain D with the third separator wage w_C.

Domains A and C are defined by exclusion. ■

Having Lemma 8.2, we can now return to the balance equation (8.5). Denoting the shares of types A, B, C and D by P_A, P_B, P_C and P_D respectively and the conditional expectation of the voluntary contributions by $\mathbf{E}[z(w)|B]$, (8.5) reduces to

$$\theta = \alpha[P_B\mathbf{E}[z(w)|B] + (P_C + P_D)\bar{z}]. \tag{8.10}$$

(The distinction between C and D is only relevant at calculating the utilities.)

To evaluate the income redistribution from the lower-earners to the higher-earners, it is worth considering the ratio of the earmarked tax rate to the maximal matching: $\theta/(\alpha\bar{z})$. This ratio lies between 0 and 1, and the lower the ratio, the stronger the redistribution within the voluntary system. Following Chapters 5 and 7, we allow for a continuum of types, with a smoothly increasing function $\delta(w)$. We have only very elementary analytical results.

Fixing the transfer rates $0 \le \tau \le \bar{\tau}$ and $\theta > 0$, for any matching rate $\alpha > 0$ denote $\bar{z}(\alpha)$ that cap which is consistent with (8.10). It is easy to see that $\bar{z}(\alpha)$ is a decreasing function. In practice, there exists frequently an upper bound on α, namely 1.

The higher the matching rate, the lower the w_A and the higher the w_B. Therefore fixing the transfer rates, raising α shifts the matched saving of the lower earners and decreases that of the higher-earners.

Conjecture 8.1. *For any pair of transfer rates* (τ, θ), *the socially optimal matching rate is maximal:* $\alpha^* = 1$ *and the corresponding cap* $\bar{z}(1)$ *is minimal.*

8.3 Numerical Illustrations

We continue the analysis with numerical illustrations. Following the convention of the book, we assume that the time spent at retirement is half as long as that of working: $\mu = 1/2$, the wage distribution is of Pareto-type with $w_{\mathrm{m}} = 1/2$. Impose the discount factor–wage function

$$\delta(w) = \delta_{\mathrm{M}} - (\delta_{\mathrm{M}} - \delta_{\mathrm{m}})e^{\eta(w_{\mathrm{m}}-w)}, \tag{5.13}$$

with $\delta_{\mathrm{m}} = 0$ and $\delta_{\mathrm{M}} = 1$. Basically, we follow the logic of Chapter 5 in general and replicate Tables 5.2 and 5.3 in particular. Luckily, the trial-and-error method (Appendix C) works for the determination of the balanced earmarked tax rate.

First, we discuss the sensitivity of the social optimum to the distribution of myopia, more precisely, to the elasticity η of the discount factor to the wage. Fixing the interest factor at $\rho[1] = 1.04$ and the matching rate at $\alpha = 1$ we shall vary η from 0.1 to 0.7. Table 8.1 shows that the socially optimal public contribution rate drops much faster than previously (in Table 5.2). At the same time, the socially optimal cap on the voluntary contributions oscillates around 0.1, probably due to rounding errors. Note that the expected saving, $\mathbf{E}m$ rises quite fast, as the elasticity grows. So does the earmarked tax rate: it grows from 0 to 0.061! As the wage elasticity rises, the relative efficiency of the voluntary system in terms of the corresponding proportional one rises steeply.

In Table 8.2, we discuss the sensitivity of the outcomes to the interest factor. For a fixed $\eta = 0.2$, as the annual interest factor $\rho[1]$ rises from 1.02 to 1.08, the socially optimal public contribution rate drops from 0.33 to 0. At the same time, the voluntary system only emerges at $\rho[1] = 1.03$,

Table 8.1 The socially optimal rates, changing elasticity

Wage elasticity discount factor, η	Mandatory contribution rate, τ_V^*	Cap on voluntary contribution, $\bar{z}^*$	Earmarked tax rate, θ^*	Expected total saving, $\mathrm{E}m^*$	Voluntary relative efficiency, $\varepsilon_{V\|P}$
0.1	0.32	0.12	0.004	0.010	1.003
0.2	0.30	0.07	0.007	0.023	1.008
0.3	0.27	0.06	0.011	0.039	1.015
0.4	0.20	0.10	0.024	0.071	1.025
0.5	0.13	0.12	0.037	0.106	1.042
0.6	0	0.14	0.057	0.164	1.072
0.7	0	0.14	0.061	0.174	1.098

Remark. $\rho[1] = 1.04$, $\alpha = 1$

Table 8.2 The socially optimal rates, changing interest factor

Annual interest factor, $\rho[1]$	Mandatory contribution rate, τ_V^*	Cap on voluntary contribution, $\bar{z}^*$	Earmarked tax rate, θ^*	Expected total saving, $\mathrm{E}m^*$	Voluntary relative efficiency, $\varepsilon_{V\|P}$
1.02	0.33	0	0	0.004	1.002
1.03	0.32	0.08	0.005	0.015	1.003
1.04	0.30	0.07	0.007	0.023	1.008
1.05	0.26	0.07	0.011	0.035	1.018
1.06	0.19	0.12	0.020	0.056	1.039
1.07	0	0.15	0.035	0.095	1.094
1.08	0	0.15	0.035	0.095	1.094

Remark. $\eta = 0.2$ and $\alpha = 1$, for ε_P, see Table 5.3

the corresponding cap rises from 0 to 0.15. Note the fast-rising earmarked tax rate: it grows from 0 to 0.035! The relative efficiency of the socially optimal multipillar pension system with respect to the mandatory one also steeply rises. The error in row 1 ($\varepsilon_{V|P} = 1.002$) stems from rounding.

The discontinuity foreshadows that similarly to the jump of the gap (Appendix I to Chapter 11), there are two branches of local optima, and the global one jumps from one to another. Considering Table 8.1, we see that around this critical value, of elasticity $\eta = 0.5$ (for $\rho[1] = 1.04$), Table 8.3 shows that there is a *plateau*, where the social welfare is practically insensitive to the value of public contribution rate and the

Table 8.3 Plateau of efficiency in the parameter space

Mandatory contribution rate, τ	Cap on voluntary contribution, $\bar{z}$	Earmarked tax rate, θ	Expected total saving, Em	Relative efficiency, $\varepsilon_{V\|P}$
0.0	0.1	0.045	0.156	1.164
	0.2	0.062	0.171	1.165
0.1	0.1	0.036	0.121	1.167
	0.2	0.050	0.135	1.166
0.2	0.1	0.028	0.090	1.165
	0.2	0.039	0.102	1.161

Remark. $\rho[1] = 1.04$, $\eta = 0.5$ and $\alpha = 1$

cap on voluntary contributions. (Similar plateau exists around a critical value of elasticity $\rho[1] = 1.06$ (for $\eta = 0.2$).) Indeed, quite different parameter sets with no public pension or strong public pension produce practically the same optimal welfare. Note that here our base is not the optimal proportional pension but the no-pension at all.

8.4 Conclusions

Voluntary pension systems appear very attractive because their use avoids coercion. However, if one takes into account that matched contributions have to be financed by earmarked taxes, part of this attraction disappears. Using proportional mandatory and voluntary pension systems, we tried to find the optimal cap and the optimal matching rate. Further models are needed to tell us: what is the optimal structure, especially leaving the realm of proportional pillars?

References

Baily, M. N., & Kirkegaard, J. F. (2009). *US Pension Reform: Lessons from other Countries.* Washington, DC: Petersons Books.

Börsch-Supan, A., Reil-Held, A., & Schunk, D. (2008). Saving Incentives, Old-Age Provision and Displacement Effects: Evidence from the Recent German Pension Reform. *Journal of Pension Economics and Finance, 7*, 295–319.
Choi, J., Laibson, D., Madrian, B., & Metrick, A. (2004). For Better or Worse: Default Effects and 401(k) Saving Behavior. In D. Wise (Ed.), *Perspectives in the Economics of Aging* (pp. 81–121). Chicago: University of Chicago Press.
Diamond, P., & Kőszegi, B. (2003). Quasi-hyperbolic Discounting and Retirement. *Journal of Public Economics, 87*, 1839–1872.
Engen, E. M., Gale, W. G., & Scholz, J. (1996). The Illusory Effects of Saving Incentives on Saving. *Journal of Economic Perspectives, 10*(4), 111–138.
Fehr, H., & Habermann, C. (2010). Private Retirement Savings and Mandatory Annuatization. *International Tax and Public Finance, 17*, 640–661.
Fehr, H., Habermann, C., & Kindermann, F. (2008). Tax-Favored Retirement Accounts: Are They Efficient in Increasing Savings and Growth? *FinanzArchiv, Public Finance Analysis, 64*, 171–198.
Findley, T. S., & Caliendo, F. N. (2009). Short Horizons, Time Inconsistency, and Optimal Social Security. *International Tax and Public Finance, 16*, 487–513.
Hinz, R., Holzmann, R., Tuesta, D., & Takayama, N. (2013). *Matching Contributions for Pensions.* Washington, DC: World Bank.
Homburg, S. (2006). Coping with Rational Prodigal: A Theory of Social Security and Saving Subsidies. *Economica, 73*, 47–58.
Hubbard, R. G., & Skinner, J. S. (1996). Assessing the Effectiveness of Saving Incentives. *Journal of Economic Perspectives, 10*(4), 73–90.
Imrohoroğlu, A., Imrohoroğlu, S., & Joines, D. H. (1995). A Life Cycle Model of Social Security. *Economic Theory, 6*, 83–114.
Laibson, D. (1997). Golden Eggs and Hyperbolic Discounting. *Quarterly Journal of Economics, 112*, 443–477.
OECD. (2005). *Tax-Favored Retirement Saving.* OECD Economic Studies (Vol. 39), Paris.
Pfarr, C., & Schneider, U. (2013). Choosing Between Subsidized and Unsubsidized Private Pension Schemes: Evidence from German Panel Data. *Journal of Pension Economics and Finance, 12*, 62–91.
Poterba, J. M., Venti, S. F., & Wise, D. A. (1996). How Retirement Saving Program Increase Saving. *Journal of Economic Perspectives, 10*(4), 91–112.
Saez, E. (2009). Details Matter: The Impact of Presentation and Information on the Take-Up of Financial Incentives for Retirement Savings. *American Economic Journal: Economic Policy, 1*(1), 204–228.
Simonovits, A. (2011). When Are Voluntary Pensions Indifferent? *Economics Letters, 111*, 153–155.

Thaler, R. H., & Benartzi, S. (2004). Save More Tomorrow: Using Behavioral Economics to Increase Employee Saving. *Journal of Political Economy, 112*, S164–S187.

9

Flexible vs. Seniority Pension Systems

9.1 Introduction

Except for Appendix F, until now we have fixed the ages of starting to work, of retirement and of death; and assumed that it is the same for every worker. In this chapter, we discuss how workers with different labor disutilities and life expectancies choose their own retirement ages under various schemes. This choice is a central issue in any pension system, and it is more and more so as the population ages, especially as the life expectancy at retirement rises (cf. Tables 1.12 and 1.13). A further complication is the widespread emergence of fragmented working careers and seniority pensions. This chapter will model these problems. We shall neglect private savings, discounting the future and heterogeneity in wages.

We only give a very short review of the related literature. Buchanan (1968) discovered the idea of *nonfinancial defined contribution* (NDC), where an unfunded public pension system emulates a funded private system. (For recent experiences with NDC, see Holzmann and Palmer 2006; Holzmann et al. 2012). Sheshinski (1978) and Crawford and Lilien (1981) were among the pioneers to determine the individually optimal retirement age (for its classic treatment, see Stock and Wise 1990; Rust and Phelan

A. Simonovits, *Simple Models of Income Redistribution*,
https://doi.org/10.1007/978-3-319-72502-4_9

1997). Gruber and Wise (1999) called attention to the impact of pension incentives and disincentives on the labor market.

A long line of papers (e.g., Fabel 1994; Diamond 2003; Eső and Simonovits 2002; Eső et al. 2011; Simonovits 2006; Bommier et al. 2006) used the tool of mechanism design to construct socially optimal and incentive compatible flexible retirement schedules for populations with heterogeneous life expectancies, when the government has no information on who has what life expectancy. Barr and Diamond (2008) underlined the importance of efficiency *and* equity. Augusztinovics and Köllő (2008, 2009) emphasized the detrimental influence of fragmented labor market careers on defined contribution pensions. Czeglédi et al. (2017) critically studied two features of the Hungarian public pension system: The seniority system for females and the elimination of early retirement, even with due deduction. Interestingly, Le Garrec and Lhuissier (2017) also modeled seniority systems but overemphasizing the role of human capital accumulation, mistakenly deplored early retirement for manual workers.

The structure of the remaining part of the chapter is as follows: Sects. 9.2 and 9.3 present the standard models of flexible (variable) retirement without fragmentation for heterogeneous labor disutilities and life expectancies, respectively (cf. also Simonovits 2003, 114–131). Section 9.4 extends the latter to seniority systems with fragmentation. Section 9.5 concludes. Appendix G generalizes the analytical results of Sect. 9.2 to realistic survival functions (cf. Banyár 2012; Simonovits 2015) and the linear benefit of Sect. 9.4 to the NDC.

9.2 Flexible Systems: Homogeneous Life Expectancy

In this section, we only consider workers with homogeneous life expectancy with uniform wage $w = 1$, who may differ in their labor disutilities. Let positive reals Q, R and D denote the ages of starting to work, of retirement and of death, respectively: $0 < Q < R < D$. (In our usual parameterization, $Q = 0$, $R = 1$ and $D = 1 + \mu$.)

It is assumed that an individual works from age Q until age R (retirement). Let R_{m} and R_{M} stand for the minimal and the maximal retirement ages, respectively: $Q < R_{\mathrm{m}} < R_{\mathrm{M}} < D$. A sufficiently high minimal retirement age prevents workers from too early retirement and poverty; while a sufficiently low maximal retirement age removes dead wood from serving without limit. The worker pays a contribution rate $\tau > 0$ while working and receives a lifetime benefit (lifetime annuity) $b(R)$ while being retired; $b(R)$ is a smooth increasing function of the retirement age.

Optimal (Variable) Retirement Age

To determine the individually optimal retirement age, one needs a lifetime utility function:

$$U(R) = (R - Q)\log(1 - \tau) - v(R) + (D - R)\log b(R), \quad (9.1)$$

where $v(R)$ is an increasing labor disutility function of the retirement age. A sufficiently strong marginal labor disutility makes the worker to retire as soon as possible and the rise in $b(R)$ makes the worker to delay retirement, possibly beyond R_{m} or even to R_{M}. To determine the optimal retirement age, we need the marginal utility of delayed retirement:

$$\begin{aligned} U'(R) = &\log(1 - \tau) - v'(R) - \log b(R) \\ &+ (D - R)\frac{b'(R)}{b(R)}, \; R \geq R_{\mathrm{m}}. \end{aligned} \quad (9.2)$$

Under standard assumptions, $U'(R)$ is decreasing. We have now

Lemma 9.1. *For any fixed contribution rate τ, the optimal retirement age $R(\tau)$ is equal to either R_{m} if $U'(R_{\mathrm{m}}) < 0$ or R_{M} if $U'(R_{\mathrm{M}}) > 0$ or it satisfies*

$$U'(R(\tau)) = 0, \qquad R_{\mathrm{m}} < R(\tau) < R_{\mathrm{M}}. \quad (9.2^{\mathrm{o}})$$

Remark. In principle, any of the three possibilities may occur. In practice, in most of the cases, either $R(\tau) = R_{\mathrm{m}}$ or $R(\tau) = R^*$—the normal retirement age to be soon introduced with linear benefit functions.

We define now the *lifetime balance* as the difference between the lifetime contributions and the lifetime benefits:

$$z(R) = \tau(R - Q) - b(R)(D - R). \quad (9.3)$$

If the (expected) age at death $\mathbf{E}D$ were known in advance, then the benefit function could be determined by (9.3) and the neutrality condition $z(R) = 0$:

$$b^{\mathrm{N}}(R) = \frac{\tau(R-Q)}{\mathbf{E}D - R}, \qquad R < \mathbf{E}D. \tag{9.4N}$$

Of course, $\mathbf{E}D$ also depends on the retirement age and the lifetime wage. The second factor is never taken into account (except in adjustment B in Chapter 14) but the first can be considered:

$$b^{\mathrm{N}}(R) = \frac{\tau(R-Q)}{\mathbf{E}_R D - R}, \qquad R < \mathbf{E}_R D. \tag{9.4N'}$$

To simplify the calculations, apart from Appendix G, we neglect the possibility of death below the maximal retirement age, therefore $\mathbf{E}_R D = \mathbf{E}D = D$, hence (9.4$N'$) reduces to

$$b^{\mathrm{N}}(R) = \frac{\tau(R-Q)}{D - R}, \qquad R < D. \tag{9.5N}$$

We shall also need the age-variant actuarial adjustment rate:

$$\frac{b^{\mathrm{N}\prime}(R)}{b^{\mathrm{N}}(R)} = \frac{d}{dR}\log b^{\mathrm{N}}(R) = \frac{1}{R-Q} + \frac{1}{D-R}. \tag{9.6N}$$

A further simplification concerns the labor disutility—retirement age function, it is assumed to be linear-quadratic:

$$v(R) = \xi(R-Q) + \chi(R-R_{\mathrm{m}})^2 \quad \text{for} \quad R \ge R_{\mathrm{m}}, \tag{9.1'}$$

where the real numbers $\xi > 0$ and $\chi > 0$ are the age-invariant and the age-variant disutility coefficients, respectively. The second is only relevant above the minimum retirement age R_{m}. We have

Theorem 9.1. *For appropriately large* ξ *and* χ, *and for a given contribution rate* τ $(0 < \tau < 1)$, *the individually optimal NDC-retirement age in (9.5N) satisfies*

$$\log(1-\tau) - \xi - 2\chi(R - R_{\mathrm{m}}) - \log\tau - \log(R - Q) + \log(D - R) + \frac{D - Q}{R - Q} = 0. \tag{9.7}$$

Proof. Substituting (9.5*N*) into (9.1) yields for $R \geq R_{\mathrm{m}}$,

$$U(R) = (R - Q)[\log(1-\tau) - \xi] - \chi(R - R_{\mathrm{m}})^2 + (D - R)[\log\tau + \log(R - Q) - \log(D - R)].$$

Taking the derivative of $U(R)$ and equating the derivative to 0 yields (9.7). ■

In general, (9.7) can only be solved numerically.

It would be attractive to study the socially optimal contribution rate for flexible (variable) retirement age with no private saving but we skip it. (Note that in previous chapters we analyzed the same issue for fixed retirement age and positive private saving!) Different workers would need different contribution rates but the contribution rate should be the same for every worker. It is easy to show that as the contribution rate rises, the individual optimal retirement age decreases if it is interior optimum. Taking the expected utilities as the social welfare function, the socially optimal contribution rate would be some average of the individual optima.

We only consider the problem when the workers have the same demographic characteristics: $Q = 20$, $D = 80$ and $R_{\mathrm{m}} = 57$, with common age-invariant labor disutility $\xi = 1$ and different age-variant labor disutilities: $\chi_1 = 0.02$, $\chi_2 = 0.03$ and $\chi_3 = 0.04$ with uniform distribution. The socially optimal contribution rate is approximately equal to the middle type's individual optimum, namely $\tau^* = 1 - b_2^* = 0.277$. Table 9.1 reports the dependence of optima on age-variant disutilities.

Table 9.1 Social optima with homogeneous life expectancies

Age-variant labor disutility, χ	Optimal	
	Retirement age, $R(\tau)$	Pension benefit, $b(\tau)$
0.02	64.2	0.775
0.03	63.4	0.723
0.04	62.7	0.684

Remark. $w = 1$, $\xi = 1$ and $\tau = 0.277$

Linear Benefit Functions

At the end of this section, we outline a practical simplification of (9.5N)—to be used in Sect. 9.4—when the hyperbolic function (9.5N) is linearized:

$$b^{\mathrm{L}}(R) = \alpha(R - Q)[1 + \eta(R - R^*)], \tag{9.4L}$$

where the real number $R^* \in (R_{\mathrm{m}}, R_{\mathrm{M}})$ is the *normal* (or statutory or full-benefit) retirement age, the real number $\alpha > 0$ is the *marginal accrual rate* and the real number $\eta > 0$ is the *actuarial adjustment rate.* The lifetime contribution and benefit to be balanced at least at the normal retirement age, we need

$$\alpha = \frac{\tau}{D - R^*}.$$

Moreover,

$$\frac{b^{\mathrm{L}\prime}(R)}{b^{\mathrm{L}}(R)} = \frac{1}{R - Q} + \frac{\eta}{1 + \eta(R - R^*)}. \tag{9.6L}$$

If we really want to approximate the hyperbolic function (9.5N) with a linear function (9.4L), then η can be chosen so that (9.6N) and (9.6L) be the same at the normal retirement age: $\eta = 1/(D - R^*)$. For $R^* = 60$, $D = 80$ and $\tau = 0.3$, $\alpha = 0.015$ and $\eta = 0.05$.

9.3 Flexible Systems: Heterogeneous Life Expectations

Except for Appendix F and Chapter 14, we had workers with a homogeneous life expectancy (LEXP); here we also distinguish two types (cf. Chapter 4). Let us assume that type L has a shorter LEXP D_L and type H has a longer LEXP D_H: $0 < D_L < D_H$, Assuming that type i's share in the population is $f_i > 0$, $f_L + f_H = 1$, the average LEXP is $\mathbf{E}D = f_L D_L + f_H D_H$. Let us assume that both types started to work at age $Q > 0$; types L and H retire at ages R_L and R_H, respectively. To avoid certain problems we assume that the shorter-lived retires earlier than the longer-lived: $R_L < R_H$ and even the longer-lived type retires before the short-lived dies: $R_H < D_L$.

Rewriting (9.4N) but changing the meaning $\mathbf{E}D$ from stochastic average within one type to statistical average for two types, the benefit functions are

$$b_i = \frac{\tau(R_i - Q)}{\mathbf{E}D - R_i}, \qquad i = L, H. \tag{9.8}$$

The corresponding lifetime balances are now

$$z_i = \tau(R_i - Q) - (D_i - R_i)b_i, \qquad i = L, H. \tag{9.9}$$

A system is called *neutral* if $z_i \equiv 0$ for $i = L, H$ and *balanced* if the average balance is zero: $\mathbf{E}z = 0$. Obviously, any neutral system is balanced but not *vice versa.*

We shall show that system (9.8) is not neutral, moreover, it is not even balanced (cf. Theorem F.2).

Theorem 9.2. *Under the flexible rule (9.8), workers with shorter LEXP lose and workers with longer LEXP gain:* $z_L > 0 > z_H$ *and due to* $R_L < R_H$, *the expected balance is negative:* $\mathbf{E}z < 0$.

Remark. In the limit case $R_L = R_H$, the expected balance is zero: $\mathbf{E}z = 0$.

Proof. Inserting (9.8) into (9.9) yields

$$z_i = \tau(R_i - Q) - \frac{\tau(R_i - Q)}{\mathbf{E}D - R_i}(D_i - R_i) = \frac{\tau(R_i - Q)(\mathbf{E}D - D_i)}{\mathbf{E}D - R_i}. \tag{9.10}$$

Using (9.8) again, (9.10) reduces to

$$z_i = (\mathbf{E}D - D_i)b_i, \qquad i = L, H. \tag{9.11}$$

Assumption $R_L < R_H$ and (9.8) imply $b_L < b_H$, i.e., (9.11) implies $z_L > 0 > z_H$. Substitute (9.11) into $\mathbf{E}z = f_L z_L + f_H z_H$,

$$\mathbf{E}z = f_L(\mathbf{E}D - D_L)b_L + f_H(\mathbf{E}D - D_H)b_H. \tag{9.12}$$

By $0 < b_L < b_H$ and $\mathbf{E}D - D_H < 0 < \mathbf{E}D - D_L$, (9.12) implies

$$\mathbf{E}z < [f_L(\mathbf{E}D - D_L) + f_H(\mathbf{E}D - D_H)]b_H = 0. \tag{9.13}$$

■

The expected loss can be eliminated (personal communication by P. Diamond) if the benefit functions are proportionally reduced by a factor ζ:

$$b_i = \frac{\zeta\tau(R_i - Q)}{\mathbf{E}D - R_i}, \qquad i = L, H.$$

A simple calculation reduces the lifetime balance to

$$z_i = \tau(R_i - Q) - \frac{\zeta\tau(R_i - Q)(D - R_i)}{\mathbf{E}D - R_i}.$$

Hence $\mathbf{E}z = 0$ implies

$$\zeta = \frac{\mathbf{E}R - Q}{\kappa}, \quad \text{where} \quad \kappa = \mathbf{E}\frac{(R_i - Q)(D_i - R_i)}{\mathbf{E}D - R_i}.$$

Table 9.2 Social optimum with heterogeneous life expectancies

Coefficient of contraction, p	Payout rate, $\tilde{\tau}$	Optimal				
		Shorter LEXP			Longer LEXP	
		Retirement age, $R_L(p)$	Pension benefit, $b_L(p)$	Lifetime balance, $z_L(p)$	Retirement age, $R_H(p)$	Pension benefit, $b_H(p)$
0.0	0.266	61.7	0.606	3.491	65.0	0.798
0.2	0.268	62.0	0.625	3.507	64.7	0.783
0.4	0.270	62.4	0.651	3.543	64.4	0.769
0.6	0.272	62.7	0.672	3.564	64.1	0.755
0.8	0.275	63.0	0.695	3.576	63.7	0.736
1.0	0.277	63.4	0.724	3.621	63.4	0.724

Remark. $\tau = 0.277$, $z_H(p) = -z_L(p)$

Finally, we illustrate our findings numerically. Rather than struggling with individual optimization of the retirement ages; as a short cut, we choose a centralized optimization of the utilitarian social welfare function. We keep $Q = 20$ and experiment with wildly heterogeneous life expectations: $D_L = 75$, $D_H = 85$. We choose $f_L = f_H = 0.5$ implying $\mathbf{E}D = 80$, we retain $\xi = 1$ and $\chi = 0.03$ but to make the model more realistic, we assume that the *threshold* ages are heterogeneous: $R_{\mathrm{m}}(k) = R_{\mathrm{m}}(p\mathbf{E}D+(1-p)D_k-Q)/(\mathbf{E}D-Q)$, where p is the factor of contraction. For example, for $p = 0$, $R_{\mathrm{m}}(k) = R_{\mathrm{m}}(D_k-Q)/(\mathbf{E}D-Q)$, while for $p = 1$, $R_{\mathrm{m}}(1) = R_{\mathrm{m}}(2) = R_{\mathrm{m}}$. With good approximation, we can retain the original contribution rate: $\tau = 0.277$.

Table 9.2 displays the dependence of the optima on the factor of contraction. As the threshold ages converge to the minimum retirement age, the shorter LEXP's retirement age converges from below to 63.4, while the longer LEXP's retirement age converges from above to 63.4 (the optimum in the middle row in Table 9.1). In conformity to Theorem 9.2, at convergence, the payout rate rises to the contribution rate. Further calculations show that if one out of million similar workers individually deviates from this optimum, they would experience a lower rather than a higher lifetime utility.

At a higher level of analysis, one may ask: how can we replace (9.9) by a more sophisticated rule, say by a menu $(b_i, R_i)_{i=1}^2$ maximizing the social welfare? Moreover, we require that the rule be such that type i choose (b_i, R_i) rather than (b_j, R_j), $j \neq i$. The theory of mechanism design gives the answer but it is beyond the scope of this book (Diamond 2003; Eső and Simonovits 2002; Eső et al. 2011).

9.4 Fragmented Labor Careers and Seniority Systems

In this section, we turn to the case, where type 1 has a continuous career and type 2 has a fragmented one (for data, see Czeglédi et al. 2017). In such a case, we have to study the seniority system as well, exempting from the benefit reduction those workers who retire below the normal retirement age but serving at least the *critical* contribution length S_o.

Denote the contribution lengths by S_1 and S_2, respectively: $S_1 \geq S_o > S_2$. Type k ($k = 1, 2$) starts working at age Q_k, retires at age R_k, and dies at age D_k; $0 < Q_k < R_k < D_k$. Due to labor market frictions, the length of contribution is a type-specific fraction of the difference between retirement age and starting age:

$$S_k = \varphi_k(R_k - Q_k), \qquad k = 1, 2, \tag{9.14}$$

where $1 - \varphi_k$ stands for the *degree of fragmentation* ($0 < \varphi_k \leq 1$). To calculate linear pension benefits (9.4L), we need the following new concept: R_o is the *critical retirement age*. Recall earlier concepts: normal retirement age R^* and $\eta > 0$ is the annual *deduction* for retiring below R^*.

The benefit rule has now two relevant branches for $R \leq R^*$.

Rule 1—seniority retirement:

$$b(R, S) = \alpha S(1 - \tau) \quad \text{if } S \geq S_o. \tag{9.15}$$

Rule 2—early retirement with deduction:

$$b(R, S) = \alpha S[1 + \eta(R - R^*)](1 - \tau) \quad \text{if } R \geq R_o \text{ and } S < S_o. \tag{9.16}$$

Remarks. 1. Rule 2 also applies to delayed retirement, i.e., $R > R^*$ but we will not discuss this case here. In early retirement, Rule 1 is always more favorable to participating workers than Rule 2.

2. Note that in the region characterized by $S_m \le S < S_o$ and $R_m \le R < R_o$, there is no retirement.
3. If $S_o \ge R^* - \min(Q_1, Q_2)$, then there is no seniority retirement.
4. If $R_o = R^*$, there is no early retirement (except for seniority).

To obtain the individually optimal retirement age, one needs a lifetime utility function:

$$U_k(R_k) = \varphi_k(R_k - Q_k)[\log(1-\tau) - \xi_k] \\ +(1-\varphi_k)(R_k - Q_k)[\log a - \xi_k] + (D_k - R_k)\log(b[R_k]),$$

where a is the value of annual aid, and ξ_k is type k's labor (and unemployment) disutility coefficient.

We need the per capita *balance* of the system, where $\mathbf{E}$ is the expectation operator:

$$\mathbf{E}z = \tau\mathbf{E}S - a\mathbf{E}(R - Q - S) - \mathbf{E}[(D - R)b(R, S)].$$

It is assumed that the system is approximately balanced, i.e., the balance is close to zero. Since we compare different parameter sets, we shall denote a generic version by x and then the corresponding social welfare function is given by

$$V(x) = \sum_{k=1}^{2} f_k U_k[x],$$

where f_k is the relative frequency of type k in the population.

To avoid the problems of ambiguity with the numerical value of the social welfare function, we shall introduce the relative efficiency of y with respect to x as

$$V(y) = V(x) + (D - Q)\log\varepsilon,$$

$$\text{i.e.,} \quad \varepsilon = \exp[V(y) - V(x)/(D - Q)].$$

Table 9.3 When the seniority system is more efficient than the flexible one

Actuarial adjustment rate, η	Critical		Contribution rate, τ	Retirement ages		Relative efficiency, ε	Balance, $\mathbf{E}z$
	Length, S_o	Ret. age, R_o		Short, R_1	High, R_2		
0.000	40.0	62.0	0.309	57.0	62.0	1.000	–0.054
0.015	40.5	61.5	0.311	57.0	61.5	0.998	–0.042
0.030	41.0	61.0	0.309	57.0	62.0	1.000	–0.054
0.045	41.5	60.5	0.303	57.6	62.0	1.000	–0.083
0.060	42.0	60.0	0.299	58.1	62.0	0.998	–0.041

We shall discuss two cases: (i) the seniority pension system yields higher *welfare* than the flexible one and (ii) the opposite case. We are unable to prove our claims, rather we illustrate them numerically. The joint parameter values are as follows: $\alpha = 0.03$; $R^* = 62$, $x = 0, 1, 2, 3, 4$ stand for the steps of transition between the seniority and the flexible systems. The critical retirement age: $R_o = R^* - 0.5x$, the seniority employment length $S_o = 40 + 0.5x$ and the deduction rate $\eta = 0.015x$. Frequencies are $f_1 = 0.6$ and $f_2 = 0.4$. The amount of aid is $a = 0.25$.

Result 1. The seniority pension system yields higher *welfare* than the flexible one when type 1 starts to work much earlier than type 2: $Q_1 < Q_2$ and her work is much more tiring: $\xi_1 > \xi_2$. Here the fragmented labor market has no role: $\varphi_1 = \varphi_2 = 1$.

Table 9.3 displays the case when type 1 is socially inferior to type 2: in years, $Q_1 = 16$ and $Q_2 = 22$, while $D_1 = 70$ and $D_2 = 80$. Labor disutilities wildly differ: $\xi_1 = 1.5$ and $\xi_2 = 0.75$.

As the system evolves from the seniority to the flexible system, type 1's optimal retirement age rises from 57 to 58.1 and type 2's retirement age remains 62 or close to it. The relative efficiency of the evolving system remains equal to or lower than the seniority system's, i.e., the seniority system is advantageous. As mentioned earlier, Le Garrec and Lhuissier (2017) drew the opposite conclusion, by claiming that even in this obvious case, the possibility of early retirement undermines the interest of workers to obtain high quality jobs.

Table 9.4 When the seniority system is less efficient than the flexible one

Actuarial adjustment rate, η	Critical		Contribution rate, τ	Retirement ages		Relative efficiency, ε	Balance, Ez
	Length, S_o	Ret. age, R_o		Short, R_1	High, R_2		
0.000	40.0	62.0	0.341	60.1	62.0	1.000	−0.077
0.015	40.5	61.5	0.338	60.6	61.5	1.004	−0.099
0.030	41.0	61.0	0.331	61.0	61.0	1.007	−0.084
0.045	41.5	60.5	0.329	60.9	60.5	1.007	−0.046
0.060	42.0	60.0	0.324	62.0	60.2	1.011	−0.047

Result 2. The seniority pension system yields *lower* welfare than the flexible one when type 1 starts to work at the same age as type 2: $Q_1 = Q_2$ and her work is much less tiring: $\xi_1 < \xi_2$. Here the fragmented labor market is important and type 2 suffers much more from it than type 1: $\varphi_1 = 1 > \varphi_2$.

Table 9.4 displays the case when type 1 is socially superior to type 2: they start to work and die at the same ages: $Q_1 = Q_2 = 20$, $D_1 = D_2 = 77$, and the degrees of fragmentation are different: $\varphi_1 = 1$ and $\varphi_2 = 0.8$.

As the system evolves from the seniority to the flexible system, type 1's optimal retirement age rises from 60.1 to 62 and type 2's retirement age smoothly sinks from 62 to 60.2. The relative efficiency of the evolving system rises from 1 to 1.011, i.e., the seniority system is *not* advantageous.

9.5 Conclusions

First we have discussed a standard model of flexible retirement. Second, we have analyzed a simplest model of a seniority pension system with heterogeneously fragmented labor careers, embedding it into a set of systems which become more and more flexible. Depending on the numerical data, the seniority system may yield higher/lower social welfare than does the flexible one. Generalizing the primitive two-type model into a full-fledged one the quantitative picture would change, but the social optimality of the seniority pension probably remains conditional.

References

Augusztinovics, M., & Köllő, J. (2008). Pension Systems and Fragmented Labor Market Careers. In R. I. Gál, I. Iwasaki, & Z. Széman (Eds.), *Assessing Intergenerational Equity* (pp. 154–170). Budapest: Akadémia.

Augusztinovics, M., & Köllő, J. (2009). Decreased Employment and Pensions. The Case of Hungary. In R. Holzmann, L. MacKellar, & J. Repansek (Eds.), *Pension Reform in Southeastern Europe. Linking Labor and Financial Market Reform.* Washington, DC: World Bank.

Banyár, J. (2012). Proposal for an Optimal Benefit Formula (in Hungarian). *Szigma, 42*, 105–124.

Barr, N., & Diamond, P. (2008). *Reforming Pensions: Principles and Policy Choices.* Oxford: Oxford University Press.

Bommier, A., Leroux, M.-L., & Lozachmeur, J.-M. (2006). Uncertain Lifetime, Redistribution and Nonlinear Pricing of Annuities. In *CESifo Area Conference*, April 20–22.

Buchanan, J. (1968). Social Insurance in a Growing Economy: A Proposal for Radical Reform. *National Tax Journal, 21*, 386–395.

Crawford, V. P., & Lilien, D. M. (1981). Social Security and Retirement Decision. *Quarterly Journal of Economics, 100*, 479–529.

Czeglédi, T., Simonovits, A., Szabó, E., & Tir, M. (2017). What Has Been Wrong with the Retirement Rules in Hungary? *Acta Oeconomica, 67*(2), 359–387.

Diamond, P. A. (2003). *Taxation, Incomplete Markets and Social Security.* Munich Lectures Cambridge, MA: MIT Press.

Eső, P., & Simonovits, A. (2002). *Designing Optimal Benefit Rules for Flexible Retirement* (Discussion Paper CMS-EMS 1353). Evanston, IL: Northwestern University.

Eső, P., Simonovits, A., & Tóth, J. (2011). Designing Benefit Rules for Flexible Retirement: Welfare and Redistribution. *Acta Oeconomica, 61*, 3–32.

Fabel, O. (1994). *The Economics of Pensions and Variable Retirement Schemes.* New York: Wiley.

Gruber, J., & Wise, D. (Eds.). (1999). *Social Security and Retirement Around the World.* Chicago: The Chicago University Press.

Holzmann, R., & Palmer, E. (Eds.). (2006). *Pension Reforms: Issues and Prospects of Nonfinancial Defined Contribution (NDC) Schemes.* Washington, DC: World Bank.

Holzmann, R., Palmer, E., & Robalino, D. (Eds.). (2012). *Nonfinancial Defined Contribution Schemes in a Changing World.* Washington, DC: World Bank.

Le Garrec, G., & Lhuissier, S. (2017). Differential Mortality, Aging and Social Security: Delaying Retirement Age When Education Spillovers Matter. *Journal of Pension Economics and Finance, 16*, 395–418.

Rust, J., & Phelan, C. (1997). How Social Security and Medicare Affect Retirement Behavior in a World of Incomplete Markets. *Econometrica, 65*, 781–831.

Sheshinski, E. (1978). A Model of Social Security and Retirement Decisions. *Journal of Public Economics, 10*, 337–360.

Simonovits, A. (2003). *Modeling Pension Systems.* Houndsmill, Basingstoke: Palgrave Macmillan.

Simonovits, A. (2006). Optimal Design of Old-Age Pension Rule with Flexible Retirement: The Two-Type Case. *Journal of Economics, 89*, 197–222.

Simonovits, A. (2015). Benefit-Retirement Age Schedules in Public Pension Systems. *Czech Economic and Financial Review, 65*, 362–376.

Stock, J. H., & Wise, D. A. (1990). Pensions, the Option Value of Work and Retirement. *Econometrica, 58*, 1151–1180.

10

Optimal Child Benefits and Income Taxes

10.1 Introduction

After the baby boom has petered out, below-reproduction fertility rates have become a great problem in a number of developed countries (Table 1.5). As a reaction, the concerned governments have expanded fertility-related transfer schemes to support families and promote fertility. Note that these schemes vary across time and space. In addition to free school and health care, *child benefit* is an important tool, the amount of which is increasing with the number of children (below working age). The child benefit system operates together with an income tax system and even interacts with the public pension system (cf. Augusztinovics 1989). In this section, we shall create and analyze such a model, when fertility is endogenous. Here the partial replacement of the basic income by the child benefit system may increase the social welfare.

Since Becker (1960) and (1991), a great number of theoretical studies have analyzed the issue of *endogenous fertility.* The basic idea is simple: the rise in the number of children diminishes the parent's consumption and its utility through raising costs but increases the utility of having children. At

A. Simonovits, *Simple Models of Income Redistribution*,
https://doi.org/10.1007/978-3-319-72502-4_10

the optimum, the two "marginal" effects cancel each other. Reformulating the theory of fertility, Becker and Barro (1988) assumed that it is the utility of the offsprings rather than their mere number that enters the parent's utility function and calculated the impact of interest rate, social security etc., on fertility.

A number of papers (from Cigno 1986 to Gábos et al. 2009) considered the positive impact of child benefits on endogenous fertility. Some studies also analyzed the interaction of public pension (and private saving) and child benefits in connection with fertility (e.g., van Groezen et al. (2003), for short, GLM) and we shall study this problem in Chapter 11.

Here we confine our attention to the two-period model of fertility distinguishing young workers raising and old workers not raising children. (Note that in his seminal paper, already Samuelson (1958) considered younger and older workers and Pestieau and Ponthiere (2014) also had two rather than one working generation but they allowed both young and old workers raise children.) We study the interaction of the financing of child benefits and the basic income and their impact on the fertility and social welfare (Simonovits 2015). This has been neglected in the *theoretical* literature.[1]

Combining fertility and wage heterogeneity, it is appropriate to assume that there are at least two types with lower/higher wages with the same relative raising costs, i.e., the absolute raising costs are proportional to the net incomes. Therefore the child benefit system (where the benefit is independent of wages) transfers resources from the rich to the poor. The redistribution is accentuated when the lower-wage types have more children than the higher-wage types have. It is plausible but still needs to be underlined that in our model (without paternalistic preference for the children) the child benefit system is socially advantageous if and only if the past average fertility is less than 1. In the complete version (Simonovits 2015) we also considered the family tax deduction system, which limits such a redistribution, excluding benefits above the tax obligation.

[1]Note that the *applied* modelers (e.g., Haan and Wrohlich 2011) analyzed these complications in much detail but they constructed the social welfare function to fit the real data rather than deriving the optimum.

We call the Reader's attention to our model's *theoretical* limitations: sterility is neglected (for asymmetric information about fertility, see Cremer et al. 2008), the labor supply is fixed (for flexible labor, see Fenge and Meier 2009) and differences in the raising costs and utility functions, especially in the parameter value of relative utility of a child are glossed over (see Hakim 2003; Simonovits 2013).[2] We emphasize again that—like in most but not all models—in our simplistic model, the common relative raising cost (the ratio of cost to net income) per child is given. The role of social norms are also neglected (cf. Lindbeck et al. 1999). Taking into account these complications presumably would not change the qualitative message of the chapter.

The remainder is organized as follows: Sect. 10.2 presents the child benefits and Sect. 10.3 numerically illustrates them. Section 10.4 concludes. Appendix H discusses the pros and cons of an approximation of the raising cost introduced in GLM and to be used in Chapter 11.

10.2 Child Benefit System

In this section, we shall consider the interaction of the child benefits and the personal income taxes. First we determine the individually optimal fertility, then deduce the macro relations.

Individually Optimal Fertility

In our model with two generations of workers, there is a unisex population, where young workers give birth to children, raise them; together with old workers they pay taxes to finance child benefits and a universal basic income (e.g., in Chapter 2).[3] For simplicity, there is neither saving nor discounting.

Every young worker in our population is characterized by her pretax wage w which is maintained for old working age, is distributed according

---

[2]Hakim (2003, p. 367) supported polarization: "The government ... should focus instead on policies to support home-centered women, who have the highest fertility rates and can most easily be persuaded to increase their family size." Simonovits (2013) opposed polarization.

[3]App and Rees (2012) and Fehr et al. (2016) considered households rather than separate parents. The latter also modeled changing family structure.

to a probability distribution function F and the distribution defines a corresponding expectation operator $\mathbf{E}$. Any young worker can freely choose the number of her children, denoted by n. As a heroic idealization, we allow for any positive real number! The transfer system has two objectives: (i) to diminish pretax wage inequalities and (ii) to finance a part of the raising costs. A worker, earning wage w, pays tax θw, $0 \le \theta \le 1$. Every worker receives a basic income γ. A young worker, who has n children, also receives child benefits φn, $\varphi > 0$ being the *child benefit rate.*[4]

Denoting the net-of-tax-rate by $\hat{\theta} = 1 - \theta$, the old worker's net income is equal to

$$z = \hat{\theta} w + \gamma \tag{10.1a}$$

and the young worker's net income is equal to

$$z + \varphi n. \tag{10.1b}$$

Neglecting the returns to scales, we assume that the raising cost is proportional to the number of children and the net income. Denoting the proportionality constant by $\pi > 0$, the raising cost is equal to $\pi n(z + \varphi n)$, therefore old and young worker's consumption are, respectively, given by

$$d = z \tag{10.2a}$$

and

$$c = (1 - \pi n)(z + \varphi n), \quad \text{where} \quad 0 < n < \frac{1}{\pi}. \tag{10.2b}$$

To avoid absurd cases, we assume that the child benefit is always nonnegative and not greater than the narrow raising cost: $0 \le \varphi \le \pi z_{\mathrm{m}}$, where z_{m} is the minimal net narrow income.

[4]The proportionality assumption may be violated in countries like Great Britain, where the second child receives much less than the first one, or in Hungary, where the second and especially the third child induces a disproportionately higher potential child-related tax benefit.

Assume that any young worker chooses her fertility to maximize an additive logarithmic utility function

$$U(c, n, d) = \log c + \zeta \log n + \log d, \tag{10.3}$$

where $\zeta > 0$ is the relative individual utility of having children with respect to that of adult consumption. This coefficient has no meaning in itself but fixing the average wage at 1 below, ζ acquires a natural meaning.

Inserting (10.2) into (10.3) yields the reduced utility function

$$U[n] = \log(z + \varphi n) + \log(1 - \pi n) + \zeta \log n + \log z. \tag{10.4}$$

We assume that the young workers neglect the impact of their fertility decisions on the tax balance described in (10.9).

Equating U's derivative to zero provides the young worker's optimality condition

$$0 = U'[n] = \frac{\varphi}{z + \varphi n} - \frac{\pi}{1 - \pi n} + \frac{\zeta}{n}. \tag{10.5}$$

At this point we shall consider the simplest, degenerated case.

Example 10.1 If there is no child benefit: $\varphi = 0$, then the balance condition (10.9′) is simply $\theta = \gamma$. The introduction of a pure basic income has no fertility effect, because the optimal fertility is independent of the net income z and inversely proportional to the raising cost π:

$$n_0 = n(w, 0, \theta) = \frac{\zeta}{\bar{\zeta}\pi}, \quad \bar{\zeta} = 1 + \zeta. \tag{10.6^o}$$

Then the young worker's consumption is equal to $c_0 = z/\bar{\zeta}$, independently of the per-child raising cost π.

Returning to the general case $\varphi > 0$, we present the explicit solution of the wage-specific fertility without considering the financial balances.

Lemma 10.1 *In a(n unbalanced) transfer system with a basic income γ and a child benefit rate φ, the optimal fertility of a young worker with a narrow* *income* $z = \hat{\theta} w + \gamma$ *is the positive root of the quadratic equation*

$$E(n, w, \varphi, \gamma) = (2 + \zeta)\pi\varphi n^2 + \bar{\zeta}(\pi z - \varphi)n - \zeta z = 0. \quad (10.6)$$

namely

$$n(w, \varphi, \gamma) = \frac{-B + \sqrt{B^2 + 4AC}}{2A}, \quad (10.7)$$

where

$$A = (2 + \zeta)\pi\varphi, \qquad B = \bar{\zeta}(\pi z - \varphi) \quad \text{and} \quad C = \zeta z. \quad (10.8)$$

Though formulas (10.7)–(10.8) are helpful in the numerical calculations, their analytical use is very limited. In contrast, (10.5) is very useful, implying a

Corollary. *The individually optimal fertility* $n(w, \varphi, \gamma)$ *is an increasing function of the benefit rate* φ*, a decreasing function of the wage* w *and of the basic income* γ*. The higher the wage, the weaker the impact of the rise in the transfer rates* φ *and* γ*.*

Indeed, consider the optimality condition (10.5) and increase φ, then the declining curve shifts to the right, leading to a higher $n(w, \varphi, \gamma)$. The opposite holds for w and γ. The higher the w, the higher the z, thus the right-hand-side of (10.5) decreases.

Macrorelations

Having finished the individual analysis, we consider the two generations with the same wage distribution (every old worker has the same wage as it had when she was young) and assume that the average wage is $\mathbf{E}w = 1$. We have four overlapping generations, where N denotes the size of generation born in the current period and N_{-i} denotes that of last but i period, $i = 1, 2, 3$. Then the current and past average fertilities are equal to $\nu = \mathbf{E}n = N/N_{-1}$ and $\nu_{-1} = \mathbf{E}n_{-1} = N_{-1}/N_{-2}$, respectively. Since pensioners are neglected, N_{-3} is irrelevant.

We shall now discuss the balance condition of the tax system in the current period. On average, the tax is the sum of the child benefit and the basic income, the former being the product of the child benefit rate and the number of children. Hence

$$(N_{-1} + N_{-2})\theta = \varphi N + (N_{-1} + N_{-2})\gamma. \tag{10.9}$$

Using definitions $N_{-1} = \nu_{-1}N_{-2}$ and $N = \nu\nu_{-1}N_{-2}$, (10.9) simplifies to the fertility equation

$$(1 + \nu_{-1}^{-1})(\theta - \gamma) = \varphi\nu(\varphi, \gamma), \tag{10.9'}$$

where $\nu(\varphi, \gamma) = \mathbf{E}n(w, \varphi, \gamma)$ is the average current fertility as a function of the child benefit rate φ and the basic income γ.

Before presenting the involved argumentation, we display another very simple special case.

Example 10.2. Assume homogeneous wages: $w \equiv 1$, and exclude basic income: $\gamma = 0$, hence $z = 1 - \theta$. To simplify the calculations, we are looking for the stationary case $n = 1$, when the balance condition (10.9′) reduces to $\varphi = 2\theta$. Substituting into (10.6) directly:

$$E(1, 1, 2\theta, 0) = 2(2 + \zeta)\pi\theta + \bar{\zeta}[\pi(1 - \theta) - 2\theta] - \zeta(1 - \theta) = 0. \tag{10.6'}$$

By simple calculation, the corresponding tax rate is given by

$$\theta_1 = \frac{\bar{\zeta}\pi - \zeta}{2 + \zeta - (3 + \zeta)\pi} > 0 \quad \text{if} \quad 0 < \pi < \frac{\zeta}{\bar{\zeta}}.$$

We return now to the general problem. For a fixed tax rate θ (suppressed), the basic income γ depends on the child benefit rate φ and the past average fertility ν_{-1}. With substitution into (10.9′), the resulting implicit equation defines $\gamma[\varphi, \nu_{-1}]$ called *balanced* basic income:

$$(1 + \nu_{-1}^{-1})(\theta - \gamma[\varphi, \nu_{-1}]) = \varphi\nu(\varphi, \gamma[\varphi, \nu_{-1}]). \tag{10.9''}$$

If $\nu_{-1} < 1$, then the multiplier of $\theta - \gamma[\varphi, \nu_{-1}]$ is greater than 2, making a positive child benefit attractive.

We are looking for the conditions guaranteeing the existence and uniqueness of the balanced income, moreover, $\gamma[\varphi, \nu_{-1}]$ is decreasing in φ. Without giving the proof (Simonovits 2015), we announce

Theorem 10.1. *Fix the past average fertility rate* $\nu_{-1} < 1$ *and let* φ_{m} *be a positive real number such that*

$$(1 + \nu_{-1}^{-1})\theta > \varphi\nu(\varphi, 0) \tag{10.10a}$$

and

$$-\varphi\nu'_{\gamma}(\varphi, \gamma) < 1 + \nu_{-1}^{-1} \tag{10.10b}$$

hold for all child benefit rates in $0 < \varphi < \varphi_{\mathrm{m}}$. *Then the balanced basic income* $\gamma[\varphi, \nu_{-1}]$ *exists, is unique and decreasing in* φ*; the average fertility* $\nu(\varphi, \gamma[\varphi, \nu_{-1}])$ *is increasing in* φ.

Remark. Condition (10.10a) comes from (10.9′) and is simple because the right hand side is an increasing function of φ. Condition (10.10b) is more complex, because the positive number on the left hand side looks much lower than the right hand side but we are not sure if this is an effective bound or not.

We can now formulate the fertility dynamics:

$$\nu[\varphi, \nu_{-1}] = \frac{(1 + \nu_{-1}^{-1})(\theta - \gamma[\varphi, \nu_{-1}])}{\varphi}, \qquad \varphi > 0. \tag{10.9‴}$$

Note that this relation is essentially independent of the utility function, only the form of $\gamma[\varphi, \nu_{-1}]$ depends on the optimization framework.

A steady-state fertility rate ν^{o} ($\nu = \nu_{-1}$) satisfies the implicit equation

$$\theta = \varphi\frac{\nu^{\mathrm{o}2}}{\nu^{\mathrm{o}} + 1} + \gamma[\varphi, \nu^{\mathrm{o}}], \qquad \text{where} \qquad \nu^{\mathrm{o}} = \mathbf{E}n[w, \varphi, \nu^{\mathrm{o}}]. \tag{10.9°}$$

We announce now the following theorem without giving a proof (Simonovits 2015).

Theorem 10.2. *Under the assumptions of (10.10a)–(10.10b), there exists a unique steady-state fertility rate, which is also an increasing function of the child benefit rate.*

Remark. For any feasible fixed child benefit rate, we conjecture that the fertility dynamics (10.9‴) converges very fast to the steady state. The convergence speed is the reciprocal of the contraction factor $|H'(\nu^{o})|$ (see its relative in (H.8) below). Extremely fast convergence is obvious for $\varphi = 0$, when the dynamics steer the fertility rate to the steady state n_0 in just one period, regardless of the past average fertility rate ν_{-1}. Our numerical experiments (Simonovits 2015) support this hypothesis for positive child benefit rates as well.

To choose the socially optimal transfer system, the government maximizes a utilitarian social welfare function (where ν_{-1} is dropped):

$$V[\varphi] = \mathbf{E}\{\log c[w,\varphi] + \zeta \log n[w,\varphi] + \log d[w,\varphi]\}. \qquad (10.11)$$

We shall prove that some positive child benefit is socially useful if the past average fertility rate is lower than 1.

Theorem 10.3. *For a given past average fertility rate $\nu_{-1} < 1$, the socially optimal child benefit rate is positive: $\varphi^* > 0$.*

Proof. The existence of the social optima is obvious. The basic idea of $\varphi^* > 0$ is borrowed from the well-known proof of the envelope-theorem. We shall show $V'[0] > 0$. Taking the derivative of V in (10.11) with respect to φ and using (10.1b) yield

$$V'[\varphi] = \mathbf{E}\frac{z'_\varphi[w,\varphi] + n[w,\varphi] + \varphi n'_\varphi[w,\varphi]}{z[w,\varphi] + \varphi n[w,\varphi]}$$

$$-\mathbf{E}\frac{\pi n'_\varphi[w,\varphi]}{1 - \pi n[w,\varphi]} + \zeta\mathbf{E}\frac{n'_\varphi[w,\varphi]}{n[w,\varphi]} + \mathbf{E}\frac{z'_\varphi[w,\varphi]}{z[w,\varphi]}.$$

Using the individual optimality condition (10.5), multiplying it by $n'_\varphi[w,\varphi]$ and applying $z'_\varphi[w,\varphi] = \gamma'[\varphi]$ [cf. (10.1a)], we obtain

$$V'[\varphi] = \mathbf{E}\frac{\gamma'[\varphi] + n[w,\varphi]}{z[w,\varphi] + \varphi n[w,\varphi]} + \mathbf{E}\frac{\gamma'[\varphi]}{z[w,\varphi]}.$$

For $\varphi = 0$, $n[w,0] = n_0$, the common denominator is $z[w,0]$ and the wage-dependent numerator of $V'[0]$ is a constant:

$$2\gamma'[0] + n_0 = n_0 - 2\frac{\nu_{-1}}{\nu_{-1}+1}n_0 = \frac{1-\nu_{-1}}{\nu_{-1}+1}n_0.$$

Therefore $V'[0] > 0$ if (and only if) $\nu_{-1} < 1$. ■

As is usual, to compare the two systems—basic income combined with child benefits and pure basic income—from a welfare point of view, we introduce the following concept: the *relative efficiency* ε of the combined system with respect to the pure basic income is equal to that positive real number, multiplying the wages of the no-benefit system by it, the welfare is equal to that of the benefit system with the original wages. Adding an argument for the average wage ε in the social welfare function, the corresponding equation for efficiency is

$$V(1,\varphi) = V(\varepsilon, 0).$$

Due to the special structure of the utility and the social welfare functions, the relative efficiency can be explicitly expressed:

$$V(\varepsilon,0) = V(1,0) + 2\log\varepsilon, \quad \text{i.e.,} \quad \varepsilon = \exp([V(1,\varphi) - V(1,0)]/2). \tag{10.12}$$

10.3 Numerical Illustrations

To help understanding the impact of the child benefit rate on the steady state and the welfare, we shall display numerically the dependence of the optimal outcomes on the balanced transfer rates. We have two types:

Table 10.1 Impact of child benefit rate on steady state

Child benefit rate, φ	Balanced basic income, $\gamma[\varphi, \nu^{o}]$	Steady-state fertility rate, ν^{o}
0	0.300	0.816
0.04	0.284	0.876
0.08	0.267	0.936
0.12	0.247	0.995
0.16	0.225	1.051

Remark. $w_L = 1/2$, $f_L = 2/3$, $\theta = 0.3$

$w_L = 0.5$ and $w_H = 2$, with a common relative raising cost $\pi = 0.35$ and population shares $f_L = 2/3$, $f_H = 1 - f_L = 1/3$. We fix the value of the tax rate at $\theta = 0.3$ and choose the preference parameter: $\zeta = 0.4$. For $\varphi = 0$, $\gamma = \theta$ and $n_L(0) = n_H(0) = n_0 = 0.814$ hold (Example 10.1).

In Table 10.1 we display the dependence of the steady state fertility rate on the child benefit rate (cf. Theorem 10.2). As the benefit rate rises from 0 to 0.16, the balanced basic income drops from 0.3 to 0.225 and the steady state fertility rate $\nu^{o}(\varphi)$ rises from $n_0 = 0.816$ to 1.051.

Moving from the steady-state analysis to the dynamic one, we should pay attention to the influence of past average fertility rate. Creating Table 10.2 we fix the past average fertility rate below 1: close to n_0, as $\nu_{-1} = 0.8$. As the child benefit rate increases, the relative efficiency increases less and less and reaches the maximum around $\varphi^* = 0.06$. Increasing φ until it almost covers the raising cost of the lower-paid type: πw_L, the fertility rate of the lower-paid increases much faster than the higher paid's: $n_L(\varphi) = 1.127 > 0.939 = n_H(\varphi)$. Note, however, that beyond the optimum, the social welfare slowly sinks, and from $\varphi = 0.12$ it drops below the no-benefit level.

It is rather risky to rely on a single parameter set in numerical investigations. Simonovits (2015) have made quite an extensive robustness analysis. For lack of space we only reproduce one run, namely when the wage distribution varies.

Creating Table 10.3, the outcomes of the socially optimal child benefit system are reported, while the low wage rises from 0.5 to 0.75 and independently, the low earners' frequency drops from 2/3 to 1/3. Note that the

Table 10.2 Impact of the child benefit rate on transition

Child benefit rate, φ	Balanced basic income, $\gamma[\varphi, \nu_{-1}]$	Fertility rate			Relative efficiency, ε
		Wage			
		Low	High	Average	
		$n_L(\varphi)$	$n_H(\varphi)$	$\nu(\varphi)$	
0.00	0.300	0.816	0.816	0.816	1.000
0.06	0.276	0.929	0.859	0.906	1.002
0.12	0.247	1.041	0.902	0.995	1.000
0.17	0.220	1.127	0.939	1.065	0.995

Remark. See Table 10.1, $\nu_{-1} = 0.8$

Table 10.3 Optimal child benefits for varying wages and frequencies

Low wage, w_L	Low earner frequency, f_L	Child benefit rate, φ^*	Balanced basic income, $\gamma[\varphi^*, \nu_{-1}]$	Fertility rate		
				Wage		
				Low	High	Average
				n_L^*	n_H^*	ν^*
0.50	0.667	0.065	0.274	0.938	0.863	0.913
	0.500	0.068	0.273	0.944	0.877	0.911
	0.333	0.071	0.271	0.950	0.890	0.910
0.75	0.667	0.070	0.272	0.920	0.879	0.906
	0.500	0.071	0.272	0.921	0.890	0.905
	0.333	0.072	0.271	0.923	0.897	0.905

Remark. $\nu_{-1} = 0.8$, $\theta = 0.3$

high wage changes according to $w_H = (1 - f_L w_L)/f_H$. If the wages rather than the frequencies are given: $w_L < 1 < w_H$, then the corresponding low-earner's frequency is determined as $f_L = (w_H - 1)/(w_H - w_L)$.

It may be surprising that the socially optimal benefit rate and the balanced basic income are insensitive to the wage and frequency distribution, they are around 0.07 and 0.27, respectively. The same invariance applies to the aggregate fertility rate (around 0.91) and the relative efficiency (around 1.002). The efficiency gain is again modest. The only noticeable change occurs within the fertilities: The lower-wage earner's fertility rate varies between 0.92 and 0.95, while the higher-wage earner's between 0.86 and 0.90. The relative efficiency is constant: $\varepsilon = 1.002$.

10.4 Conclusions

We have studied a model of child benefits and deviated from earlier models in two dimensions: (i) Sharing the burden of child benefits between young and old workers (parent and grandparents), we obtained a dynamic rather than a static model. (ii) Making the consumption of children proportional to net incomes, the young worker's consumption is nonlinear in the fertility rate. To analyze a nonlinear dynamic model rather than a linear static one made the task quite difficult. Finally, we were able to prove that under the plausible assumption that the past average fertility rate is lower than 1, a suitably chosen positive child benefit rate is socially optimal. In the full version of this chapter (Simonovits 2015), we extended the analysis to the system of family tax deduction. To our surprise, the ranking of the two family transfer systems is not straightforward: depending on the parameter values of the model, each can be better than the other.

We warn the Reader on the limits of the model. We have used the simplest utility function pair, two logarithmic functions. Even at the modest generalization into CRRA (cf. e.g., Greenwood et al. 2005), the independence of the fertility rate of the wage in Example 10.1 (no child benefit) disappears, therefore the saving of Theorem 10.1 requires further, nontrivial assumptions. The neglect of the negative impact of taxation on labor supply and of tax reporting further weakens the force of our numerical examples. The inclusion of underreporting with tax morale (Sect. 2.3) and flexible labor supply with labor disutility (e.g., Sects. 2.2 and 6.3) would make the model more realistic and determine the optimal tax rate, would more fully highlight the differences between the two transfer systems. But these modifications would complicate the analysis, therefore we have not used them here. The heterogeneity of the relative raising cost also deserves an examination.

References

App, P., & Rees, R. (2012). *Optimal Taxation, Child Care and Models for Households* (Discussion Paper 6823). Bonn: IZA.

Augusztinovics, M. (1989). The Costs of Human Life. *Economic Systems Research, 1*, 5–26.

Becker, G. S. (1960). An Economic Analysis of Fertility. In R. Esterline (Ed.), *Demographic and Economic Change in Developed Countries*. Princeton: Princeton University Press.

Becker, G. S. (1991). *A Treatise on the Family*, an enlarged edition. Cambridge, MA: Harvard University Press.

Becker, G. S., & Barro, R. (1988). A Reformulation of the Economic Theory of Fertility. *Quarterly Journal of Economics, 103*, 1–25.

Cigno, A. (1986). Fertility and the Tax-Benefit System. *Economic Journal, 96*, 1035–1051.

Cremer, H., Gahvari, F., & Pestieau, P. (2008). Pensions with Heterogeneous Individuals and Endogenous Fertility. *Journal of Population Economics, 21*, 961–981.

Fehr, H., Kallweit, M., & Kindermann, F. (2016). Household Formation, Female Labor Supply and Saving. *Scandinavian Journal of Economics, 118*, 868–911.

Fenge, R., & Meier, R. (2009). Are Family Benefits and Fertility Related Pensions Perfect Substitutes? *International Tax and Public Finance, 16*, 137–163.

Gábos, A., Gál, R. I., & Kézdi, G. (2009). The Effects of Child-Related Benefits and Pensions on Fertility by Birth-Order. *Population Studies: A Journal of Demography, 16*, 215–231.

Greenwood, J., Sheshadri, A., & Vandenbroucke, G. (2005). The Baby Boom and Baby Bust. *American Economic Review, 95*, 183–207.

Haan, P., & Wrohlich, K. (2011). Can Child Care Policy Encourage Employment and Fertility. *Labour Economics, 18*, 498–512.

Hakim, C. (2003). A New Approach to Explaining Fertility Patterns: Preference Theory. *Population and Development Review, 29*, 349–374.

Lindbeck, A., Nyberg, S., & Weibull, J. W. (1999). Social Norms and the Welfare State. *Quarterly Journal of Economics, 114*, 1–35.

Pestieau, P., & Ponthiere, G. (2014). Policy Implications for Changing Longevity. *CESifo Economic Studies, 60*, 178–212.

Samuelson, P. A. (1958). An Exact Consumption-Loan Model of Interest with or Without the Social Contrivance of Money. *Journal of Political Economy, 66*, 467–482.

Simonovits, A. (2013). *Savings, Child Support, Pensions and Endogenous (and Heterogeneous) Fertility* (IE-CERS-HAS Working Paper 35).
Simonovits, A. (2015). *Socially Optimal Child-Related Transfers with Endogenous Fertility* (IE-CERS-HAS Working Paper 37).
van Groezen, B., Leers, T., & Meijdam, L. (2003). Social Security and Endogenous Fertility: Pensions and Child Benefits as Siamese Twins. *Journal of Public Economics, 87*, 233–251.

11

Child Support, Pension and Fertility

11.1 Introduction

Chapter 10 discussed the impact of child benefits on fertility. In this chapter, we add the pensions and study their interaction with child benefits. In addition to the pioneering paper of Cigno (1986), see Kovács (2012) for the Hungarian debate about a parental pension bonus and Simonovits (2013) for its theoretical critique. Some studies have already analyzed the interaction of public pension (and private saving) and child benefits in connection with fertility. Among them, we shall make van Groezen et al. (2003) (for short, GLM) the basis of our investigation. (They considered a small open economy but van Groezen and Meijdam (2008) also discussed a large closed economy.) While GLM studied an infinite series of overlapping generations, we rest satisfied with a single representative generation, whose members support their children and parents. (This model is not only simpler but also more realistic, giving up the fiction of secular time-invariance and gets rid of the very sensitive social discount factor.) In the simplest setting, the appropriate increase in fertility rate through child benefits raises the pension benefits, while the introduction of fertility-related pensions can also raise fertility.

A. Simonovits, *Simple Models of Income Redistribution*,
https://doi.org/10.1007/978-3-319-72502-4_11

Studying a model with general rather than logarithmic utility function, Cremer et al. (2008) also took into account that the government has no information on raising cost differences. Applying the methods of mechanism design, they also analyzed the problems of moral hazard (when parents have no full control over their fertility) and of adverse selection (when low-cost type pretend to be high-cost type). They found that under adverse selection, "linking benefits to fertility rate penalizes high-cost individuals" and this is undesirable. In order to simplify the analysis, we shall neglect heterogeneity (but see Simonovits (2013) for heterogeneous fertility rates with fertility-dependent pensions and Chapter 10 with wage and age heterogeneity). Anyway, we leave aside moral hazard and adverse selection. Leroux and Pestieau (2014) extended the analysis to the in-kind transfers as well.

Taking into account the credit constraint, we meet again the phenomenon *jump the gap* mentioned in Chapters 4 and 8; there are two local welfare maxima: the no-transfer case and the no-saving case. In the interesting case, when the latter gives a higher maximum than the former, the nonoptimal government's transfer has to be sufficiently high to ensure higher welfare than the no-transfer case does.

The structure of the chapter is as follows: Sect. 11.2 presents the model of child support and pensions. Section 11.3 displays the numerical illustrations. Appendix I (located in Appendices) discusses jumping the gap.

11.2 The Model

With the extension to pensions, the fertility model becomes quite complex, especially taking care of the existence of credit constraint.

It is heroically assumed that the tax and contribution rates do not influence the labor supply which is equal to unity (cf. Sects. 2.2 and 6.2 for the opposite case). Furthermore, in our small open economy, the world interest rate determines the domestic interest rate. To stay as close as possible to GLM, we retain their unitary length ratio: $\mu = 1$, though the generalization to $\mu \leq 1$ would be straightforward.

We add new notations and equations to the old ones (introduced in Chapter 10) and modify others. Uniform total wage: $w = 1$, pension contribution (rate): τ, tax (rate): θ, saving: s. Following the approximation discussed in Appendix H to Chapter 10, we take the cost of raising a child independent of the net wage: p, per child benefit: φ, fertility rate, i.e., the number of children per parent (half the total fertility rate): n, the pay-as-you-go benefit: b; all positive real numbers. We retain the heroic assumption of the literature: the number of children can be any positive real!

Worker's (c) and pensioner's consumptions (d) are, respectively, equal to

$$c = 1 - \tau - \theta - s - (p - \varphi)n \quad \text{and} \quad d = \rho s + b. \tag{11.1}$$

The new lifetime utility function is a discounted utility plus the utility of having children:

$$U(c, n, d) = \log c + \zeta \log n + \delta \log d, \tag{11.2}$$

where ζ is the coefficient of the relative utility of having children and δ is the discount factor; $\zeta > 0$ and $0 \leq \delta \leq 1$.

Introducing the net-of-contribution rate $\hat{\tau} = 1 - \tau$ and inserting (11.1) into (11.2) yield the reduced utility function:

$$U[s, n] = \log(\hat{\tau} - \theta - s - (p - \varphi)n) + \zeta \log n + \delta \log(\rho s + b). \tag{11.3}$$

Denoting the individual optimum by $c(\tau, \theta), n(\tau, \theta), d(\tau, \theta)$ we define a *paternalistic* social welfare function by replacing the discount factor δ with 1 in (11.2). Then our social welfare function is an undiscounted utility:

$$V(\tau, \theta) = \log c(\tau, \theta) + \zeta \log n(\tau, \theta) + \log d(\tau, \theta). \tag{11.4}$$

As is usual in this type of models, the workers neglect the impact of their decisions on the balances described in (11.6). Filling the gap left in GLM, from now on we exclude negative savings and distinguish two cases: either slack or tight credit constraint.

To learn if the credit constraint is slack or tight, we have to determine the *separatrix curve* θ_τ which separates the two domains in the (τ, θ)-plane. Delaying the proof, we only present

Lemma 11.1. *(a) The separatrix curve θ_τ is given by*

$$\theta_\tau = \frac{[\delta p - \zeta\rho^{-1}\tau]\hat{\tau}}{\delta p + \rho^{-1}\tau}, \quad \textit{where} \quad 0 \leq \tau < \zeta^{-1}\delta p\rho.$$

(b) The separatrix curve starts from $\theta_0 = 1$ and ends at $\theta_{\tau_M} = 0$, where $\tau_M = \zeta^{-1}\delta p\rho$; and θ_τ is declining in $[0, \tau_M]$.
(c) If $0 \leq \tau < \tau_M$ and $0 < \theta < \theta_\tau$, then $s(\tau, \theta) > 0$: slack.
(d) If $0 \leq \tau \leq \tau_M$ and $\theta_\tau \leq \theta \leq \hat{\tau}$, then $s(\tau, \theta) = 0$: tight.
(e) If $\tau_M < \tau \leq 1 - \theta$, then $s(\tau, \theta) = 0$: tight.

Slack Credit Constraint (S)

We continue the analysis with the slack credit constraint. Copying GLM, we take the partial derivatives of (11.3) with respect to s and n yielding the first-order necessary conditions for optimum:

$$0 = U_s'[s, n] = \frac{-1}{\hat{\tau} - \theta - s - (p - \varphi)n} + \frac{\delta\rho}{\rho s + b} \tag{11.5a}$$

and

$$0 = U_n'[s, n] = \frac{-(p - \varphi)}{\hat{\tau} - \theta - s - (p - \varphi)n} + \frac{\zeta}{n}. \tag{11.5b}$$

For the time being, we do not exclude negative savings. Equations (11.1) and (11.5) imply

Lemma 11.2. *The conditionally optimal consumption pair and fertility are*

$$c(\tau, \theta) = \frac{\hat{\tau} - \theta + \rho^{-1}b}{1 + \delta + \zeta}, \quad d(\tau, \theta) = \delta\rho c(\tau, \theta)$$

$$\text{and} \quad n(\tau, \theta) = \frac{\zeta}{p - \varphi}c(\tau, \theta).$$

In this model, the tax rate θ and pension b depend on fertility rate n, therefore we introduce the transfer balance equations:

$$\theta = \varphi n \tag{11.6a}$$

and

$$b = \tau n. \tag{11.6b}$$

In words: (a) the tax rate is equal to the product of the child benefit rate and fertility rate; (b) the pension benefit is equal to the product of the contribution and fertility.

There is a general presumption—which we follow—that these two transfer systems should be balanced separately but in some countries this is not the case. For example, countries like Denmark, operate flat public pensions and finance the system from personal income taxes rather than from pension contributions. On the other hand, there are countries like Hungary, which use pension contributions for correcting distortions in their personal income tax systems.

The introduction of child benefit rate φ reduces the *private* cost of raising a child from p to $p - \varphi$. If (11.6a) holds, there is no income effect. The introduction of the contribution rate τ diminishes the young-age consumption by the same amount and increases the old-age consumption according to $b = \tau n$ [(11.6b)]. In a stationary economy with $n = 1$, the two changes cancel each other; for falling/growing population, the reduction of young-age consumption is greater/lower than the increase of the old-age consumption. Using the concept of dynamic efficiency: $\rho > n$, the comparison above changes. As is known, in a dynamically efficient economy, the introduction of a pay-as-you-go pension is suboptimal etc., except for excessive myopia (Appendix D).

Inserting the transfer equations (11.6a)–(11.6b) into (11.5a)–(11.5b) yields the final optima (see GLM):

Theorem 11.1. *(a) When the credit constraint is slack (Lemma 11.1c), then the individually optimal young-age consumption and fertility rate are given respectively:*

$$c_S(\tau,\theta) = \frac{\hat{\tau} - \theta[1 - \tau/(p\rho)]}{1 + \delta + \zeta - \zeta\tau/(p\rho)} \tag{11.7a}$$

and

$$n_S(\tau,\theta) = \frac{\zeta\hat{\tau} + (1+\delta)\theta}{(1+\delta+\zeta)p - \zeta\rho^{-1}\tau}. \tag{11.7b}$$

(b) *For a given contribution rate τ, the optimal fertility rate is an increasing function of the tax rate θ. For a given tax rate θ, the optimal fertility rate is a decreasing/increasing function of the contribution rate if the tax rate is lower/higher than the critical tax rate*

$$\theta_\zeta = \frac{(1+\delta+\zeta)p\rho - \zeta}{1+\delta}.$$

Remark. If $\theta_\zeta < 0$, then the first case (decreasing fertility rate: normal) is empty; if $\theta_\zeta > \theta(\tau)$, then the second case (increasing fertility rate: paradox) is empty. Denoting by τ_ζ the root of $\theta_\zeta = \theta(\tau_\zeta)$, to be called critical contribution rate, normalcy prevails in interval $\tau_\zeta < \tau < 1$.

Proof. Combining (11.5a) and (11.5b) leads to

$$\frac{p\delta\rho}{\rho s + \tau n} = \frac{p}{\hat{\tau} - s - pn} = \frac{\zeta}{n} + \frac{\delta\tau}{\rho s + \tau n}.$$

With rearrangement,

$$s = \zeta^{-1}\rho^{-1}[p\delta\rho - (\delta+\zeta)\tau].$$

Rewrite (11.5a) as $(\rho s + \tau n) = \delta\rho(\hat{\tau} - s - pn)$ or $\rho(1+\delta)s = \delta\rho\hat{\tau} - (p\delta\rho + \tau)n$. Inserting s into our last equation leads to (11.7b) and via $n_S(\tau,\theta)$ to (11.7a). ■

Though we are unable to give a full picture of the dependence of social welfare on the transfer rates in the slack region, we prove that the no-transfer system is a (local) maximum for a large domain of the parameter space.

Theorem 11.2. *If the worker's child preference is not excessive: $\zeta < 2$, then the no-transfer system $(\tau_S^*, \theta_S^*) = (0, 0)$ is a local maximum, where the optimal outcomes are*

$$c_S^* = \frac{1}{1+\delta+\zeta}, \qquad d_S^* = \frac{\delta\rho}{1+\delta+\zeta}, \quad n_S^* = \frac{\zeta}{(1+\delta+\zeta)p}. \tag{11.7*}$$

Remarks. 1. The assumption $\zeta < 2$ is quite mild. In fact, for $\tau = 0 = \theta$, the locally optimal fertility rate is

$$n_S^* = \frac{\zeta}{(1+\delta+\zeta)p}.$$

For example, for $\zeta = 2$, $p = 1/3$ and $\delta = 1$, the slack-optimal fertility rate is too high: $n_S^* = 1.5$.

2. Tables 11.1 and 11.2 suggest that probably our local maximum is also a global one in the slack region.

Proof. In this proof, we shall drop the subindex S and study the behavior of the social welfare function (11.4). Take the partial derivatives with respect to the two transfer rates:

$$V_\tau'(\tau,\theta) = \frac{c_\tau'(\tau,\theta)}{c(\tau,\theta)} + \zeta\frac{n_\tau'(\tau,\theta)}{n(\tau,\theta)} + \frac{d_\tau'(\tau,\theta)}{d(\tau,\theta)}$$

and

$$V_\theta'(\tau,\theta) = \frac{c_\theta'(\tau,\theta)}{c(\tau,\theta)} + \zeta\frac{n_\theta'(\tau,\theta)}{n(\tau,\theta)} + \frac{d_\theta'(\tau,\theta)}{d(\tau,\theta)}.$$

Using $d = \delta\rho c$, the first and the third terms are equal in both equations. Moreover, using (11.7a) and (11.7b) at $\tau = 0 = \theta$

$$\frac{c_\tau'(0,0)}{c(0,0)} = \frac{\zeta p^{-1}\rho^{-1} - (\bar{\xi}+\delta)}{\bar{\xi}+\delta} < 0$$

$$\text{and} \quad \frac{n_\tau'(0,0)}{n(0,0)} = \zeta^{-1}\frac{c_\tau'(0,0)}{c(0,0)}.$$

Hence

$$V'_\tau(\tau,\theta) = 3\frac{c'_\tau(0,0)}{c(0,0)} < 0.$$

By the linearity of $c(0,\theta)$ and $n(0,\theta)$, the elasticities are equal to 1 and −1, respectively, i.e., $V'_\theta(0,0) = -2 + \zeta < 0$ etc.

The second-order conditions are omitted. ■

Tight Credit Constraint (T)

We turn now to the tight credit constraint: $s = 0$. We have to replace condition $U'_s[s,n] = 0$ [(11.5a)] by $U'_s[0,n] < 0$ and then (11.5b) becomes $U'_n[0,n] = 0$. By easy calculation we obtain

$$(p-\varphi)n = \zeta c = \zeta[\hat{\tau} - \theta - (p-\varphi)n].$$

Inserting the budget condition $\theta = \varphi n$, and notation $\bar{\zeta} = 1 + \zeta$, we end up with

Theorem 11.3. *(a) When the credit constraint is tight (Lemma 11.2d and e), the optimal fertility rate and the corresponding young-age consumption are respectively equal to*

$$n_{\mathrm{T}}(\tau,\theta) = \frac{\zeta\hat{\tau} + \theta}{\bar{\zeta} p} \quad \text{and} \quad c_{\mathrm{T}}(\tau,\theta) = \frac{\hat{\tau} - \theta}{\bar{\zeta}}. \tag{11.8}$$

(b) The optimal fertility rate is a decreasing function of the contribution rate τ and an increasing function of the tax rate θ.

(c) For $0 < \zeta < 1$, the equal increase of the transfer rates increases the optimal fertility rate: $\Delta\tau = \Delta\theta > 0$ implies $\Delta n_{\mathrm{T}}(\tau,\theta) > 0$; for $\zeta > 1$, the opposite holds: $\Delta n_{\mathrm{T}}(\tau,\theta) < 0$.

Remark. It is obvious that the special value $\zeta = 1$ plays a critical role: $\Delta\tau = \Delta\theta > 0$ implies $\Delta n_{\mathrm{T}}(\tau,\theta) = 0$. Unfortunately, we have no empirical knowledge about the realistic value of this parameter.

Finally we are able to give the

Proof of Lemma 11.1. Inserting formulas (11.7a), (11.7b) and (11.8) respectively for $n_S(\tau, \theta)$ and $n_T(\tau, \theta)$ into the separatrix, $n_S(\tau, \theta) = n_T(\tau, \theta)$ results in

$$\frac{\zeta\hat{\tau} + (1+\delta)\theta}{(1+\delta+\zeta)p - \zeta\rho^{-1}\tau} = \frac{\zeta\hat{\tau} + \theta}{\bar{\zeta} p}.$$

With rearrangement, $[\zeta\hat{\tau} + (1+\delta)\theta]\bar{\zeta} p = [\zeta\hat{\tau} + \theta][(1+\delta+\zeta)p - \zeta\rho^{-1}\tau]$. After simplification, $\theta(\tau)$ is obtained. For $\theta > \theta(\tau)$, $s(\tau, \theta) = 0$; for $\theta < \theta(\tau)$, $s(\tau, \theta) > 0$.

The separatrix in Lemma 11.1 is a fraction: its numerator is the product of two decreasing positive functions and its denominator is an increasing positive function, therefore the fraction is also declining. ■

Next we determine the socially optimal pair of contribution and tax rates in the tight region.

Theorem 11.4. *In the region of tight credit constraint, the socially optimal contribution and tax rates are equal to each other:*

$$\tau_T^* = \theta_T^* = \frac{1}{3+\zeta} \tag{11.9}$$

and the corresponding outcomes are equal to

$$n_T^* = \frac{\zeta}{(1+\zeta)p}, \qquad c_T^* = \frac{1}{3+\zeta}, \qquad d_T^* = \frac{1}{(3+\zeta)^2 p}. \tag{11.8*}$$

Remarks. 1. It is easy to show that the optimal pair of transfer rates in (11.9) generate tight credit constraint.

2. It is natural that the optimal fertility rate in (11.8*) is a decreasing function of the relative utility of children (ζ) but it is surprising that the two optimal transfer rates are equal to each other and are independent of any other parameter value.
3. In both regions, the socially optimal child support is always lower than the expenditure on children: $0 \le \varphi < p$.

Proof. Our starting point is as follows:

$$V\{\tau,\theta\} = \log\frac{\hat{\tau}-\theta}{\bar{\zeta}} + \zeta\log\frac{\zeta\hat{\tau}+\theta}{\bar{\zeta}p} + \log\frac{\tau(\zeta\hat{\tau}+\theta)}{\bar{\zeta}p} \to \max.$$

Using the identity $\log(x/y) = \log x - \log y$, the constant denominators can be dropped. Returning to $\hat{\tau} = 1-\tau$, we have then an equivalent problem:

$$\tilde{V}\{\tau,\theta\} = \log(1-\tau-\theta) + \bar{\zeta}\log(\zeta(1-\tau)+\theta) + \log\tau \to \max.$$

Taking the partial derivatives of $\tilde{V}$ with respect to τ and θ and equate the derivatives to zero yield the first-order necessary conditions:

$$0 = \tilde{V}'_\tau = \frac{-1}{1-\tau-\theta} - \frac{\bar{\zeta}\zeta}{\zeta(1-\tau)+\theta} + \frac{1}{\tau} \tag{11.10}$$

and

$$0 = \tilde{V}'_\theta = \frac{-1}{1-\tau-\theta} + \frac{\bar{\zeta}}{\zeta(1-\tau)+\theta}. \tag{11.11}$$

From (11.11),

$$\theta = \frac{1-\tau}{2+\zeta} = \kappa(1-\tau). \tag{11.12}$$

Inserting back (11.12) into (11.10),

$$\frac{-1}{(1-\kappa)(1-\tau)} - \frac{\bar{\zeta}\zeta}{(\zeta+\kappa)(1-\tau)} + \frac{1}{\tau} = 0.$$

Hence Theorem 11.4 is obtained. ■

Comparing the presumed welfare maxima of the two regions, the following quantity plays an important role. The *critical* discount factor $\delta(\zeta,\rho)$ is defined as the discount factor (depending on the raising cost, the relative child utility and the interest factor) for which the two systems achieve the same social welfare (cf. (11.7*) and (11.8*)). The function $\delta(\zeta, \rho)$ is to be determined from the following implicit equation:

$$V(0,0) = V(\tau_{\mathrm{T}}^{*}, \theta_{\mathrm{T}}^{*})$$

but it would not be helpful.

Obviously, if $0 < \delta < \delta(\zeta, \rho)$, then the T-optimum is better than the S-optimum, and vice versa. From now on we shall confine our attention to the T-case, which is probably the more relevant and definitely the simpler case.

As has already been mentioned several times, the numerical value of the social welfare function has no economic content. To obtain meaningful numbers, we shall occasionally compare the welfare provided by a (τ, θ)-system with the no-transfer system's (0, 0) as follows. Let us define the *relative efficiency* of the former with respect to the latter by the positive number $\varepsilon(\tau, \theta)$ if multiplying the unit wage by ε in the no-transfer system, the welfare would reach that value provided by the transfer system with unitary wages. In formula:

$$V[\varepsilon, 0, 0] = V[1, \tau, \theta].$$

Due to the simple utility function (11.2), the optimal fertility rate is independent of the wage and the optimal consumption pair are homogeneous linear functions of the wage. Therefore

$$\begin{aligned} &2\log\varepsilon(\tau,\theta) + \log c(0,0)) + \zeta\log n(0,0) + \log d(0,0) \\ &\quad = \log c(\tau,\theta) + \zeta\log n(\tau,\theta) + \log d(\tau,\theta). \end{aligned}$$

Hence $\log\varepsilon(\tau, \theta)$ or $\varepsilon(\tau, \theta)$ can simply be determined:

$$\begin{aligned} &2\log\varepsilon(\tau,\theta) + V[1,0,0] = V[1,\tau,\theta] \\ &\text{i.e.}\quad \varepsilon(\tau,\theta) = \exp[(V[1,\tau,\theta] - V[1,0,0])/2]. \end{aligned}$$

Table 11.1 Critical discount factor function $\delta[1]_{\zeta,\rho[1]}$

Coefficient of relative utility, ζ	Compounded		Optimal steady state fertility rate	
	Interest factor, $\rho[1]$	Critical discount factor, $\delta(\zeta, \rho[1])$	Slack, n_S^*	Tight, n_T^*
0.3	1.02	0.938	0.593	1.126
	1.03	0.927	0.611	
	1.04	0.916	0.625	
0.4	1.02	0.943	0.727	*1.176*
	1.03	*0.931*	*0.753*	
	1.04	0.920	0.771	
0.5	1.02	0.946	0.846	1.224
	1.03	0.934	0.877	
	1.04	0.924	0.897	

Remark. $p = 0.35$, $\zeta = 0.4$

11.3 Numerical Illustration

Here we numerically illustrate the simplest case of homogeneous fertility rate and proportional pensions. Assume a 30-year long period between accumulation and decumulation. To give room for an unfunded pension system, we assume $\delta\rho < 1$. Three tables show respectively the critical discount factor, the dependence of fertility rate and relative efficiency as a function of the two transfer rates. The last table displays the problem called jump the gap, where the contribution and the tax rates are equal.

Table 11.1 displays the critical discount factor for a fixed raising cost $p = 0.35$ for selected points of a grid. For a fixed coefficient ζ, the higher the interest factor, the lower the critical value. For example, for $\zeta = 0.4$, as the annual interest factor $\rho[1]$ rises from 1.02 to 1.04, the annual critical discount factor $\delta(0.4, \rho[1])$ drops from 0.943 to 0.920. In parallel, the steady-state slack fertility rate rises from $n_S^* = 0.727$ to 0.771, while $n_T^* = 1.176$ remains invariant. Similarly, fixing $\rho[1] = 1.03$, as ζ rises from 0.3 to 0.5, the critical $\delta(\zeta, 1.03)$ rises from 0.927 to 0.934, basically invariant.

Table 11.2 Transfer rates and fertility rate (ν)

Contribution rate (τ)	Tax rate (θ)				
	0.0	0.1	0.2	0.3	0.4
0.0	0.771	0.980	1.188	1.397	1.606
0.1	0.717	0.932	1.143	1.347	1.551
0.2	0.653	0.857	1.061	1.265	1.469
0.3	0.571	0.776	0.980	1.184	1.388
0.4	0.490	0.694	0.898	1.102	1.306

Remark. $p = 0.35$, $\rho[1] = 1.03$ and $\zeta = 0.4$

Choose the middle (italicized) row as a basis in Table 11.1: $\zeta = 0.4$, but with some slight modification: $\rho[1] = 1.03$ (the annual interest rate being 0.88%), and $\delta[1] = 0.9$ (i.e., the annual discount rate of 10%), well below the critical value 0.931.

Changing the contribution and the tax rates, their impact can be studied also numerically. First, we present the separatrix (discussed in Lemma 11.1). It declines from 1 to 0 while the contribution rate τ rises from 0 to 0.17. Second, from Theorem 11.1, $\tau^* = \theta^* = 0.294$, close 0.3, appearing in Tables 11.2 and 11.3.

To stay close to the real world, we limit the contribution and the tax rates by 0.4–0.4, respectively. Starting with the optimal fertility rate, the first line of Table 11.2 (no-pension) shows a marked rise in fertility rate in parallel with the tax rate from 0.771 (at $\theta = 0$) to 1.606 (at $\theta = 0.4$). The first column (not considering the column of contribution rates) of Table 11.2 (no child benefit) displays a marked sink in fertility rate while the contribution rate rises: from 0.771 (at $\tau = 0$) to 0.571 (at $\tau = 0.4$). Similar tendencies can be observed in the other lines and columns, respectively, though for low enough tax rates (with positive savings) the fertility rate is paradoxically an increasing function of the contribution rate but it cannot be seen here.

Next, we display the dependence of the relative efficiency of the transfer system on the transfer rates. The first line of Table 11.3 (no-pension system) displays the drop in the relative welfare as the tax rate rises: from 1 (at $\theta = 0$) to 0.695 (at $\theta = 0.4$). The first column of Table 11.3 (no child benefit) displays the drop in the relative welfare as the contribution rate rises: from 1 (at $\tau = 0$) to 0.879 (at $\tau = 0.4$). No other column

Table 11.3 Transfer rates and relative efficiency (ε)

Contribution rate (τ)	Tax rate (θ)				
	0.0	0.1	0.2	0.3	0.4
0.0	1.000	0.944	0.872	0.788	0.695
0.1	0.916	0.871	0.859	0.892	0.899
0.2	0.878	0.994	1.068	1.103	1.095
0.3	0.916	1.050	1.129	*1.153*	1.116
0.4	0.879	1.024	1.097	1.097	1.009

Remark. See Table 11.2

Table 11.4 The impact of the equal transfer rates

Transfer rates, $\tau = \theta$	Fertility rate, n^*	Saving, s^*	Young-age	Old-age	Relative efficiency, ε
			Consumption		
			c^*	d^*	
0.00	0.771	0.055	0.675	0.134	1.000
0.05	0.850	0.033	0.619	0.123	0.936
0.10	0.932	0.008	0.566	0.113	0.871
0.15	1.000	0	0.500	0.150	0.958
0.20	1.061	0	0.429	0.212	1.068
0.25	1.122	0	0.357	0.281	1.134
0.30	*1.184*	*0*	*0.286*	*0.355*	*1.153*
0.35	1.245	0	0.214	0.436	1.117
0.40	1.306	0	0.143	0.522	1.009

Remark. See Table 11.2

and only the next row, however, show similar monotonicity. The entry of the fourth line and the fourth column (italicized) contains the approximately maximal efficiency, namely 1.153 at $(\tau, \theta) = (0.3, 0.3)$. In this sense, the social optimum is achieved for the careful harmonization of the contribution and the tax rates.

To get a more detailed picture than in Table 11.3, we repeat the calculations in Table 11.4 along the diagonal with $\tau = \theta$ with half the earlier step-size but display not only the fertility rate and the relative efficiency but also the young- and the old-age consumption. First of all, note that the optimal saving is only positive for low enough contribution and tax rates, namely around $\tau = \theta = 0.1$. The relative efficiency reaches its maximum close to 0.3 (italicized).

11.4 Conclusions

Simplifying the fertility model of Chapter 10, we have extended the investigation to the Siamese twins of child benefits and pensions. Distinguishing slack and tight credit constraints, we had to find and compare the foregoing two optima. Simonovits (2013, Sect. 3) extended the analysis to the interaction of pensions and child benefits. It turned out that introducing fertility-related pensions without activating the incentives only increases the inequality of pensions but decreases the social welfare. Also activating the pension incentives, the average fertility rate increases but the social welfare may lag behind the undifferentiated case.

References

Cigno, A. (1986). Fertility and the Tax-Benefit System. *Economic Journal, 96*, 1035–1051.

Cremer, H., Gahvari, F., & Pestieau, P. (2008). Pensions with Heterogeneous Agents and Endogenous Fertility. *Journal of Population Economics, 21*, 961–981.

Kovács, E. (2012). Hungary Contemplating a Parental Bonus in the Pension System. *Acta Oeconomica, 62*, 529–535.

Leroux, M.-L., & Pestieau, P. (2014). Social Security and Family Support. *Canadian Journal of Economics, 14*, 115–149.

Simonovits, A. (2013). *Savings, Child Support, Pensions and Endogenous (and Heterogeneous) Fertility* (IE-CERS-HAS Working Paper 35).

van Groezen, B., Leers, Th., & Meijdam, L. (2003). Social Security and Endogenous Fertility: Pensions and Child Benefits as Siamese Twins. *Journal of Public Economics, 87*, 233–251.

van Groezen, B., & Meijdam, L. (2008). Growing Old and Staying Young: Population Policy in an Aging Closed Economy. *Journal of Population Economics, 21*, 573–588.

12

Models of Political Economy

12.1 Introduction

Until now, we have exclusively relied on the method of social welfare maximization, but approaching the end of the book at least we have to touch its rival, namely Political Economy. In doing so, we have to confine ourselves to the median voter approach (Black 1948; Mas-Colell et al. 1995). (Relying on the concept of fiscal fairness, Scheve and Stasavage (2016) gave an alternative explanation connected with mass wars.) Assume that two parties compete for the votes of an odd number of voters. The issue of the voting here is the value of the transfer rate, either personal income tax rate or pension contribution rate. Every voter's utility function is first increasing, then decreasing with the transfer rate (single-peaked). Then relying on the notion of Nash-equilibrium, both parties propose that transfer rate which maximizes the utility function of the median voter. Of course, in such a situation, the voters choose their parties according to secondary issues. This theory is frequently if not always relevant.

The structure of this chapter is as follows: Sect. 12.2 discusses voting on taxation under flexible labor supply and taxation morale, respectively. Section 12.3 outlines few voting models on pensions.

A. Simonovits, *Simple Models of Income Redistribution*,
https://doi.org/10.1007/978-3-319-72502-4_12

12.2 Voting on Taxation

Taxation Under Flexible Labor Supply

Romer (1975) initiated the study of *majority voting* on linear income taxes—an alternative to welfare analysis. In such a political economy framework, Meltzer and Richard (1981) proved an interesting, intuitively appealing result: the greater the pretax income inequality, the greater redistribution will be chosen by the median voter. (Note that there is a huge literature showing that rising inequality may not increase the support for redistribution, Ashok et al. (2015) being a most recent source.)

This section modifies the Rawlsian model of taxation discussed in Sect. 2.2 into a voting model. We have $I = 2M - 1$ voters, $M > 1$, with increasing wage rates $w_1 < \cdots < w_M < \cdots < w_{2M-1}$ and voter M is called the median voter. (Note the different notations for the median wage w_M here and the maximal wage w_{M} in other chapters.) As a normalization, we take the average wage as unity: $(w_1 + \cdots + w_{2M-1})/(2M - 1) = 1$ and assume that the median wage is less than the average wage: $w_M < 1$. Recall that l is the labor supply and the workers vote on their preferred personal income tax rate θ. We copy the utility function of a worker with wage rate w:

$$U(w, c, l) = 2c - wl^2. \tag{2.2}$$

Using Lemma 2.1, we see that for a given tax rate θ, the maximum of the voter w's utility function

$$U[\theta, w, l^*] = 2\theta(1 - \theta) + w(1 - \theta)^2 = w + 2(1 - w)\theta - (2 - w)\theta^2 \tag{12.1}$$

has a single peak in the tax rate θ. Therefore the median voter theorem applies.

Theorem 12.1. *In the model of Sect. 2.2 with flexible labor supply, the median voter selects the following tax rate:*

$$\theta_M^* = \frac{1 - w_M}{2 - w_M} < \frac{1}{2} \tag{12.2}$$

and the competing two parties adopt it.

Remarks. 1. Our model harmonizes with Meltzer and Richard's (1981) finding if the pretax earning inequality is measured by the difference between the average and the median wages $1 - w_M$. Table 1.3 contains data on w_M for selected countries. Of course, other indicators may show different rankings.

2. Since the minimal wage is lower than the median wage: $w_1 < w_M$, therefore $\theta_M^* < \theta_1$, i.e., the median voter's tax rate is lower than the Rawlsian optimum.
3. Our model helps explain the connection between the extension of voting rights and the rise in the average income tax rate. If there is a minimum wage/income threshold below which the citizen cannot vote, then the median income of voters obviously rises with the threshold, diminishing the preferred tax rate. Even if every adult has a voting right, the participation rate generally rises with the income. Note, however, that other factors also play important roles in the determination of the tax rates (see e.g., Table 1.2).

Taxation Under Tax Morale

Here we discuss the role of tax morale (Sect. 2.3) in the majority voting. Now the tax morale η replaces the role of labor disutility and if voter i hides e_i from his wage w_i, then his quasi-linear utility function is equal

$$U_i(c_i, e_i) = 2c_i - \eta w_i^{-1} e_i^2, \qquad i = 1, 2, \ldots, 2M - 1. \tag{2.12}$$

We shall transform the truncated social welfare function maximization into a median voter framework. The tax morale should be constrained so that the tax rate lies between 0 and 1.

Again, every worker's indirect utility satisfies the single-peaked condition [cf. (2.17)] and the optimal tax rate corresponds to that of Theorem 2.3, only the M-minimal average wage W_M is replaced by the median one w_M, and the critical tax morale η_M with its counterpart η^o. We have

Theorem 12.2. *In the model of Sect. 2.3, assume that the tax morale is higher than 1 and lower than the critical value* η^o*:*

$$1 < \eta < \eta^o = \frac{2 - w_M}{1 - w_M}. \tag{12.3}$$

Then the median voter's preferred tax rate is positive and is given by

$$\theta^* = \frac{1 - w_M}{2 - w_M}\eta. \tag{12.4}$$

Remarks. 1. We substantiated Meltzer and Richard (1981) again, now in a model with tax morale.

2. Since the M-minimal average wage is generally lower than the median wage: $W_M < w_M$, therefore $0 < \theta^* < \theta_M^*$, i.e., the M-optimum tax rate is higher than the median voter's. Also, the bounds mean much stronger restrictions in the political economy model than in the welfare maximization model. If the cutoff index J is high, so $W_J \approx w_M$, then the J-optimal solution is close to the median voter's one.
To make a numerical illustration, Tables 2.4 and 2.5 are used. For example, for $\eta = 2$, $w_M = 0.8$ yields the same tax rate $\theta^* = 0.571$ as the cutoff index $J = 3$ for social welfare maximization.

12.3 Voting on Pensions

Background

For a long time, there has been an almost unanimous agreement among economists that the pending population aging will significantly raise the pension and health expenditures in terms of GDP (cf. Disney 1996). Galasso and Profeta (2004), for short, GP cite OECD calculations of

2002, determining the contributions of the old-age dependency ratio, and the components of the pension rule to the increase in the ratio of pension expenditure to the GDP. OECD (2013) provides the latest projections: The share of public pension expenditure in the GDP will rise from 10.3 (2010) to 12.7%, a much smaller change than the drop of the support ratio from 3.9 (2012) to 1.9 (2060). Since in most developed countries, pensions and health care are largely publicly financed and they form the dominant part of social expenditures, the welfare state will face unusual financial difficulties (for numbers, see Tables 1.16 and 1.17).

Various studies have attempted to explain the positive correlation between population aging and the size of the welfare state, where the size of the unfunded pension system may be decisive (e.g., Mulligan and Sala-i-Martin 1999; GP 2004), an excellent early survey was given by Galasso and Profeta (2002).

Starting with Browning (1975), many economists proved this relationship analytically. (For example, Breyer and Stolte (2001, p. 409) applied endogenous labor supply, when "the burden of demographic change may fall completely or predominantly on the pensioners.") The simplest possible neoclassical explanation applies an overlapping cohorts model with flat earnings and flat old-age benefits. As the population ages, the median voter gets closer to the retirement age, and his interest shifts from the contribution side to the benefit side. These results can also be confirmed in a model with heterogeneous earnings and partially earnings-related benefits (Casamatta et al. 2000; hereafter CCP), where intergenerational redistribution is complemented by intragenerational one (for a summary, see Simonovits 2003b).

This perspective has been questioned by Razin et al. (2002), for short: RSS. They formulated a very peculiar Overlapping Generations (OLG) voting model and proved analytically that the older the population, the smaller (rather than the larger) the welfare state. In this section, we reformulate RSS and show how limited is the validity of their conclusions. It is another question that RSS claimed empirical verification but inadvertently included dependent children to the category of pensioners (Bryant 2003 and Simonovits 2003a, 2007). Therefore their index of aging was misleading; while between 1970 and 1992 in the United States, the old-age dependency ratio increased from 19 to 22%, the total dependency ratio fell from 48 to 41%. Therefore their indicator showed just the opposite what they claimed: during the period between 1960 and 1992, the size of the welfare state grew, while the population aged.

A Generalized Model

Turning to RSS's theoretical model, first we list six basic assumptions of RSS in our modification:

A1. The old receive a flat benefit b and the workers receive a given share of the old's benefit χb, where χ is a given *Y/O benefit ratio*, $\chi \geq 0$. In RSS, $\chi = 1$, which is an excessive assumption.
A2. Each period, the workers expect that they will receive old-age benefit in the future equaling to a given share ψ of the present old-age benefit. This ratio will be called the *strength of link* between average present tax and future benefits. If the strength of link is zero, then we return to RSS (which is also an excessive assumption); if it is unity, then we obtain CCP and GP. (We have already dissected this questionable assumption made Feldstein (1985) in Appendix D.)
A3. The lifetime total earning of any worker is a (non-strictly) decreasing function of the tax rate.
A4. The pensioners vote for a tax rate, ensuring maximal old-age benefit and every worker votes for a tax rate maximizing his own expected lifetime income.
A5. There are more workers than pensioners and the median voter's optimal tax rate is chosen (who is a worker).
A6. The relevant parameters of the economy (i.e., wages and interest rate) are independent of the old-age dependency ratio.

Let e be a scalar between 0 and 1, showing the earning ability type of the individuals. The corresponding distribution function is denoted by F. Let τ be the tax rate on the (lifetime) total wage w, which in turn depends on the type e and the tax rate τ in the following way: $w(e, \tau)$. By convention, w is a decreasing function of e and a (possibly non-strictly) decreasing function of τ (A3).

Then the *average (lifetime) total wage* is equal to

$$W(\tau) = \int w(e, \tau) dF \tag{12.5}$$

and the *average payroll tax* is equal to

$$R(\tau) = \tau W(\tau).$$

We want $R(\tau)$ be a concave function of τ; furthermore, $R(\tau)$ first increase and later decrease. First we determine $R'(\tau)$:

$$R'(\tau) = W(\tau) + \tau W'(\tau). \tag{12.6}$$

We need the *dependency ratio* μ. In the model, there are neither children nor unemployed, nor nonemployed working-age people, nor working old-age people, therefore there is no need for adjectives like old-age or demographic. Since every worker supports μ pensioners, the per-worker macrobalance of the welfare system is as follows:

$$\chi b + \mu b = R(\tau), \quad \text{i.e.,} \quad b(\tau) = \frac{R(\tau)}{\chi + \mu}. \tag{12.7}$$

Voting on the tax rate, every pensioner maximizes his old-age benefit $b(\tau)$. Since $R(\tau)$ as well as $b(\tau)$ is inverse U-shaped, there is a unique and interior optimum for the pensioners: τ_{R}, $0 < \tau_{\mathrm{R}} < 1$.

Until now, time has not played any role. Now we denote current and future contribution rates by τ and $\tilde{\tau}$, respectively. A worker of ability e, born in period 0, maximizes his lifetime net income Y. Denoting by ρ the compounded interest factor, the reciprocal of the interest factor will be called the *discount factor*: $\delta = 1/\rho$. Then the *lifetime net income* is equal to

$$Y(e, \tau, \tilde{\tau}) = (1 - \tau) w(e, \tau) + \chi b(\tau) + \delta b(\tilde{\tau}).$$

We assume that every worker expects to receive an old-age benefit equal to ψ-times the present old-age benefit (A2), i.e., he maximizes his *expected lifetime net income*

$$\mathbf{Y}(e,\tau) = (1-\tau)w(e,\tau) + (\chi + \delta\psi)b(\tau) \tag{12.8}$$

rather than his net lifetime income. (Recall that in RSS, $\psi = 0$; while in CCP and GP, $\psi = 1$.) Before substituting (12.7) into (12.8), we introduce a new notation for the multiplier of revenue R on income $\mathbf{Y}$:

$$\phi = \frac{\chi + \delta\psi}{\chi + \mu}. \tag{12.9}$$

Then (12.7)–(12.9) yield

$$\mathbf{Y}(e,\tau) = (1-\tau)w(e,\tau) + \phi R(\tau). \tag{12.10}$$

By the concavity of the objective functions, the theory of the median voter can be applied. Note that the median voter is a worker (A5), whose ability is denoted by e_M. Since the system is progressively redistributive, it is the poorer workers, who may support it. Therefore the median voter is defined by the implicit relation $\mu + 1 - F(e_M) = F(e_M)$, i.e.,

$$F(e_M) = \frac{\mu + 1}{2}.$$

To avoid theoretical complications and imitating the reality, we also assume that for any $e < e_M$ (the unskilled workers in RSS), and for any τ, $w(e,\tau) \equiv w_{\mathrm{m}} > 0$. Thus the median voter is unskilled for every contribution rate and his net wage is $(1-\tau)w_{\mathrm{m}}$. (For example, for $\mu = 0.5$, $F(e_M) = 0.25$.)

To have a nonzero transfer system, the median voter has to vote at least for a small transfer system. Thus he should be interested in some form of redistribution. This depends on the *ratio of the minimum earning to the average one* in the ideal economy without transfers: $\Omega = w_{\mathrm{m}}/\tilde{w}(0) < 1$ and the other parameters of the model.

Theorem 12.3. *Under assumptions A1–A3, the median voter's optimal contribution rate is positive if and only if the Y/O benefit ratio is high enough:*

$$\chi > \chi^{\mathrm{o}} = \frac{(\Omega\mu - \delta\psi)_+}{1-\Omega}, \tag{12.11}$$

where x_+ is the positive part of x. Then the optimal contribution rate is determined by

$$\phi R'(\tau_{\mathrm{o}}) = w_{\mathrm{m}} \tag{12.12}$$

and it is less than the pensioners' optimum: $0 < \tau_{\mathrm{o}} < \tau_{\mathrm{R}}$.

Remarks. 1. Since Ω refers to the imaginary economy without transfers, it is very difficult to guess the interval of its reasonable values. The trial with $\Omega = 0.5$ and $\psi = 0$ leads to $\bar{\chi} = \mu$, but much higher critical values are also conceivable. For example, if $w_{\mathrm{m}} > 2/3$, then $w^*(0) > 2/3$, hence $\Omega > 2/3$, thus $\mu = 1/2$ leads to $\bar{\chi} > 1$, i.e., RSS's model becomes empty: assumption A1 is not sufficient to have a positive contribution rate.

2. Note that the critical value of the Y/O benefit rate is a decreasing function of ψ, it may be even negative. This is the case for $\psi = 1$ if $\rho < \nu$ or equivalently $\delta > \mu^{-1}$ (dynamic inefficiency, Samuelson, 1958). We shall assume, however, that dynamic efficiency holds, $\delta < \mu^{-1}$, then for high enough Ωs or low enough ψs, the critical value is still positive.

Proof. Using the assumption that the median voter is unskilled, and taking the derivative of $\mathbf{Y}$ with respect to τ, (12.10) leads to

$$\mathbf{Y}'_\tau(e_M, \tau) = -w_{\mathrm{m}} + \phi R'(\tau). \tag{12.13}$$

This implies (12.12). By (12.9), (12.11) is equivalent to $w_{\mathrm{m}} < \phi w^*(0)$. Together with (12.13) and (12.6), (12.11) implies $\mathbf{Y}'_\tau(e_M, 0) > 0$, i.e., $\tau_{\mathrm{o}} > 0$. Note that $R'(\tau_{\mathrm{R}}) = 0$ and (12.13) lead to $\mathbf{Y}'_\tau(e_M, \tau_{\mathrm{R}}) = -w_{\mathrm{m}} < 0$ which implies $\tau_{\mathrm{o}} < \tau_{\mathrm{R}}$. ■

It is time to turn to the main topic of RSS, which is the *impact of population aging on the size of the welfare state.* Following RSS, we shall study the dependence of the contribution rate determined by the median voter on the dependency ratio. We shall generalize A6 as follows: A6*: Except for the interest rate ρ or equivalently, the discount factor δ, all the other parameters and functions (χ, w_{m}, $w(e, \tau)$, etc.) are independent of the dependency ratio. As is known, in reality, $\rho'(\mu) \le 0$, i.e., $\delta'(\mu) \ge 0$.

Theorem 12.4. *Under the assumptions of Theorem 12.3 with $\psi \ge 0$, $\chi > \chi^{\mathrm{o}} \ge 0$ and assumption A6*, the contribution rate determined by the median voter is counterintuitively a decreasing function of the dependency ratio μ if and only if the discount factor δ is a sufficiently mildly increasing function of the dependency ratio:*

$$\psi(\chi + \mu)\delta'(\mu) < \chi + \psi\delta(\mu). \tag{12.14}$$

Remarks. 1. It is well-known that aging *does* influence important parameters. As the World Bank (1994, p. 35) emphasized, falling fertility rate, i.e., rising old-age dependency may lead to dramatic improvements in education and consequently, in productivity. Similarly, if every worker receives child benefit φ per child, then his or her child benefit is given by $\Phi(\mu) = \mu^{-1}\varphi$ (see Chapters 10 and 11; in a 3-generations unisex model, each worker has $1/\mu$ children). It is equally well known that in isolation, aging will depress the (real) interest rate. (The marginal productivity of a rising per capita capital will decline.) Following RSS, we neglect the first two dependencies, but differing from RSS, we stress the existence of connection $\rho(\mu)$, or equivalently, $\delta(\mu)$.

2. Theorem 12.4 shows that a slight modification of A2 and A6 may turn a decreasing contribution rate–dependency rate function into an increasing one. If we introduced child benefit $\Phi(\mu) = \varphi/\mu$, then the generalization of (12.14) would even be more restrictive than (12.14) is.
3. Recall the Remark to Theorem 5.1: the maximal contribution rate is an increasing function of the dependency rate and this maximum is the social optimum for sufficiently myopic population!

Proof. By the implicit function theorem,

$$\tau_o'(\mu) = -\frac{\phi'(\mu)R'(\tau_o)}{\phi(\mu)R''(\tau_o)}.$$

Taking into account $R'' < 0 < R', \phi$, our formula implies that $\tau_o'(\mu) < 0$ is equivalent to $\phi' < 0$. Taking the derivative of (12.9) by μ implies (12.14). ■

At the end of the subsection, let us mention several simple but often neglected problems with the application of such models.

i. If the Y/O benefit ratio is low enough and the poorest workers are very risk averse, then their optimal saving intention may be negative. Having met credit constraints, they have to maximize lifetime utility rather than the lifetime income. Then the set of workers, who form a majority with the pensioners, does not contain the poorest workers (CCP, footnote 1 on p. 507) and the paradox may disappear even for inflexible interest rate. This may happen when the benefit is earnings-related or the earning distribution is different from that used in RSS. At the same time, CCP also mentioned the possibility of the paradox without calling it a paradox, and did not work it out.
ii. Social security offers *insurance* against certain risks (longevity, inflation, etc.) which cannot be easily insured on the market (cf. Sects. 3.3 and 3.4). As is well known (e.g., Mitchell et al. 1999), people are ready to pay much more for getting social insurance than the deterministic equivalent of the service.
iii. The participation rate in voting strongly depends on age. "The turnout in US elections is sharply increasing in age, rising from 45% for the 20-year old to 75% for the 65-year old" (Hassler et al. 2003, p. 96).

12.4 Conclusions

In Sect. 12.2, we presented the simplest taxation models of the median voter where workers react to taxation with restrained labor supply and tax evasion. In Sect. 12.3, we generalized and criticized RSS pension model and qualified their paradox: the older the population, the smaller the welfare state. Their empirical corroboration rested on a simple confusion between old-age dependency rate (which increased) and the total dependency rate (which decreased) between 1970 and 1992.

Cremer and De Donder (2016) analyzed a much more realistic model: In addition to the heterogeneous wages and the size of the social security system, they also considered life expectancy heterogeneity (Appendix F) and the degree of redistribution (see Sect. 4.3 and Chapter 6). Applying a two-dimensional voting model, they proved the difference between the public pension systems of France and Great Britain. Unfortunately, they neglected the credit constraints and historical developments (path dependence).

References

Ashok, V., Kuziemko, L., & Washington, E. (2015). Support for Redistribution in an Age of Rising Inequality: New Stylized Facts and Some Tentative Explanations. *Brookings Papers on Economic Activity. Spring*, 367–433.

Black, D. (1948). On the Rationale of Group Decision Making. *Journal of Political Economy, 56*, 23–34.

Breyer, F., & Stolte, K. (2001). Demographic Change, Endogenous Labor Supply and the Political Feasibility of a Pension Reform. *Journal of Population Economics, 14*, 409–424.

Browning, E. K. (1975). Why the Social Insurance Budget Is Too Large in a Democracy. *Economic Inquiry, 13*, 373–388.

Bryant, J. (2003, June). Modelling the Effect of Population Ageing on Government Social Expenditures (New Zealand Treasury Discussion Paper 03/15). Wellington.

Casamatta, G., Cremer, H., & Pestieau, P. (2000). The Political Economy of Social Security. *Scandinavian Journal of Economics, 102*(3), 503–522.

Cremer, H., & De Donder, P. (2016). Life Expectancy Heterogeneity and the Political Support for the Collective Annuities. *Scandinavian Journal of Economics, 118*, 594–615.

Disney, R. (1996). *Can We Afford to Get Older? A Perspective on the Economics of Aging*. Cambridge, MA: MIT Press.

Galasso, V., & Profeta, P. (2002). The Political Economy of the Social Security: A Survey. *European Journal of Political Economy, 18*, 1–29.
Galasso, V., & Profeta, P. (2004). Lessons for an Aging Society: The Political Sustainability of Social Security Systems. *Economic Policy, 38*, 63–115.
Hassler, J., Mora, J. V. R., Storesletten, K., & Zilibotti, F. (2003). The Survival of the Welfare State. *American Economic Review, 93*, 87–112.
Mas-Colell, A., Whinston, M. D., & Green, J. (1995). *Microeconomic Theory*. New York: Oxford University Press.
Meltzer, A. H., & Richard, S. F. (1981). The Rational Theory of the Size of the Government. *Journal of Political Economy, 89*, 914–927.
Mitchell, O. S., Poterba, J. M., Warshawski, M. J., & Brown, J. R. (1999). New Evidence on Money's Worth of Individual Annuities. *American Economic Review, 89*(5), 1299–1318.
Mulligan, C. B., & Sala-i-Martin, X. (1999). Gerontocracy, Retirement, and Social Security. *NBER WP 7117*, Cambridge, MA.
OECD. (2013). *Glance at Pensions*. Paris.
Razin, A., Sadka, E., & Swagel, P. (2002). The Aging Population and the Size of the Welfare State. *Journal of Political Economy, 110*, 900–918.
Romer, T. (1975). Individual Welfare, Majority Voting and the Properties of a Linear Income Tax. *Journal of Public Economics, 4*, 163–185.
Samuelson, P. A. (1958). An Exact Consumption-Loan Model of Interest with or Without the Social Contrivance of Money. *Journal of Political Economy, 66*, 467–482.
Scheve, K., & Stasavage, D. (2016). *Taxing the Rich: A History of Fiscal Fairness in the United States and Europe*. New York: Russell Saga Foundation.
Simonovits, A. (2003a). A Note on Population Aging and the Size of the Welfare State (CEU, Department of Economics Working Paper 4). Budapest.
Simonovits, A. (2003b). *Modeling Pension Systems*. Houndsmill, Basingstoke: Palgrave, Macmillan.
Simonovits, A. (2007). Can Population Aging Imply a Smaller Welfare State? *European Journal of Political Economy, 23*, 534–541.
World Bank. (1994). *Averting Old-Age Crisis*. Washington, DC: World Bank.

13

Imperfect Knowledge of Transfer Rules: Irrational Inattention

13.1 Introduction

Following the dominant approach, as a rule, in the book, we assumed that the workers perfectly know the transfer rules. In this late chapter, we give up this approach and adopt a more realistic one, namely that workers imperfectly know the transfer rules. We do not investigate the causes of imperfect knowledge, we just accept the fact. (To avoid misunderstanding, we do not apply the assumption of excessive underestimation of future benefit commonly used in Feldstein (1985) and Razin et al. (2002), which is closer to a trick than to description, see Appendix D and Chapter 12, respectively.) We cite selectively only a few sources. Note that in some cases, imperfect knowledge can be rational inattention (Sims 2003) but in our cases it is irrational.

Slemrod (2006, p. 57) examined the role of misconceptions in support for regressive tax reform. He used "data from an exceptionally detailed survey of attitudes toward taxation in the United States to investigate the relative importance of one particular misconception—that high-income people would pay more tax under an apparently regressive reform, mostly because many people believe that the distribution of the burden of the

A. Simonovits, *Simple Models of Income Redistribution*,
https://doi.org/10.1007/978-3-319-72502-4_13

existing income tax is regressive—in explaining public support for the flat[-rate] tax and a retail sales tax."

Ballard-Rosa et al. (2015) (see Scheve and Stasavage 2016, p. 212) reported a recent study of the preferred marginal income tax rate for six income categories. They presented progressive schedules but even the preferred top rate is lower than the actual one. "One possible reason people don't want higher tax rates is that the individuals in our survey fail to understand how high inequality is today and how much it has increased in recent years." Table 1.9 reports the huge differences on actual, presumed and preferred wealth distribution among the US citizens.

Gustman and Steinmeier (2005) also studied the imperfect knowledge of social security and private pension. Barr and Diamond (2008, p. 48, Box 4.2) enlisted the following items of imperfect "consumer" information. (a) Poor sense of risk and uncertainty (e.g., life annuity), (b) workers are poorly informed about complex products like private DC plans, (c) private DB plans also contain details most workers do not understand. They also mentioned a related problem, namely that of processing information.

Ágoston and Kovács (2007) interviewed several hundred Hungarians asking them how they saved for their future. On average, the interviewees had correct projections on their future pensions and their aspired old-age consumption, and wanted to save accordingly, but after breaking the population into groups according to earnings, the future is less rosy.

Benitez-Silva et al. (2009) interviewed several hundred US citizens about the basic Social Security rules and it turned out that a large part of the interviewees had very scant information about the rules. For example, only half of them knew the exact value of the minimal retirement age (62); only two-thirds knew the interval spanned by the rising normal retirement age (65–67); only a quarter knew the minimal number of years needed to have a benefit (10). The foregoing authors have created two models: (i) with perfect information and (ii) with imperfect information. In the model with perfect information they were able to replicate the retirement age distribution of the US workers but they could improve the explanation by relying on imperfect information.

Finseraas and Jakobssen (2013) interviewed Norwegians about their knowledge of the respective pension system and discovered that increased information had no impact on retirement plans. Lusardi and Mitchell

(2014) is the most recent and authoritative overview of financial literacy, surveying facts as well as theories.

Perhaps the most spectacular error, stemming from imperfect information, occurred in the so-called mis-selling campaign, where millions of British employees opted out from the State Earnings-Related Pension Scheme into the newly emerging personal pension (with individual account). "Over time it became clear that many people who have made such a move were predictably worse off as a result" (Barr and Diamond 2008, Box 9.2, 157–158).

Dushi and Honig (2015) analyzed "how much do respondents in the health and retirement study know about their contributions to tax-deferred contribution plans?" The message is simple: very little.

The next item is a little bit different from the previous ones: Csontos et al. (1998) interviewed Hungarian citizens about their tax awareness and their attitudes to the reform of the welfare state. The majority of the interviewees knew relatively little about the transfer programs in health care, education and pensions. It is not surprising that they were not partners in the discussion of the reform of the welfare state.

The structure of the remainder of the chapter is as follows. Section 13.2 presents a simple model of inattention in voting on tax (a counterpart of Sect. 12.3). Section 13.3 creates a framework for the pension rules. Section 13.4 models the decision of entering the Hungarian mandatory private pillar forsaking one part of their benefits earned in the old system. By overestimating the private system's advantages over the pay-as-you-go system much more workers entered into the mixed system than it would have been reasonable. Section 13.5 analyzes a model, where workers underestimate the actuarial adjustment rate and retire earlier than would be rational. Section 13.6 concludes.

13.2 Underestimating the Collected Taxes

The simplest case of irrational inattention is when the median voter underestimates the collected taxes, financing the basic income, and voting for less than the proper value. We rely again on the taxation model of Sect. 2.2. Let ψ be a real between 0 and 1, showing the degree of underestimation.

Then the revenue function $\theta(1-\theta)$ is replaced by $\psi\theta(1-\theta)$ and (12.1) becomes

$$U_M[\theta, l(\theta)] = 2\psi\theta(1-\theta) + w_M(1-\theta)^2.$$

Taking its partial derivative by θ yields the modified optimality condition:

$$0 = U'_{M,\theta}[\theta, l(\theta)] = 2\psi[1-2\theta] - 2w_M(1-\theta).$$

Hence we arrived to the modified Theorem 12.1:

Theorem 13.1. *If the median voter's underestimation factor ψ of collected taxes satisfies $w_M < \psi \leq 1$, then the median voter's preferred tax rate is given by*

$$\theta_M = \frac{\psi - w_M}{2\psi - w_M}.$$

Remark. As expected, within limits, the lower the underestimation factor ψ, the lower the preferred tax rate. At the lowest point, the tax rate becomes zero.

13.3 Pension Framework

In this section, we create a general framework to analyze the impact of imperfect knowledge of the pension rules. Let x be the individual decision vector (e.g., labor supply, tax evasion, private saving), scalars c and d be the consumption of the worker and the pensioner. The later consumption depends on the pension rules and both consumptions depend also on the individual decision: $c = C(x)$ and $d = D(x)$, where the impact of the rule is suppressed. The lifetime utility of the worker depends on the two consumptions and the decision: $U(c, d, x)$. (For example, in addition to his consumption pair (c, d), the young-age utility also depends on his labor supply and tax evasion but both subutilities are only implicitly dependent on saving.) Substituting $c = C(x)$ and $d = D(x)$ into $U(c, d, x)$ yields the reduced utility function

$$U[x] = U(C(x), D(x), x).$$

In the following, it is assumed that all the foregoing functions are smooth and the optimum is interior (except for Sect. 13.5). If the worker knew the actual pension rule, then his optimal decision would be x^{o} such that

$$\begin{aligned} U'[x] &= U'_c(C(x), D(x), x)C'(x) + U'_d(C(x), D(x), x)D'(x) \\ &\quad + U'_x(C(x), D(x), x) = 0. \end{aligned}$$

Under suitable conditions, there is a unique solution to this optimality condition, x^{o}.

In practice, the worker may know the true C but he does not know the true pension function D. Rather, he mistakes $\tilde{D}$ for D, $\tilde{D} \neq D$. Repeating the calculations executed above, the distorted reduced utility function is

$$\tilde{U}[x] = U(C(x), \tilde{D}(x), x)$$

and the corresponding distorted optimum $\tilde{x}^{\mathrm{o}}$ satisfies

$$\begin{aligned} \tilde{U}'[x] &= U'_c(C(x), \tilde{D}(x), x)C'(x) + U'_d(C(x), \tilde{D}(x), x)\tilde{D}'(x) \\ &\quad + U'_x(C(x), \tilde{D}(x), x) = 0. \end{aligned}$$

Rather than analyzing the general problem, we shall discuss two special models.

13.4 Hidden Loss at Entering the Mixed System

The World Bank (1994) initiated some form of partial privatization of public pension systems, especially in ex-post socialist countries and Latin America. This section discusses a peculiarity of the Hungarian structural reform of 1998. Basically, those entering the mixed system voluntarily (having already started working) had lost a quarter of their earlier pension rights but could expect higher yields in the private part (Simonovits 1999). (In all the subsequent reforms executed in other East and Central European countries, those entering the mixed system retained the proportional part of their previous benefits earned in a mono system.) Most Hungarian workers overestimated the relative gains of the new private pillar and even such workers entered whose expected loss would have been much greater than their gain. (We use past conditional, because the private pillar was closed down at the end of 2010, two years earlier than the payout phase had been planned to start: the whole issue lost its relevance.) As to be expected, the share of entrants decreased with age (see Fig. 10.1 of Simonovits 2003). Eventually about half of the workers entered voluntarily into the mixed system.

Here is the simplest model to explain the phenomenon excessive joining (a more complex one was presented in Simonovits (2003), using real data presented in its Table 5.2). The length of the working period is taken as unity and the share of time spent in the monopillar, a proxy for age at 1998, is denoted by T, $0 < T < 1$. The contribution rate is τ, the presumed relative gain in the private pillar with respect to the public one is $\alpha > 0$ and the share of the private pillar in the total one is q, $0 < q < 1$. By definition, the gain of a worker, earning unitary wages, is $\alpha q\tau(1 - T)$ and his loss is $q\tau T$. At the critical age, the two quantities are equal:

$$\alpha q\tau(1 - T) = q\tau T.$$

Hence a simple calculation yields

Theorem 13.2. *A worker is indifferent between joining or not the mixed system, if his age T_α is critical:*

$$T_\alpha = \frac{\alpha}{1+\alpha}.$$

Note that the values of τ and q are indifferent with respect to T_α.

If we neglect the variation in the cohort-sizes and the rising wage–age schedule, moreover, we assume that only the presumed relative gain determined the critical age, then the fact that half of the workers voluntarily entering the mixed system implies a critical age 1/2, i.e., $\alpha = 1$. Taking into account that during the 13 years of its existence the private system had only produced about 10% real gains, while the pay-as-you-go system also produced a significant gain (see Appendix D), one can conclude that a huge majority of the joiners significantly overestimated the relative gain (for details, see Simonovits 2011).

At the end, we note that there were many voluntary participants who did not know about the low and entered without making any calculation. Depending on their share, the presumed gain of entry is lower than determined above.

13.5 Underestimating the Delayed Retirement Credit

We apply now the imperfect knowledge to the issue of flexible retirement system, studied already in Chapter 9. To avoid repetition, we only shortly refer to the antecedents.

Let positive reals Q, R and D denote the ages of entering into work, of retirement and of death, respectively: $0 < Q < R < D$. We copy the linear benefit function

$$b^L(R) = \alpha(R - Q)[1 + \eta(R - R^*)], \tag{9.4L}$$

where the real number $R^* \in (R_{\mathrm{m}}, R_{\mathrm{M}})$ is the normal retirement age, the real number $\alpha > 0$ is the marginal accrual rate and the real number $\eta > 0$ is the true adjustment rate. By error, the worker underestimates η by a factor ψ, therefore its presumed lifetime utility function is

$$\begin{aligned}\tilde{U}[R] &= (R - Q)[\log(1 - \tau) - \chi] \\ &\quad + (D - R)\log(\alpha(R - Q)[1 + \psi\eta(R - R^*)]).\end{aligned}$$

Rephrasing Theorem 9.1, we have

Theorem 13.3. *If the worker underestimates the adjustment rate η by a factor of ψ, then the distorted interior optimal retirement age is determined by*

$$\tilde{U}'[R] = \log(1-\tau) - \chi - \log(\alpha(R-Q)[1+\psi\eta(R-R^*)])$$
$$+(D-R)\left[\frac{1}{R-Q} + \frac{\psi\eta}{1+\psi\eta(R-R^*)}\right] = 0. \qquad (13.5)$$

Remark. If $\tilde{U}'[R_{\mathrm{m}}] < 0$, then the worker retires at the earliest age: $R_{\tilde{\eta}} = R_{\mathrm{m}}$. It is difficult to analyze (13.5), therefore we rely on numerical illustration.

Example 13.1. $Q = 20$, $D = 80$, $\tau = 0.2$, $\chi = 1.2$. Working with $\eta = 0.05$, the underestimation factor ψ decreases from 1 to 0 with step-size 0.2. For the true rate, the optimal retirement age is about 65.6 years, but for $\psi = 0.4$ (row 4), $\tilde{\eta} = 0.2$, the distorted retirement age is only $\tilde{R} = 63.8$ and the presumed and true benefits are equal to 0.471 and 0.521, respectively. Table 13.1 displays further values.

Table 13.1 The impact of the underestimating delayed retirement rate

Underestimated rate, $\tilde{\eta}$	Retirement age (years), $R_{\tilde{\eta}}$	Presumed	Actual	Lifetime balance, z
		Benefit		
		$\tilde{b}$	b	
0.05	65.6	0.584	0.584	0.715
0.04	65.2	0.546	0.570	0.611
0.03	64.7	0.510	0.552	0.494
0.02	63.8	0.471	0.521	0.316
0.01	62.4	0.434	0.475	0.122
0.00	59.9	0.399	0.397	0.000

Remark. Benefits and balances are given in annual average total wage, $\eta = 0.06$

13.6 Conclusions

Departing from the main line of the book, in this chapter, we have modeled three cases, where the individuals (or even the government) did not know the actual transfer rules. As a result, they acted suboptimally. In the first model, they underestimated the collected taxes and voted for suboptimal tax rates. In the second model, the workers overestimated the relative gains of joining the mandatory private funded system and—knowing or not knowing the loss of entering into the private pillar—even such workers had entered, who should not have to. In the third model, the workers underestimated the delayed retirement credit and retired suboptimally early. The detailed discussion of imperfect information is an important topic but should be left to future studies.

References

Ágoston, K. C., & Kovács, E. (2007). The Specifics of Hungarian Self-Reliance (in Hungarian). *Hungarian Economic Review, 54,* 560–578.

Ballard-Rosa, C., Martin, L., & Scheve, K. (2015). *The Structure of American Income Tax Policy Preferences.* Stanford: Stanford University.

Barr, N., & Diamond, P. (2008). *Reforming Pensions: Principles and Policy Choices.* Oxford: Oxford University Press.

Benitez-Silva, H., Demiralp, B., & Liu, Z. (2009). *Social Security Literacy and Retirement Well-Being (Discussion Paper).* Ann Arbor: University of Michigan.

Csontos, L., Kornai, J., & Tóth, I. G. (1998). Tax Awareness and the Reform of the Welfare State. *Economics of Transition, 6,* 287–312.

Dushi, I., & Honig, M. (2015). How Much Do Respondents in the Health and Retirement Study Know About Their Contributions to Tax-Deferred Contribution Plans? A Cross-Cohort Comparison. *Journal of Pension Economics and Finance, 14,* 203–239.

Feldstein, M. S. (1985). The Level of Social Security Benefits. *Quarterly Journal of Economics, 100,* 302–320.

Finseraas, H., & Jakobssen, N. (2013). Does Information About the Pension System Affect Knowledge and Retirement Plans? *Evidence from a Survey Experiment, Journal of Pension Economics and Finance, 13,* 250–271.

Gustman, A. I., & Steinmeier, T. L. (2005). Imperfect Knowledge of Social Security and Pension. *Industrial Relations, 44*, 373–397.

Lusardi, A., & Mitchell, O. (2014). The Economic Importance of Financial Literacy: Theory and Evidence. *Journal of Economic Literature, 52*, 5–44.

Razin, A., Sadka, E., & Swagel, P. (2002). The Aging Population and the Size of the Welfare State. *Journal of Political Economy, 110*, 900–918.

Scheve, K., & Stasavage, D. (2016). *Taxing the Rich: A History of Fiscal Fairness in the United States and Europe*. New York: Russell Sage Foundation.

Simonovits, A. (1999). The New Hungarian Pension System and Its Problems. In K. Müller & H.-J. Wagener (Eds.), *Transformation of Social Security: Pensions in Central-Eastern Europe* (pp. 211–230). Heidelberg: Physica.

Simonovits, A. (2003). *Modeling Pension Systems*. Houndsmill, Basingstoke: Palgrave Macmillan.

Simonovits, A. (2011). The Mandatory Private Pension Pillar: An Obituary. *International Social Security Review, 64*(3), 81–98.

Sims, A. C. (2003). Implications of Rational Inattention. *Journal of Monetary Economics, 50*, 665–690.

Slemrod, J. (2006). The Role of Misconceptions in Support for Regressive Tax Reform. *National Tax Journal, 59*, 57–75.

World Bank. (1994). *Averting Old-Age Crisis*. Washington, DC: World Bank.

14

Wage-Dependent Longevity and Pension Benefits

14.1 Introduction

We have already discussed heterogeneous longevity in Appendix F to Chapter 4 (with heterogeneous wages) and Chapter 9 (with homogeneous wages). Due to its paramount importance, now we return to this issue. The basic problem is that in a number of countries, the heterogeneity in longevity has always been significant and during the last decades it has been dramatically increasing (Auerbach et al. 2017). Then the optimality of a strong link between unadjusted *lifetime* contributions and *annual* benefits is not straightforward (Liebmann 2002 and Fehr et al. 2013).

Section 14.2 is a direct continuation of Ayuso et al. (2016). We only cite their *hypothetical* implicit tax/subsidy rates for lifetime income quintiles in the United States for male and female cohorts of 1930 and 1960 if an NDC worked there. Note that in our hypothetical world, shorter-lived, poorer quintiles subsidized the longer-lived, richer quintiles in both cohorts but the redistribution dramatically grew during the last 30 years.

Section 14.3 extends the calculation to the variable retirement ages without considering gender differences asymmetric information and adverse selection.

A. Simonovits, *Simple Models of Income Redistribution*,
https://doi.org/10.1007/978-3-319-72502-4_14

Table 14.1 Implicit tax/subsidy rates (%) for lifetime income quintiles in the United States with NDC

Quintile	1	2	4	5
Male				
Cohort 1930	−5.3	−3.2	6.0	12.8
Cohort 1960	−21.9	−15.3	13.2	16.2
Female				
Cohort 1930	−0.3	−3.1	3.1	11.7
Cohort 1960	−12.7	−8.3	2.2	29.3

*R*emark. Ayuso et al. (2016, Table 2, p. 7) (cf. Whitehouse and Zaidi 2008)

Section 14.4 discusses indexation of benefits. We call attention to Barr and Diamond (2008, Subsection 5.1.4) which starts with the indexation of covered wages in calculating the initial benefits (valorization) and indexing of benefits in payment (or in progress). Concentrating on the latter, they analyze the advantages and disadvantages of price and wage indexation: the price indexing defends the workers against drop in real benefit, for a given starting value it is less costly to the government than wage indexing but for growing real wages it results in relative decrease of pension to wages. Price indexation is better for short lived pensioners than others. These features are modeled in the foregoing section. Feldstein (1990), Legros (2006), Weinzierl (2014) are also recommended.

The structure of the chapter is as follows: Sect. 14.2 presents three adjustments to the unadjusted nonfinancial defined contribution (NDC) pension system when wages do not change in time and age: (A) proportional reduction of all the benefits to eliminate aggregate loss; (B) calculating with wage-specific rather than average life expectancies and (C) combining NDC with a flat benefit. Section 14.3 considers heterogeneous retirement ages as well (Chapter 9). Section 14.4 analyzes the impact of indexation on redistribution (Table 14.1).

14.2 Time- and Age-Invariant Wages and Common Retirement Ages

In this section, we concentrate on the case, where workers born in a given year earn heterogeneous wages but these wages do not change with time/age in real terms. Our main interest lies with the impact of wage-dependent longevities on the benefits.

Annual wages have a density function $f(w)$ and a distribution function $F(w)$, where $f(w) = F'(w)$. We need the following notations: contribution rate τ, retirement age R, starting age Q, remaining life expectancy at retirement of a worker with wage w, $e_R(w)$, where for a fixed R, $e_R(\cdot)$ is increasing. Then the traditional NDC benefit is calculated with *average* remaining life expectancy $e_R = \mathbf{E}_w e_R(w)$:

$$b^N(w, R) = \frac{\tau w(R - Q)}{e_R}. \qquad (14.1N)$$

We shall need the lifetime net contribution

$$z = \tau w(R - Q) - b(w, R)e_R(w). \qquad (14.2)$$

Substituting (14.1N) into (14.2) yields

$$\begin{aligned} z^N(w, R) &= \tau w(R - Q) - \frac{\tau w(R - Q)}{e_R} e_R(w) \\ &= \frac{\tau w(R - Q)}{e_R}[e_R - e_R(w)]. \end{aligned}$$

Using (14.1N) again results in

Theorem 14.1. *At traditional NDC (14.1N), the wage-dependent lifetime net contribution is equal to the product of the NDC benefit and of the difference between the average and the wage-dependent remaining life expectancies:*

$$z^N(w, R) = b^N(w, R)[e_R - e_R(w)]. \qquad (14.3N)$$

For continuous or symmetric distribution functions, we can define the *separator wage* w_R at which the wage-specific remaining life expectancy is equal to the average one: $e_R(w_R) = e_R$. (Note that e_R is *not a separator!*) An easy implication is as follows:

$$e_R(w) < e_R(w_R) \quad \text{if} \quad w < w_R, \qquad e_R(w) > e_R(w_R) \quad \text{if} \quad w > w_R.$$

In certain cases, the quantity w_R might be independent of R and simply be equal to the average wage, namely $w_R = \mathbf{E}w = 1$.

Theorem 14.1 have a

Corollary. *Under (14.1N), (a) for earners with below-average life expectancy, the lifetime net contribution is positive (losers); for earners with above-average life expectancy, the lifetime net contribution is negative (gainers). (b) The expected lifetime net contribution is negative.*

Proof. (a) See (14.3N).

(b) Divide the wage distribution into two parts: below and above the separator wage. Since $b^N(\cdot, R)$ is an increasing function, it can be replaced by $b(w_R, R)$ for the average life expectancy, thus increasing $z^N(w, R)$ for positive values and decreasing $z^N(w, R)$ for negative values, hence $\mathbf{E}z = b(w_R, R)\mathbf{E}e_R(w) = 0$. ■

Peter Diamond (private communication) suggested the simple *adjustment* for eliminating the aggregate loss; to contract all the benefits with the same factor ζ:

$$b^A(w, R) = \frac{\zeta \tau w(R - Q)}{e_R} = \zeta b^N(1, R)w. \tag{14.1A}$$

Inserting (14.1A) into (14.2) yields

$$z^A(w, R) = b^N(1, R)w[e_R - \zeta e_R(w)]. \tag{14.3A}$$

Taking expectations and equaling it to zero:

$$0 = \mathbf{E}z^A(w, R) = b^N(1, R)\mathbf{E}\{w[e_R - \zeta e_R(w)]\},$$

hence

$$\zeta^A = \frac{e_R}{\mathbf{E}[we_R(w)]}. \tag{14.4A}$$

Note that if we replace the assumption that $e_R(w)$ is an increasing function by the weaker assumption that w and $e_R(w)$ are positively correlated, i.e., (using $\mathbf{E}w = 1$) $\mathbf{E}[we_R(w)] > e_R$, then $\zeta^A < 1$.

Theorem 14.1A. *At the proportionally adjusted NDC (14.1A), the lifetime net contribution is equal to the product of the unadjusted NDC benefit and of the difference between the average and the contracted wage-dependent remaining life expectancy (14.3A), where the contracting factor ζ is determined in (14.4A).*

Following Ayuso et al. (2016), we shall discuss two further corrections to eliminate, dampen or reverse this type of redistribution. Adjustment B simply divides the pension wealth with the wage-specific life expectancy $e_R(w)$ rather than with the average e_R. Then

$$b^B(w, R) = \frac{(R - Q)w}{e_R(w)} \quad \text{and} \quad z^B(w, R) = 0. \tag{14.1B}$$

In this modification, the adjustment factor depends on the wage: $\zeta^B(w) = e_R(w)/e_R$ but it is difficult to sell politically adjustment B.

Adjustment C linearly combines the A-adjusted NDC benefit and the flat one, where the latter is equal to $\zeta b^{\text{o}} = \zeta b(1, R)$ and the non-negative weights are α and $1 - \alpha$, respectively:

$$b^C(w, R) = \zeta\alpha b^N(w, R) + (1-\alpha)\zeta b^{\text{o}}, \qquad 0 \le \alpha \le 1. \tag{14.1C}$$

Substituting (14.1C) into (14.2) yields

$$z^C(w, R) = b^{\text{o}}we_R - [\alpha\zeta b^{\text{o}}w + (1 - \alpha)\zeta b^{\text{o}}]e_R(w).$$

Taking the expectation and making it zero:

$$0 = \mathbf{E}_w z^C(w, R) = b^{\text{o}}e_R - \alpha\zeta b^{\text{o}}\mathbf{E}[we_R(w)] - (1 - \alpha)\zeta b^{\text{o}}e_R.$$

Hence the α-dependent contraction factor ζ^C is now equal to

$$\zeta^C = \frac{e_R}{(1-\alpha)e_R + \alpha \mathbf{E}[we_R(w)]}. \tag{14.4C}$$

Note that for $\alpha = 1$, (14.1C)–(14.4C) reduces to (14.1B).

Diminishing the value of α, the direction of the redistribution changes. In summary,

Theorem 14.1B. *The benefit rule (14.1B) eliminates the perverse redistribution. The benefit rule (14.1C) and (14.4C) weakens or even reverses perverse redistribution.*

At the end of this section, we illustrate our results on a simple numerical example. Number of types: $I = 3$ with equal weights 1/3, contribution rate $\tau = 0.25$. $Q = 20$, $R = 60$, $\alpha = 0.5$ in adjustment C. To make the results of the calculations simple, we use symmetric earnings and remaining life expectancies, their values are given in columns 1 and 2 of Table 14.2, respectively. Note that in ANDC, the absolute value of the loss of the low-earner is much lower than the gain of the high-earner, the adjustment factor $\zeta^A = 0.952$. Benefit adjustment B eliminates all redistribution, while the adjustment C with $\alpha = 0.5$ replaces redistribution from the low LEXP to the high LEXP by redistribution to the other direction, furthermore, the adjustment factor is higher than before: $\zeta^C = 0.976$.

Table 14.2 NDC's variations: Homogeneous retirement age

Wage, w_i	LEXP at ret., e_i	Adjusted NDC				
		Benefit-A, b_i^A	Balance-A, z_i^A	Benefit-B, b_i^B	Benefit-C, b_i^C	Balance-C, z_i^C
0.5	17	0.238	0.952	0.294	0.366	−1.220
1.0	20	0.476	0.476	0.500	0.488	0.244
1.5	23	0.714	−1.429	0.652	0.610	0.976

Remark. $Q = 20$, $R = 60$, $\alpha = 0.5$; $z_1^B = z_2^B = z_2^B = 0$

14.3 Heterogeneous Retirement Ages

Now we turn to a less important but relevant issue: we extend the analysis to the case where the retirement ages are also heterogeneous. Avoiding complex lifetime utility maximization, especially when the government does not know the life expectancies (Diamond 2003, etc.), we simply assume the more one earns, the later dies, therefore later retires: $R(w)$ is an increasing function.

We have to repeat all the calculations for our heterogeneous retirement ages.

Start with the NDC:

$$b^N(w, R(w)) = \frac{\tau w[R(w) - Q]}{e_{R(w)}}, \tag{14.5N}$$

where $e_{R(w)}$ is the average remaining life expectancy for retirement age $R(w)$, independent of w. Because longer-lived and higher-paid workers also retire later, under (14.5N), the benefit is again an increasing function of the wage. Therefore the corollary can be generalized and the average loss remains.

Turning to the proportionally adjusted NDC:

$$b^A(w, R(w)) = \frac{\zeta\tau w[R(w) - Q]}{e_{R(w)}}. \tag{14.5A}$$

In contrast, earning w and retiring at age $R(w)$, on average, she will live in retirement for $e_{R(w)}(w)$. Substituting (14.5A) into (14.3A) yields

$$z^A(w, R(w)) = \frac{\tau w[R(w) - Q]}{e_{R(w)}}[e_{R(w)} - \zeta e_{R(w)}(w)]. \tag{14.6A}$$

Taking the expected value in (14.6A) and equalizing it to zero:

$$0 = \mathbf{E}z^A(w, R(w)) = \tau\mathbf{E}\left\{\frac{w[R(w) - Q]}{e_{R(w)}}[e_{R(w)} - \zeta e_{R(w)}(w)]\right\},$$

hence ζ is determined from

$$\mathbf{E}[w[R(w)-Q]] = \zeta^A \mathbf{E}\left\{\frac{w[R(w)-Q]}{e_{R(w)}} e_{R(w)}(w)\right\}. \tag{14.7A}$$

As in Sect. 14.2, there are the same two simple corrections to eliminate or dampen this type of redistribution. Rule B simply divides the accumulated virtual wealth by wage-specific $e_{R(w)}(w)$ rather than the average $e_{R(w)}$. Then

$$b^B(w,R) = \frac{\tau w[R(w)-Q]}{e_{R(w)}(w)} \quad \text{and} \quad z^B(w,R(w)) = 0. \tag{14.5B}$$

This solution is difficult to sell politically, therefore we propose a more sophisticated one: partly preserve (14.5A) and combine it with a flat one. Introducing a scalar α for the weight of the ANDC, $0 \le \alpha \le 1$, the second modified benefit is equal to

$$b^C(w,R) = \alpha \frac{\zeta \tau w[R(w)-Q]}{e_{R(w)}} + (1-\alpha)\zeta b^{\mathrm{o}}. \tag{14.5C}$$

Substituting (14.5C) into (14.2) yields

$$\begin{aligned} z^C(w,R(w)) = {} & \tau w[R(w)-Q] - \alpha \frac{\zeta \tau w[R(w)-Q]}{e_{R(w)}} e_{R(w)}(w) \\ & -(1-\alpha)\zeta b^{\mathrm{o}} e_{R(w)}(w). \end{aligned}$$

Taking expectation and equaling it to zero:

$$\begin{aligned} 0 = {} & \tau \mathbf{E}[w[R(w)-Q]] - \alpha \zeta \tau \mathbf{E} \frac{w[R(w)-Q] e_{R(w)}(w)}{e_{R(w)}} \\ & -(1-\alpha)\zeta b^{\mathrm{o}} \mathbf{E} e_{R(w)}(w), \end{aligned}$$

i.e.,

$$\tau \mathbf{E}[w[R(w)-Q]] \\ =\zeta^C\left\{\alpha\tau\mathbf{E}\frac{w[R(w)-Q]e_{R(w)}(w)}{e_{R(w)}}+(1-\alpha)b^{\mathrm{o}}\mathbf{E}e_{R(w)}(w)\right\}. \tag{14.6C}$$

The α-dependent contraction factor ζ^C is uniquely determined from (14.6*C*).

Note that for $\alpha = 1$, (14.6*C*) reduces to (14.6*A*). Diminishing the value of α, the direction of the redistribution changes.

Theorem 14.2. *With heterogeneous retirement ages, benefit rule (14.5A)–(14.7A) eliminates the aggregate loss. Benefit rule (14.5B) eliminates the perverse redistribution. Benefit rule (14.5C)–(14.6C) weakens or even reverses perverse redistribution.*

At the end of this section, we again illustrate our results on a simple numerical example. For heterogeneous retirement ages, the simplest generalization of the function $e_{60}(w) = 20 + 6(w - 1)$ is as follows:

$$e_R(w) = 80 - R + 6(w - 1).$$

Assuming that citizens spend 2/3 of their adult lives with work, $R_1 = 58$, $R_2 = 60$ and $R_3 = 62$.

Table 14.3 NDC's variations: Heterogeneous retirement ages

Wage, w_i	Retire age, R_i	LEXP at ret., $e_{R_i}(w_i)$	Adjusted NDC: Benefit-A, b_i^A	Balance-A, z_i^A	Benefit-B, b_i^B	Benefit-C, b_i^C	Balance-C, z_i^C
0.5	58	19	0.203	0.897	0.25	0.349	−1.890
1.0	60	20	0.470	0.609	0.50	0.488	0.236
1.5	62	21	0.822	−1.506	0.75	0.671	1.654

Remark. See Table 14.2. $R_i - Q = 2[D_i - Q]/3$, $i = 1, 2, 3$

Table 14.3 reports the new results. With retirement ages depending on life expectancies, the ANDC contraction coefficient ζ^A drops from 0.952 to 0.939 but the error of the ANDC diminishes, for example, the loss z_1^A decreases from 0.952 to 0.897. With adjustment B, only the early and late retirement ages influence the benefits. Due to the proportionality of active and passive adult years, $b_i^B = 0.5w_i$ holds. With adjustment C, the gain z_1^C jumps from +1.22 to +1.89, while the absolute value of the loss z_3^C drops from 0.976 to 1.654.

14.4 Partial Wage Indexation of Benefits

In the previous sections of the present chapter, we have neglected the secular rise of real wages and the conflict between the rise and the less than full wage indexation of benefits in progress. Here we model the impact of the conflict on the gains and losses. Let us assume that the real wages and the newly granted pension benefits grow uniformly with a factor $g > 1$ but the pension in progress may grow more slowly than the wages.

Consider a worker with initial wage w_Q who retires at the common age $R > Q$ (both positive integers), her last year real wage $w_{R-1} = w_Q g^{R-Q-1}$. Due to valorization (or indexing of initial benefits), her NDC wealth is equal to $W_R = (R - Q)w_{R-1}$ but her expected liability (discounted by the growth factor g) is equal to

$$W_R = \sum_{j=R}^{D-1} g^{-j+R} b_j,$$

where $D = R + e_R$ is life expectancy at birth, and b_j is the real value of the benefit at age $j = R, \ldots, D-1$, $D > R$ is also an integer.

Suppose that there is a scalar ι between 0 and 1, the *wage share in benefit indexation.* Then

$$b_j = b_{j-1} g^{\iota}, \quad \text{where} \quad j = R, \ldots, D-1.$$

(Note that in reality, the growth factor is the weighted average of wage's and price's growth factor, i.e., $\iota g + 1 - \iota = (g - 1)\iota + 1$.) Inserting this formula to the previous one yields

$$(R - Q)w_{R-1} = b_R \sum_{j=R}^{D-1} g^{-(1-\iota)(j-R)}.$$

To avoid superfluous separation of the analysis for $\iota = 1$ and $0 \leq \iota < 1$, we shall introduce notation $e_R^{(\iota)}$ for the sum:

$$\text{either} \quad e_R^{(\iota)} = e_R \quad \text{for} \quad \iota = 1$$
$$\text{or} \quad e_R^{(\iota)} = \frac{1 - g^{-(1-\iota)e_R}}{1 - g^{-(1-\iota)}} \quad \text{for} \quad 0 \leq \iota < 1.$$

Then the unadjusted NDC benefit is equal to

$$b^N(w_{R-1}, R) = \frac{\tau(R - Q)w_{R-1}}{e_R^{(\iota)}}. \tag{14.8N}$$

Note that the higher the wage share in indexation ι, the greater the indexed remaining life expectancy $e_R^{(\iota)}$ and the lower the starting benefits $b^N(w, R)$.

To take into account the heterogeneity in life expectancy, we postulate a distribution F for closing wages w_{R-1} and we assume that there is no seniority wage rise, real wages rise with calendar time but at the same growth factor g for everybody. We are interested in the impact of wage share in indexation on the lifetime redistribution.

To avoid too much repetition, we only explore adjustment A here. We shall consider the partial wage indexation with correction A, the initial benefit being

$$b^A(w_{R-1}, R) = \zeta^A \frac{\tau(R - Q)w_{R-1}}{e_R^{(\iota)}}. \tag{14.8A}$$

Introducing notation

$$\begin{aligned} e_R^{(1)}(w_{R-1}) &= e_R(w_{R-1}) \\ \text{or} \quad e_R^{(\iota)}(w_{R-1}) &= \frac{1-g^{-(1-\iota)e_R(w_{R-1})}}{1-g^{-(1-\iota)}} \quad \text{for} \quad 0 \le \iota < 1, \end{aligned} \tag{14.9A}$$

the lifetime net balance is now

$$\begin{aligned} z^A(w_{R-1}, R) &= \tau(R-Q)w_{R-1} - \zeta^A b^N(w_{R-1}, R)e_R^{(\iota)}(w_{R-1}) \\ &= b^N(1, R)w_{R-1}[e_R^{(\iota)} - \zeta^A e_R^{(\iota)}(w_{R-1})]. \end{aligned} \tag{14.10A}$$

Taking the expectations and equalizing the result to zero:

$$0 = \mathbf{E}z^A(w_{R-1}, R) = b^N(1, R)\mathbf{E}w_{R-1}[e_R^{(\iota)} - \zeta^A e_R^{(\iota)}(w_{R-1})]. \tag{14.11A}$$

Hence

$$\zeta^A = \frac{e_R^{(\iota)}}{\mathbf{E}[w_{R-1}e_R^{(\iota)}(w_{R-1})]}. \tag{14.12A}$$

Theorem 14.3A. *For indexed benefits, the adjusted NDC formula is given by (14.8A) and the correction coefficient is provided by (14.9A) and (14.12A).*

We complete the present section with a numerical illustration. In details, let $w_{R-1}(i) = 0.5, 1, 1.5$ again. Table 14.4 reports the results for wage indexation: $\iota = 1$, combined wage-price indexation: $\iota = 0.5$ and price indexation: $\iota = 0$. It is quite surprising that the adjustment factor ζ^A is hardly sensitive to the type of indexation, it varies between 0.952 and 0.963. As the wage share in indexation diminishes, for every type, the initial benefit uniformly rises (and the final benefit, not shown, decreases). It is noteworthy that with wage indexation, not only the ex ante short-lived but also the average worker contributes to the ex ante long-lived worker's benefit. On the other hand, with price indexation, the opposite holds.

Table 14.4 The impact of indexation on initial benefits and balances (A)

Wage, $w_{i,R-1}$	Remaining LEXP, e_i	Indexation					
		Wage		Wage-price		Price	
		Benefit, $b^1_{i,R-1}$	Balance, $z^1_{i,R-1}$	Benefit, $b^{0.5}_{i,R-1}$	Balance, $z^{0.5}_{i,R-1}$	Benefit, $b^0_{i,R-1}$	Balance, $z^0_{i,R-1}$
0.5	17	0.238	0.952	0.263	0.870	0.289	0.791
1.0	20	0.476	0.476	0.525	0.420	0.577	0.369
1.5	23	0.714	−1.429	0.788	−1.290	0.866	−1.161

14.5 Conclusions

We have discussed three related models of NDC with three different benefit adjustments. In model 1, the workers only differ in wages and life expectancies but retire at the same age. Due to the positive correlation between wages and life expectancies, the unadjusted NDC does not only strongly redistribute from the short-lived poor to the long-lived rich but also implies aggregate loss. In model 2, we assume additionally that longer-lived workers also retire later, increasing the perverse redistribution. In both models, we experimented with explicit income redistribution in the pension formula. In model 3, we return to common retirement age but introduce secular real wage rise. Diminishing the wage share in indexation, the initial benefits rise and the direction of the redistribution is reversed.

In all the three models, we assumed that the workers do not react to the retirement rules and the government chooses the rules *ad hoc.* Introducing individual and social optimization may change our results. Especially the introduction of progressivity may weaken the incentives to retire later. Only better models can corroborate our findings.

References

Auerbach, A., et al. (2017). *How the Growing Gap in Life Expectancy May Affect Retirement Benefits and Reforms* (NBER WP 23329). Cambridge, MA.

Ayuso, M., Bravo, J. M., & Holzmann, R. (2016). *Addressing Longevity Heterogeneity in Pension Scheme Design and Reform* (IZA Discussion Paper 10378).

Barr, N., & Diamond, P. (2008). *Reforming Pensions: Principles and Policy Choices.* Oxford: Oxford University Press.

Diamond, P. (2003). *Taxation, Incomplete Markets and Social Security.* Munich Lectures. Cambridge, MA: MIT Press.

Fehr, H., Kallweit, M., & Kindermann, F. (2013). Should Pensions Be Progressive? *European Economic Review, 63,* 94–116.

Feldstein, M. S. (1990). Imperfect Annuity Markets, Unintended Bequest, and the Optimal Age Structure of Social Security Benefits. *Journal of Public Economics, 41,* 31–43.

Holzmann, R., & Palmer, E. (Eds.). (2006). *Pension Reforms: Issues and Prospects of Nonfinancial Defined Contribution (NDC) Schemes.* Washington, DC: World Bank.

Legros F. (2006). NDCs: A Comparison of French and German Point Systems. In Holzmann and Palmer (Eds.) (pp. 203–238).

Liebmann, J. B. (2002). Redistribution in the Current U.S. Social Security System. In M. A. Feldstein & J. B. Liebmann (Eds.), *The Distributional Aspects of Social Security and Social Security Reform* (pp. 11–48). Chicago: Chicago University Press.

Weinzierl, M. (2014). *Seesaws and Social Security Benefits Indexing* (pp. 137–196). Fall: Brookings Papers on Economic Activity.

Whitehouse, E., & Zaidi, A. (2008). *Socioeconomic Differences in Mortality: Implications for Pension Policy* (OECD Social, Employment and Migration Working Papers 70). Paris: OECD.

15

Dynamic Extensions

15.1 Introduction

In the whole book we have mostly confined our attention to static models. At the end of the book we discuss complications caused by dynamic extensions. One may think that all pension models (including the models already discussed in the book) are dynamic. Indeed, in every pension model there are at least two periods, referring to young and old ages, respectively. Moreover, mechanism design (started with Mirrlees 1971; Diamond and Mirrlees 1978) used the techniques of dynamic optimization!

Nevertheless, in genuine dynamic models, in addition to age, calendar time also plays an important role. The rule which transforms contributions into benefits is not confined to a single time period, as above. On the contrary, current contributors will be future beneficiaries *ad infinitum*. In this sense, the child benefit model of Chapter 10 is truly dynamic, since past fertility influences current fertility but there was no continuation.

Section 15.2 studies the interaction of taxation with government debt. Section 15.3 discusses the propagation of a tax reduction in the whole pension system. Section 15.4 presents the simplest version of Samuelson (1958) *overlapping generations* model. Section 15.5 concludes.

A. Simonovits, *Simple Models of Income Redistribution*,
https://doi.org/10.1007/978-3-319-72502-4_15

15.2 Budget Balances and Government Debt

In our static models, tax revenues and expenditures were identical. In this section, we study the dynamic case, when the divergence between revenues and expenditures (budget balances) gives rise to government debt.

Working with years, we shall index them as $t = 1, 2, \ldots$. Denote the end-of-year *debt* by D_t, the *primary balance* of the revenues and of noninterest expenditures by E_t. Introducing the interest factor ρ_t, we have the following identity:

$$D_t = D_{t-1} + (\rho_t - 1)D_{t-1} - E_t = \rho_t D_{t-1} - E_t, \qquad t = 1, 2, \ldots, \tag{15.1}$$

where D_0 is the initial value of the government debt. (If there was no debt before, we assume that $D_0 = 0$ but it may be a positive number as well.)

To get rid of exponentially growing variables, we introduce the growth equation of output: $Y_t = g_t Y_{t-1}$, where g_t stands for the growth factor of output. Dividing both sides of (15.1) by Y_t results in a relative dynamics:

$$\frac{D_t}{Y_t} = \frac{\rho_t}{g_t}\frac{D_{t-1}}{Y_{t-1}} - \frac{E_t}{Y_t}. \tag{15.2}$$

Note the advantage of working with interest and growth factors rather than interest and growth rates, respectively.

It is worth introducing separate notations for these output ratios and for the relative interest factor (the ratio of interest factor to the growth factor):

$$d_t = \frac{D_t}{Y_t}, \qquad e_t = \frac{E_t}{Y_t} \quad \text{and} \quad R_t = \frac{\rho_t}{g_t}. \tag{15.3}$$

Inserting (15.3) into (15.2) yields

$$d_t = R_t d_{t-1} - e_t, \qquad t = 1, 2, \ldots. \tag{15.4}$$

Assuming time-invariant primary balance rates $e_t = e$ and relative interest factors $R_t = R$, (15.4) simplifies to a simple recursion:

$$d_t = Rd_{t-1} - e, \quad \text{where} \quad d_0 = \frac{D_0}{Y_0} \quad \text{is given.} \tag{15.5}$$

Note, however, that bringing back inflation, the formula would change.

We have the following elementary theorem:

Theorem 15.1. *Assume time-invariance. (a) If $R \neq 1$, then there exists a steady-state value of the debt ratio:*

$$d^{\mathrm{o}} = \frac{e}{R-1}. \tag{15.6}$$

(b) The explicit formula for debt ratio is given by

$$d_t = d^{\mathrm{o}} + R^t(d_0 - d^{\mathrm{o}}), \qquad t = 1, 2, \ldots. \tag{15.7}$$

(c) The debt dynamic is (relatively) stable if and only if

$$R < 1. \tag{15.8}$$

Remarks. 1. To have a positive steady-state debt in (15.6), either $e > 0$ and $R > 1$ (unstable) or $e < 0$ and $R < 1$ (stable) needed.

2. Note that the traditional budgetary balance is equal to the primary balance less the interest paid after the debt: $\mathbf{e} = e - (\rho - 1)d^{\mathrm{o}}$. In the so-called Maastricht treaty, $-\mathbf{e} < 0.03$ and $d^{\mathrm{o}} < 0.6$ are required.

Proof. (a) To determine the steady state, insert $d_t = d_{t-1} = d^{\mathrm{o}}$ into (15.5):

$$d^{\mathrm{o}} = Rd^{\mathrm{o}} - e. \tag{15.9}$$

Hence we obtain (15.6).

(b) Deduct (15.9) from (15.5): $d_t - d^{\mathrm{o}} = R(d_{t-1} - d^{\mathrm{o}})$ yielding (15.7).

(c) It is easy to see that $\lim_{t\to\infty} d_t = d^{\mathrm{o}}$ if and only if $R < 1$. ■

Table 1.8 displays debt ratios for selected countries before and after the Great Recession, together with the corresponding GDP growth index.

We only mention another dynamic issue in taxation, the so-called POUM-hypothesis: the *prospect of upward mobility* may prevent the poor from supporting redistribution consistent with static models but "in U.S. data recent the POUM effect is probably dominated by the demand for social insurance" (Benabou and Ok 2001, p. 447).

15.3 Propagation of a Tax Rate Reduction

Due to the dynamic nature of pension calculation, at least in Hungary, the pension contribution is proportional to the gross (i.e., total) wage, while the benefit is proportional to the net wage. (In fact, we should have distinguished the employee and the employer's contribution but we combine the two.) We have now a single pension cohort (aged 3) but two worker cohorts (aged 1 and 2), the length of a period is now 2 decades. Having a proportional transfer system, we need not model wage distribution. Assume that in period t, the single (flat) personal income tax rate is θ_t and the net-of-tax-rate is $\hat{\theta}_t = 1 - \theta_t - \tau_t$. Then the entry pension in period t is given by

$$b_t = \beta(\hat{\theta}_{t-1} g w_{t-1} + \hat{\theta}_{t-2} g^2 w_{t-2}) \tag{15.10}$$

as if g were an interest factor. Taking into account that $g w_{t-1} = g^2 w_{t-2} = w_t$, formula (15.10) simplifies to

$$b_t = \beta(\hat{\theta}_{t-1} + \hat{\theta}_{t-2}) w_t. \tag{15.11}$$

Note that the balance equation is now

$$b_t = 2\tau_t w_t. \tag{15.12}$$

Inserting (15.11) into (15.12) yields

$$\tau_t = \frac{1}{2}\beta(\hat{\theta}_{t-1} + \hat{\theta}_{t-2}) = \beta - \frac{1}{2}\beta(\theta_{t-1} + \theta_{t-2} + \tau_{t-1} + \tau_{t-2}). \tag{15.13}$$

(15.13) is a second-order inhomogeneous linear difference equation for the contribution rate.

Theorem 15.2. *(a) If the personal income tax rate θ_t is time-invariant, then the steady-state contribution rate should be equal to*

$$\tau(\theta) = \frac{\beta(1-\theta)}{1+\beta}. \tag{15.14}$$

(b) If the tax rate θ_t becomes constant after $t > 0$, then the contribution rate converges to $\tau(\theta)$.

Proof. (a) Substituting $\tau_{t-k} = \tau$ and $\theta_{t-k} = \theta$ (for $k = 0, 1, 2$) into (15.13) yields $\tau = \beta(1 - \theta - \tau)$, i.e., (15.14).
(b) Having introduced the deviation $\hat{\tau}_t = \tau_t - \tau(\theta)$, (15.13) simplifies to

$$\hat{\tau}_t = -\frac{1}{2}\beta(\hat{\tau}_{t-1} + \hat{\tau}_{t-2}). \tag{15.15}$$

Using the method invented by Euler in the eighteenth century, we are looking for the basic solution in the form of $\hat{\tau}_t = \xi\lambda^t$ with undetermined constants $\xi \neq 0$ and λ. Substituting it into (15.15) yields

$$\xi\lambda^t = -\frac{1}{2}\beta(\xi\lambda^{t-1} + \xi\lambda^{t-2})$$

or equivalently

$$\lambda^2 + \frac{1}{2}\beta(\lambda + 1) = 0. \tag{15.16}$$

Since $\beta < 1$, the discriminant of this quadratic equation is negative ($4D = \beta^2 - 2\beta < 0$) and we have two conjugate complex roots λ_1 and $\lambda_2 = \overline{\lambda_1}$. Finding conjugate coefficients ξ_1 and $\xi_2 = \overline{\xi_1}$, the general solution to (15.16) is

$$\hat{\tau}_t = \xi_1\lambda_1^t + \overline{\xi}_1\overline{\lambda}_1^t = \tau(\theta_1) + |\lambda_1|^t A\cos(\varphi t + \delta), \qquad t = 0, 1, \ldots.$$

Hence the given initial conditions τ_{-1} and τ_0 (real numbers) determine ξ_1 and thus A, φ and δ (also real numbers).

Table 15.1 Transient behavior at the reduction of the PI tax rate

Period, t	Tax rate, θ_t	Contribution rate, τ_t	Benefit, b_t
0	0.2	0.267	0.533
1	0.1	0.292	0.533
2	0.1	0.285	0.571
3	0.1	0.306	0.611
4	0.1	0.302	0.604
5	0.1	0.298	0.596
6	0.1	0.300	0.600

Since $|\lambda_1|^2 = \beta/2 < 1$, the steady state is stable but the convergence is achieved with oscillations. ■

To provide a numerical illustration, assume that $\beta = 0.5$, $\theta_0 = 0.2$ and it drops to $\theta_1 = 0.1$ and stays there forever. We also assume that at the start $\tau_{-1} = \tau_0 = \tau(\theta_0)$ and look at the transient behavior. Note that here the length of one period is about 20 years, therefore the stabilization of the new steady state is a prolonged process, raising the contribution rate from 0.267 to 0.3, while lifting the benefit from 0.533 to 0.6 (Table 15.1).

15.4 Overlapping Generations

The model of Overlapping Generations is probably one of the most important models of modern economics. It was invented by Samuelson (1958) and its main novelty lies in deriving the interest rate dynamics in a simplest way as a general equilibrium model with rational expectations. Note that here the basic simplification of halving the second period (already discussed in Chapter 4) breaks down and we have to return to the unrealistic equality of the lengths of working period and of retirement period. Diamond (1965) extended the analysis from an exchange model to a production model, introducing debt dynamic as well. Gale (1973) was perhaps the first who gave a precise mathematical formulation of the original model and who generalized it into a multi-generational model. Following Simonovits (2003, Appendix B), first we solve the interest rate dynamics without assuming optimization and second we sharpen our result by introducing optimization. Augusztinovics (2000) gave a good survey on the relation between theory and reality of overlapping generations.

No Optimization

The calendar time is discrete, is denoted by $t = 0, 1, 2, \ldots$. Each period two generations live together: the young (indexed by $i = 1$) and the old (indexed by $i = 2$). The interest factor from period t to $t+1$ is denoted by ρ_{t+1}. The income is time-invariant but is age-dependent: y_1, y_2; savings are time- and age-variant: $(s_{i,t})$. For mathematical convenience, here we drop our requirement of positivity.

We assume that the young enters the labor force without receiving a bequest and the old exits without leaving any bequest. By definition, every young starting to work in period t has the following lifetime budget constraint:

$$\rho_{t+1}s_{1,t} + s_{2,t+1} = 0. \tag{15.17}$$

We assume that every old has ν young children (a mother–daughters, a father–sons), where ν is a positive real. We consider an exchange economy, therefore the cross-sectional total saving is equal to zero:

$$\nu s_{1,t} + s_{2,t} = 0. \tag{15.18}$$

Before introducing optimization, we assume that the young has a perfect forecast (i.e., rational expectations) on the next period interest factor, and his saving depends on it: $s_{1,t} = s(\rho_{t+1})$, where $s(\cdot)$ is an exogenously given increasing function.

Substituting this function into (15.17) yields

$$s_{2,t+1} = -\rho_{t+1}s_{1,t} = -\rho_{t+1}s(\rho_{t+1}). \tag{15.19}$$

Considering the cross-sectional saving equation (15.18), we need $s_{2,t}$ rather than $s_{2,t+1}$. Heuristically, we replace $t+1$ by t in (15.19) and insert the new function into (15.18):

$$S(\rho_t, \rho_{t+1}) = \nu s(\rho_{t+1}) - \rho_t s(\rho_t) = 0, \qquad t = 0, 1, 2, \ldots, \tag{15.20}$$

where $S(\cdot, \cdot)$ is the total saving function per pensioner with arguments current and future interest factors. This is a first-order nonlinear implicit scalar difference equation, with a given initial condition ρ_0.

Before turning to the dynamics, we make an elementary but important observation on the *steady states,* defined as rest points.

Theorem 15.3. *The dynamic system described by $S(\rho_t, \rho_{t+1}) = 0$ has two steady states: ρ_B with $s_1^B = s_2^B = 0$ (called balanced or autarch) or $\rho_G = \nu$ (called golden rule).*

Proof. For any steady state $\rho_0 = \rho_1 = \rho^{\mathrm{o}}$,

$$S(\rho^{\mathrm{o}}, \rho^{\mathrm{o}}) = (\nu - \rho^{\mathrm{o}})s(\rho^{\mathrm{o}}) = 0. \tag{15.20^{o}}$$

Obviously, $\nu = \rho^{\mathrm{o}}$ or $s(\rho^{\mathrm{o}}) = 0$. ■

We only mention that the balanced and the golden-rule states represent the funded and the unfunded pension systems, respectively.

By the implicit function theorem, (15.20) has a solution $\{\rho_t\}_{t=0}^{\infty}$ around both steady states, at least at the start. As we have seen in Appendix C, the resulting dynamics $\rho_t = g(\rho_{t-1})$ is locally asymptotically stable if $|g'(\rho^{\mathrm{o}})| < 1$. Again, by the stated theorem,

$$g'(\rho^{\mathrm{o}}) = -\frac{S_1'}{S_2'},$$

where

$$S_1'(\rho^{\mathrm{o}}, \rho^{\mathrm{o}}) = -s(\rho^{\mathrm{o}}) - \rho^{\mathrm{o}} s'(\rho^{\mathrm{o}}) \quad \text{and} \quad S_2'(\rho^{\mathrm{o}}, \rho^{\mathrm{o}}) = \nu s'(\rho^{\mathrm{o}}). \tag{15.21}$$

Substituting (15.21) into $g'(\rho^{\mathrm{o}})$ yields

$$g'(\rho^{\mathrm{o}}) = \frac{s(\rho^{\mathrm{o}}) + \rho^{\mathrm{o}} s'(\rho^{\mathrm{o}})}{\nu s'(\rho^{\mathrm{o}})} = \frac{s(\rho^{\mathrm{o}})}{\nu s'(\rho^{\mathrm{o}})} + \frac{\rho^{\mathrm{o}}}{\nu}. \tag{15.22}$$

We have to substitute the two steady states separately into (15.22):

$$g'(\nu) = \frac{s(\nu)}{\nu s'(\nu)} + 1. \tag{15.22G}$$

and

$$g'(\rho_B) = \frac{\rho_B}{\nu}. \tag{15.22B}$$

We have arrived to

Theorem 15.4. *(Gale 1973) (a) The golden-rule steady state is locally stable if*

$$s(\nu) < 0 \quad \textit{and} \quad -2\nu s'(\nu) < s(\nu).$$

(b) The balanced steady state is locally stable if $\rho_B < \nu$.

Remarks. 1. Condition (b) is well-known as the necessary and sufficient condition that at a steady state of overlapping cohorts, the pay-as-you-go pension system is more efficient than the funded one (cf. Samuelson 1958; Aaron 1966). Note, however, that for the actual transition from a pay-as-you-go system to the funded system, the negation of this condition does not tell anything (Orszag and Stiglitz 2001).

2. The first pair of condition is quite involved. We shall see that for a specific utility function of Cobb–Douglas type, this is just the opposite of the second condition.

Optimization

It is high time to add lifetime utility function to the model. We introduce the consumption pair (c, d), and for the time being, drop the time indices. Recall

$$c = y_1 - s \quad \text{and} \quad d = y_2 + \rho s.$$

(Note that unlike in Chapters 10 and 11, here we keep neglecting the parents' expenditures on their children's consumption.) To determine the young's saving, we posit our usual discounted Cobb–Douglas utility function:

$$U(c, d) = \log c + \delta \log d. \tag{3.2}$$

Repeating the calculation done there, we have

$$s(\rho) = \frac{\delta y_1}{1+\delta} - \frac{y_2}{\rho(1+\delta)}. \tag{15.23}$$

By (15.23), $s(\rho_B) = 0$ yields

$$\rho_B = \frac{y_2}{\delta y_1}.$$

The stability condition of ρ_B simplifies to $y_2 < \nu\delta y_1$. (15.23) implies: $s(\nu) > 0$ if and only if $\nu\delta y_1 > y_2$. The same way, the stability condition of ρ_G simplifies to $y_2 > \nu\delta y_1$, just the negation of the first.

Returning to the dynamics, (15.23) becomes

$$s(\rho_{t+1}) = \frac{\delta y_1}{1+\delta} - \frac{y_2}{(1+\delta)\rho_{t+1}}. \tag{15.24}$$

Substituting (15.24) into (15.20)

$$\nu\left(\frac{\delta y_1}{1+\delta} - \frac{y_2}{(1+\delta)\rho_{t+1}}\right) - \rho_t\left(\frac{\delta y_1}{1+\delta} - \frac{y_2}{(1+\delta)\rho_t}\right) = 0,$$

$$t = 0, 1, 2, \ldots. \tag{15.25}$$

With simple calculations, we obtain the following difference equation:

$$\rho_{t+1} = g(\rho_t) = \frac{\nu y_2}{\nu\delta y_1 + y_2 - \delta y_1 \rho_t}, \qquad t = 0, 1, 2, \ldots.$$

This is the simplest deduction of the interest rate dynamics from first principles.

Table 15.2 Stable and unstable paths in OLG

Period, t	Paths of interest factors		
	$\rho(1)$	$\rho(2)$	$\rho(3)$
−1	0.1	1.900	2.020
0	0.690	1.667	2.041
1	0.866	1.500	2.085
2	0.937	1.333	2.186
3	0.969	1.200	2.457
4	0.985	1.111	3.684
5	0.993	1.059	
6	0.996	1.030	
7	0.998	1.015	
8	0.999	1.008	
9	1	1.004	

Finally, we illustrate a simple dynamics (15.25) for the case $\rho_B < \nu$, when ρ_B is stable. We work with $y_1 = 2/3$, $y_2 = 1/3$, $\delta = 1/2$ (annually $\delta[1] = 0.977$) and $\nu = 2$ (annually $\nu[1] = 1.023$). Note that for any initial interest factor in $(0, \rho_G)$, the path fast converges to ρ_B. On the other hand, initial interest factors slightly above ρ_G generate unviable paths with $\rho_5 < -1$ (Table 15.2).

15.5 Conclusions

In the bulk of the book we worked with static models. In this chapter, we brought in the dynamics. First, we presented a simple debt model which replaces balanced budgets with positive and negative balances. Second, we modeled the propagation of the reduction of personal income tax. Third, we outlined a most important macromodel, the so-called overlapping generations model. We note again that this OLG model is just the first step into the world of dynamic pension models. We have already mentioned Auerbach and Kotlikoff (1987), which generalized this model into a multi-cohort model with 55 year-groups, with annual replacement of the oldest cohort. Not only the interest rate is endogenous but the wage rate also depends on the capital stock. To mention a rather new model,

Fehr et al. (2013) considered the optimal progressivity of the German pension system in a calibrated dynamic general equilibrium model.

References

Aaron, H. J. (1966). The Social Insurance Paradox. *Canadian Journal of Economics and Political Science, 32*, 371–374.

Auerbach, A. J., & Kotlikoff, L. J. (1987). *Dynamic Fiscal Policy*. Cambridge: Cambridge University Press.

Augusztinovics, M. (2000). The Dynamics of Retirement Savings-Theory and Reality. *Structural Change and Economic Dynamics, 11*, 111–128.

Benabou, R., & Ok, E. A. (2001). Social Mobility and the Demand for Redistribution: The POUM Hypothesis. *Quarterly Journal of Economics, 116*, 447–487.

Diamond, P. A. (1965). National Debt in a Neoclassical Growth Model. *American Economic Review, 55*, 1126–1150.

Diamond, P., & Mirrlees, J. (1978). A Model of Social Insurance with Variable Retirement. *Journal of Public Economics, 10*, 295–336.

Fehr, H., Kallweit, M., & Kindermann, F. (2013). Should Pensions Be Progressive? *European Economic Review, 63*, 94–116.

Gale, D. (1973). Pure Exchange Equilibrium of Dynamic Economic Models. *Journal of Economic Theory, 6*, 12–36.

Mirrlees, J. A. (1971). An Exploration in the Theory of Optimum Income Taxation. *Review of Economic Studies, 38*, 175–208.

Orszag, P., & Stiglitz, J. E. (2001). Rethinking Pension Reform: Ten Myths about Social Security Systems. In R. Holzmann & J. E. Stiglitz (Eds.), *New Ideas about Old-Age Security: Toward Sustainable Pension Systems in the 21st Century*. Washington, DC: World Bank.

Samuelson, P. A. (1958). An Exact Consumption-Loan Model of Interest with or Without the Social Contrivance of Money. *Journal of Political Economy, 66*, 467–482.

Simonovits, A. (2003). *Modeling Pension Systems*. Houndmills and Basingstoke: Palgrave Macmillan.

16

Conclusions

We have discussed a couple of simple intra- and intergenerational transfer models and we hope that the Reader has gained some new insights into their working as well as the underlying principles of existing transfer systems. Here we only highlight some results and draw conclusions before the Reader turns to the Appendices.

Due to original income differences, the introduction of well-designed personal income taxes raises social welfare. Since labor disutility and tax morale decrease labor supply and reported income, respectively, the tax rates should be moderate.

Due to individual myopia, the government must operate a public pension system. But the system must leave enough room for private savings, sometimes in the form of voluntary pensions. Introducing means-testing or caps, the various aims can be combined.

The impact of fertility on transfers is a well-understood field. Much less clear is the impact of transfers on fertility. Even in our very simple framework, small details like formulating the raising function of children can have great impact on our results.

In the bulk of the book we worked in a static framework, with exogenous interest and wage rates; rational workers, but at the end of the book we

A. Simonovits, *Simple Models of Income Redistribution*,
https://doi.org/10.1007/978-3-319-72502-4_16

relaxed some of these assumptions: irrational inattention was modeled, dynamics was introduced and interest rates were endogeneized.

We have deliberately not discussed any complex transfer model. These omissions are only listed here.

i. Except for Sect. 4.3, models based on *asymmetrical information* have been neglected. Note that the very first application of mechanism design was connected to the pioneering model of Mirrlees (1971) on designing optimal personal income tax. Since Diamond and Mirrlees (1978), the role of this method in disability pension design has been well-known. Diamond (2003) gave a guided tour to the interaction of taxation and pension in this framework. In other studies, with or without coauthors, we have also applied this tool to the socially optimal design of variable (flexible) retirement: Eső and Simonovits (2002), Simonovits (2003, 2006, 2015) and Eső et al. (2011).
ii. Sophisticated multi-cohort general equilibrium models have already been mentioned in various chapters. Other forms of complexity, namely in behavioral economics were alluded to (cf. Pickhard and Prinz 2013) and two of our papers, namely Méder et al. (2012) and Király and Simonovits (2018) applied *agent-based modeling* to tax evasion and voluntary pension savings, respectively.

I have generally refrained from the detailed presentation of the nonelementary models in this small book because it would have gone much beyond the modest aims of the book. (To name the basic ones: highlighting taxes to finance intragenerational transfers and mandatory or voluntary pensions fighting myopia in the simplest set-ups.) It goes without saying that elementary models can only provide elementary wisdom and at the end of the day, sophisticated models are superior to our elementary ones.

References

Diamond, P. A. (2003). *Taxation, Incomplete Markets and Social Security*. Munich Lectures. Cambridge, MA: MIT Press.

Diamond, P., & Mirrlees, J. (1978). A Model of Social Insurance with Variable Retirement. *Journal of Public Economics, 10*, 295–336.

Eső, P., & Simonovits, A. (2002). *Designing Optimal Benefit Rules for Flexible Retirement (Discussion Paper CMS-EMS 1353)*. Evanston, IL: Northwestern University.

Eső, P., Simonovits, A., & Tóth, J. (2011). Designing Benefit Rules for Flexible Retirement: Welfare and Redistribution. *Acta Oeconomica, 61*, 3–32.

Király, B., & Simonovits, A. (2018). Learning to Save in a Voluntary Pension System: Toward an Agent-Based Model. *Journal of Economic Interaction and Coordination*, 1–25.

Méder, Z., Simonovits, A., & Vincze, J. (2012). Tax Morale and Tax Evasion: Social Preferences and Bounded Rationality. *Economic Analysis and Policy, 42*, 171–188.

Mirrlees, J. A. (1971). An Exploration in the Theory of Optimum Income Taxation. *Review of Economic Studies, 38*, 175–208.

Pickhard, M., & Prinz, A. (2013). Behavioral Dynamics of Tax Evasion-A Survey. *Journal of Economic Psychology, 39*, 45–60.

Simonovits, A. (2003). Designing Optimal Linear Rules for Flexible Retirement. *Journal of Pension Economics and Finance, 2*, 273–293.

Simonovits, A. (2006). Optimal Design of Old-Age Pension Rule with Flexible Retirement: The Two-Type Case. *Journal of Economics, 89*, 197–222.

Simonovits, A. (2015). Benefit-Retirement Age Schedules in Public Pension Systems. *Czech Economic and Financial Review, 65*, 362–376.

Appendices

Appendix A to Chapter 2. When the Socially Optimal Income Tax Schedule is Linear

As was mentioned in the Introduction, there has been a lively discussion on the optimality of the linear personal income tax: Mankiw et al. (2009) claimed optimality, while Diamond and Saez (2011) refuted it. Though we agree with the latter, for pedagogical reasons, we analyze a simple case when the former claim seems to be true.

Before turning to the discussion of our minimodel we recapitulate Domonkos's (2016) analysis of the determinants of tax policy preferences in post-socialist Eastern Europe. His starting point is that in the foregoing region, most countries replaced their strongly progressive personal income tax systems with a flat-rate tax but some of them later on turned to the original system. Table A.1 reproduces Table 1 of Domonkos. Note the major differences in the single tax rates across time and space.

Using multilevel modeling, Domonkos (2016, p. 127) gave the following explanation for this process. "[S]ocio-economic and demographic variables, such as household income, occupational social class and age, are important in determining PIT preferences. However, beliefs about

A. Simonovits, *Simple Models of Income Redistribution*,
https://doi.org/10.1007/978-3-319-72502-4

Table A.1 The diffusion of flat-rate tax in Eastern Europe

Country (year of introduction)	Marginal rates (before)	Further measures
Estonia (1994)	26 (16, 24, 33)	Reduced to 21% in 2008
Latvia (1994)	25 (10, 25)	Decrease to 24% in 2013
Lithuania (1994)	33 (10,..., 33)	Gradual decrease to 15% by 2009
Russia (2001)	13 (12, 20, 30)	–
Ukraine (2004)	13 (10,..., 40)	Minor modifications
Slovakia (2004)	19 (10,..., 38)	Introduction of a second rate of 25%: 2013
Romania (2005)	16 (18,..., 40)	–
Bulgaria (2008)	10 (20, 22, 24)	–
Czechia (2008)	15 (12, ..., 32)	Additional 7% on high incomes
Hungary (2011)	16 (20, 40)	Transitional progressivity eliminated

Remark. Domonkos (2016, p. 135, Table 1). *In Hungary, no exemption exists for low incomes. Very regressive tax exemptions between 2011 and 2013 for families with three or more children

fairness and perceptions of corruption also play a significant role.... The public in less developed post-socialist countries are more in favor of non-redistributive forms of taxation... ."

Returning to modeling, we continue the analysis of optimal taxation under tax morale (Sect. 2.3). We consider workers with heterogeneous wages. Labor supply is uniformly equal to unity but a worker with gross wage w hides e from his wage, therefore, his reported income is $y = w - e$. To improve on the income distribution, the government operates a transfer system. We replace the linear tax–reported income function with a general smooth tax–reported income function $t(y)$ which continues paying every worker a *basic income* $\gamma \geq 0$.

Every sensible progressive tax system satisfies the following three conditions: (a) the tax is nonnegative but less than or equal to the pretax income; (b) a one euro rise in the pretax income raises the tax but at most by one euro; (c) the marginal rate defined in (b) is either constant or increasing in the pretax income. In formula:

$$0 \leq t(y) \leq y, \qquad 0 \leq t'(y) \leq 1 \quad \text{and} \quad t''(y) \geq 0. \tag{A.1}$$

The worker earning w has a *consumption*

$$c = w - t(y) + \gamma. \tag{2.11$'$}$$

With a common tax morale $\eta > 0$, the utility function of worker earning w is given by

$$U(w, c, e) = 2c - \eta w^{-1} e^2. \tag{2.12$'$}$$

Then the reduced utility function is given by

$$U[w, e] = 2[w - t(w - e) + \gamma] - \eta w^{-1} e^2. \tag{A.2}$$

The optimality condition $U_e' = 0$ simplifies to

$$0 = U_e'[w, e] = 2t'(w - e) - 2\eta w^{-1} e,$$

hence the wage-dependent optimal unreported income satisfies

$$e[w] = \eta^{-1} w t'(w - e[w]). \tag{A.3}$$

Under suitable assumptions, there exists a unique solution to this parametric fixed-point problem: $e[w]$.

Returning to the optimal reported income and the tax:

$$y[w] = w - e[w] \quad \text{and} \quad t[w] = t(w - e[w]). \tag{A.4}$$

The simplest social welfare function is the basic income, which is equal to the expected tax revenue:

$$\gamma(t) = \mathbf{E}t[w].$$

The government has to choose a tax–reported-income schedule $t^*(y)$ which maximizes the tax revenue: γ.

Though we do not consider the problem of asymmetric information (cf. Mirrlees 1971), we find it too difficult to solve explicitly even our simpler model. Rather, we experiment with the simplest smooth nonlinear function, which is quadratic:

$$t(y) = \theta_1 y + \theta_2 y^2 \tag{A.5}$$

with parameters $\theta_1, \theta_2 \geq 0$. To satisfy (A.1), we have to restrict the parameter values as follows:

$$0 \leq \theta_1 + \theta_2 y \leq 1 \quad \text{and} \quad 0 \leq \theta_1 + 2\theta_2 y \leq 1. \tag{A.6}$$

The second implies the first condition. We do not know yet the reported income–wage schedule $y[w]$ but for a strong tax morale (A.6) is quite close to the stronger condition

$$\theta_1 + 2\theta_2 w \leq 1. \tag{A.6$'$}$$

Our inequality highlights a serious pitfall of such a tax-schedule: the pretax wage cannot be too high!

By a simple calculation, the optimal evasion and reported income—as functions of the two tax rates—are, respectively, equal to

$$\begin{aligned} e[\theta_1, \theta_2, w] &= \frac{\theta_1 + 2\theta_2 w}{\eta w^{-1} + 2\theta_2} \quad \text{and} \\ y[\theta_1, \theta_2, w] &= w - e[\theta_1, \theta_2, w] = \frac{\eta - \theta_1}{\eta w^{-1} + 2\theta_2}. \end{aligned} \tag{A.7}$$

The government's aim is to maximize the average revenue:

$$\mathbf{E}t[\theta_1, \theta_2, w] = \mathbf{E}\frac{\eta\theta_1 - \theta_1^2}{\eta w^{-1} + 2\theta_2} + \mathbf{E}\frac{\theta_2(\eta - \theta_1)^2}{(\eta w^{-1} + 2\theta_2)^2}. \tag{A.8}$$

Note that for the linear case ($\theta_2 = 0$), with $\mathbf{E}w = 1$, (A.8) simplifies to

$$\mathbf{E}t[\theta_1, 0, w] = \theta_1 - \eta^{-1}\theta_1^2 \tag{A.9}$$

whose maximum is reached at $\theta_1^* = \eta/2$ (cf. (2.15)).

Table A.2 The impact of two tax rates on the tax revenue $\mathbf{E}t$

Linear rate, θ_1	Quadratic rate (θ_2)				
	0	0.1	0.2	0.3	0.4
0.0	0	0.082	0.105	0.112	0.113
0.1	0.090	0.136	0.144	0.141	0.136
0.2	0.160	0.177	0.171	0.161	0.151
0.3	0.210	0.204	0.188	0.172	0.159
0.4	0.240	0.216	0.194	0.175	0.159
0.5	*0.250*	0.215	0.188	0.168	0.152
0.6	0.240	0.200	0.172	0.152	0.137
0.7	0.210	0.171	0.146	0.128	0.114

Remark. $\eta = 1$

Even for a binary random wage variable, it is quite difficult to determine the quadratic optimum. We cannot prove that in our framework the socially optimal quadratic schedule is linear but we announce it as

Conjecture A.1. *If the workers have utility functions (2.12′) and the government maximizes the basic income, then the socially optimal quadratic tax function is linear:* $\tilde{\theta}_2^* = 0$ *and* $\tilde{\theta}_1^* = \eta/2$. *The italicized entry is the optimum.*

We rest content with the usual simple numerical example. Tax morale: $\eta = 1$, wages: $w_L = 1/2$, $w_H = 2$, frequencies: $f_L = 2/3$, $f_H = 1/3$. To visualize the dependence, in Table A.2, both tax rates vary by 0.1, running θ_1 from 0 until 0.7 (row) and θ_2 from 0 until 0.4 (column). Note that for low linear rates, the presence of the quadratic rate is helpful, but from $\theta_1 = 0.3$ it becomes detrimental. This result survives for much finer resolution as well.

Appendix B to Chapter 3. Cobb–Douglas vs. CRRA (CES) Utility Functions

In this book, we mostly work with (two-term) Cobb–Douglas utility functions. On the one hand, this is a very handy assumption which yields explicit formulas and utterly simplifies the calculations. On the other hand, this specification excludes complications which are very important in theory as well as in applications. In this appendix, we shall solve a constrained utility maximization problem under a more general CRRA (constant relative risk aversion or equivalently, CES = constant elasticity of substitution) utility function just to show the difference. The assumption of general, nonparametric utility functions is often useful (e.g., Diamond 2003 and Salanié 2011), and sometimes is applied in this book, too (Chapter 5).

Let x and y be two positive numbers, representing the volumes of two consumer goods, respectively. The prices of the two goods are positive reals p and q, respectively, and the income is denoted by a positive real m.

The consumer has a CRRA utility function:

$$U(x, y) = \sigma^{-1}[\alpha x^{\sigma} + (1-\alpha)y^{\sigma}], \quad 0 < \alpha < 1 \quad \text{and} \quad \sigma < 1, \quad \sigma \neq 0. \tag{B.1}$$

Note that for $\sigma = 0$, this is equivalent to a Cobb–Douglas utility function:

$$U(x, y) = \alpha \log x + (1-\alpha)q \log y.$$

The real number σ shows the curvature of the utility function, while the real number α is connected to the relative preference for x.

The budget constraint is

$$px + qy = m. \tag{B.2}$$

Theorem B.1. *For a CRRA utility function (B.1) with constraint (B.2), the optimal demand pair are*

$$x(p, q) = \frac{m}{p + \varphi^{-\kappa} p^{\kappa} q^{1-\kappa}} \quad \text{and} \quad y(p, q) = \frac{m}{q + \varphi^{\kappa} p^{1-\kappa} q^{\kappa}}, \tag{B.3}$$

where

$$\kappa = 1/(1-\sigma) \quad \text{and} \quad \varphi = \alpha/(1-\alpha). \tag{B.4}$$

As a special case of CRRA, we have

Example B.1. For a Cobb–Douglas utility function, i.e., for $\sigma = 0$ ($\kappa = 1$), the optimal demand pair are

$$x(p, q) = \frac{\alpha m}{p} \quad \text{and} \quad y(p, q) = \frac{(1-\alpha)m}{q}.$$

Note that the cross-price elasticities are zero: $x(p, q)$ does not depend on q, while $y(p, q)$ does not depend on p. Consequently, the expenditure shares for x and y are independent of the prices: $px/m = \alpha$ and $qy/m = 1 - \alpha$. To eliminate these imperfections may require CRRA rather than Cobb–Douglas utility functions.

Proof. Introduce the Lagrange function with multiplier λ:

$$L(x, y) = U(x, y) - \lambda(px + qy - m).$$

Inserting U into L:

$$L(x, y) = \sigma^{-1}[\alpha x^{\sigma} + (1-\alpha)y^{\sigma}] - \lambda(px + qy - m).$$

Apply the necessary first-order conditions:

$$L'_x(x, y) = \alpha x^{\sigma-1} - \lambda p = 0$$
$$\text{and} \quad L'_y(x, y) = (1-\alpha)y^{\sigma-1} - \lambda q = 0.$$

Hence,

$$\lambda = \alpha p^{-1} x^{\sigma-1} = (1-\alpha)q^{-1} y^{\sigma-1}.$$

Using our notations κ and φ (B.4), y can be simply expressed by x:

$$\alpha p^{-1} y^{1-\sigma} = (1-\alpha)q^{-1} x^{1-\sigma}, \quad \text{i.e.,} \quad y = \varphi^{-\kappa} p^{\kappa} q^{-\kappa} x.$$

Inserting (x, y) into the budget condition (B.2) implies

$$m = px + q\varphi^{-\kappa} p^{\kappa} q^{-\kappa} x,$$

yielding x in (B.3). Relying on symmetry, y is obtained in (B.3).

Remark. It is worth comparing the two cases of $0 < \sigma < 1$ and $\sigma < 0$. The key to the comparison lies in the transformation

$$1 - \kappa = \frac{1 - \sigma - 1}{1 - \sigma} = \frac{-\sigma}{1 - \sigma}.$$

If $0 < \sigma < 1$, then $1 - \kappa < 0$, therefore the demand $x(p, q)$ is an increasing function of the other price (q) which is a paradox. Here, the utility function is defined for the corner solutions: for example, if $y = 0$, then $x = m/p$ and the corresponding utility is equal to

$$U(m/p, 0) = \frac{\alpha m^\sigma}{\sigma p^\sigma}.$$

Similarly, for the other corner solution,

$$U(0, m/q) = \frac{(1 - \alpha)m^\sigma}{\sigma q^\sigma}.$$

It can be shown that the corner solutions are inferior to the local maximum, therefore the local maximum is also a global one.

If $\sigma < 0$, then $1 - \kappa > 0$, therefore the demand $x(p, q)$ is a decreasing function of the other price (q). The utility function is not defined for the corner solution.

Appendix C to Chapter 3. Numerical Methods for Finding Roots

In the whole book, we often solve numerically parametric nonlinear equations for a whole range of the parameter values. Then, the primitive method of tabulating the corresponding function and stop at the root would be most inconvenient. In this appendix, we shall present three well-known and efficient methods for finding the approximate root of a nonlinear scalar–scalar equation: (i) the trial-and-error method, (ii) Newton–Raphson's tangent method and (iii) the chord method. To avoid difficulties, we assume that the underlying function is monotone increasing/decreasing in the foregoing interval.

i. The trial-and-error method (successive approximation)

We have a smooth scalar–scalar function f, mapping interval $[0, 1]$ into interval $[-1, 1]$. By the intermediate-value theorem, there exists a scalar $x^* \in [0, 1]$ called the root of f for which

$$f(x^*) = 0. \tag{C.1}$$

We shall rewrite equation (C.1) as a fixed-point problem:

$$x^* = g(x^*), \quad \text{where} \quad g(x) = x - f(x). \tag{C.2}$$

Trivially, (C.1) and (C.2) are equivalent to each other.

There is a powerful theorem guaranteeing the existence and the uniqueness of the fixed point in (C.2), moreover, it provides a numerical method for its computation. To formulate it, we need a definition.

Definition *(Contraction).* A scalar–scalar function g mapping $[a, b]$ into itself is called *contraction* if there exists a positive scalar $q < 1$ for which any pair (x, y), $(a \leq x < y \leq b)$ satisfy

$$|g(x) - g(y)| \leq q|x - y|. \tag{C.3}$$

Theorem C.1 (Fixed-point theorem for contraction). *Let g be a contraction on interval $[a, b]$. Then g has a unique fixed point $x^* = g(x^*)$ which can be approximated by the trial-and-error method for any initial state x_0:*

$$x_{t+1} = g(x_t), \quad \text{where} \quad t = 0, 1, 2, \ldots \tag{C.4}$$

and the error converges to zero exponentially:

$$|x_t - x^*| \leq \frac{q^t}{1-q}|x_0 - g(x_0)|. \tag{C.5}$$

Proof. Let t and v be two integers, $v > t$. Using the triangle inequality and the definition of contraction for the telescopic sum

$$x_v - x_t = x_v - x_{v-1} + \cdots + x_{t+1} - x_t$$

yield inequalities

$$\begin{aligned} |x_v - x_t| &\leq |x_v - x_{v-1}| + \cdots + |x_{t+1} - x_t| \\ &\leq (q^{v-t} + \cdots + 1)|x_{t+1} - x_t|. \end{aligned}$$

Using the formula for the infinite geometric progression (majoring the finite one) and the definition of contraction yield

$$|x_v - x_t| \leq \frac{1}{1-q}|x_{t+1} - x_t| \leq \frac{q^t}{1-q}|x_1 - x_0|. \tag{C.6}$$

Inequality (C.6) shows that $\{x_t\}_{t=0}^{\infty}$ is a Cauchy-sequence, i.e., it is convergent, i.e., there exists at least one fixed point. By continuity, its limit obviously satisfies the fixed-point condition: $x^* = g(x^*)$.

If there were another fixed point, say $y^* = g(y^*) \neq x^*$, then applying (C.3) again,

$$|x^* - y^*| = |g(x^*) - g(y^*)| \leq q|x^* - y^*| < |x^* - y^*|,$$

a contradiction.

Taking the limit in (C.6) by v results in (C.5). ∎

We shall give a sufficient condition for the contracting property.

Corollary. *Assume that g is a smooth function which maps $[a, b]$ into itself. If $|g'(z)| \leq q < 1$ for $a \leq z \leq b$ and an appropriate constant q, then g is a contraction, i.e., the trial-and-error method works.*

Proof. Indeed, using the Lagrange intermediate-value theorem, for any (x, y), there exists a z between x and y such that

$$g(x) - g(y) = g'(z)(x - y).$$

Taking absolute values, and applying $|g'(z)| \leq q$ yield

$$|g(x) - g(y)| = |g'(z)||x - y| \leq q|x - y|,$$

i.e., (C.3) holds. ∎

ii. **Newton–Raphson's tangent method**

There is a special variant of the method above, discovered by Newton around 1670 and improved by Raphson around 1690. Consider (C.1) and linearize f around the t-th approximation:

$$f(x) \approx f(x_t) + f'(x_t)(x - x_t).$$

We have to assume that x^* is a simple root, i.e., $f'(x^*) \neq 0 = f(x^*)$. Denoting the next approximation of the root by x_{t+1} results in

$$f(x_{t+1}) \approx 0 = f(x_t) + f'(x_t)(x_{t+1} - x_t). \tag{C.8}$$

Rearranging (C.8) implies

$$x_{t+1} = x_t - \frac{f(x_t)}{f'(x_t)}. \tag{C.9}$$

Theorem C.2. *If f'' is bounded, then there is an interval $J = (x^* - h, x^* + h)$ such that*

$$|f(x)f''(x)| \leq q[f'(x)]^2, \qquad 0 < q < 1, \quad \text{and} \quad x \in J, \tag{C.10}$$

then iteration (C.9) converges to the root x^*.

Proof. Starting from (C.9), introduce notation

$$g(x) = x - \frac{f(x)}{f'(x)}$$

and calculate g's derivative around x^*:

$$g'(x) = 1 - \frac{f'(x)f'(x) - f(x)f''(x)}{[f'(x)]^2} = \frac{f(x)f''(x)}{[f'(x)]^2}.$$

By (C.10), $|g'(x)| \leq q < 1$ in J, i.e., Corollary to Theorem C.1 applies. ∎

iii. **The chord method**

But there are cases, where Newton–Raphson's method does not work, e.g., at multiple roots with $f'(x^*) = 0$. Then there is a slower but safer algorithm called the chord method. The idea is simple. If there are two subsequent approximations x_t, x_{t+1} such that either $f(x_t) < 0 < f(x_{t+1})$ or $f(x_t) > 0 > f(x_{t+1})$, then there exists a newer approximation x_{t+2} such that its error is smaller than the greater previous one:

$$|x_{t+2} - x^*| < \max(|x_t - x^*|, |x_{t+1} - x^*|)$$

with two alternatives:

(i)

$$\begin{aligned} &\text{either } f(x_t) < f(x_{t+2}) < 0 < f(x_{t+1}) \\ &\text{or} \quad f(x_t) < 0 < f(x_{t+2}) < f(x_{t+1}) \end{aligned}$$

(ii)

$$\begin{aligned} &\text{either } f(x_t) > f(x_{t+2}) > 0 > f(x_{t+1}) \\ &\text{or} \quad f(x_t) > 0 > f(x_{t+2}) > f(x_{t+1}). \end{aligned}$$

For example, $x_{t+2} = (x_t + x_{t+1})/2$ or a finer linear interpolation.

Appendix D to Chapter 3. Feldstein's Undervaluation of Social Security

In this appendix (cf. Simonovits 2017), we revisit Feldstein's (1985) seminal paper (Sects. I and II with homogeneous workers), where he undervalued the optimal Social Security benefits. As was stated in the Introduction, the basic idea was fruitful: the representative worker strongly discounts the utility of old-age consumption and the government tries to mitigate this negligence by introducing a mandatory pension system. But in his analysis, Feldstein committed several errors: (i) he chose a Lernerian rather than the standard Samuelsonian social welfare function; (ii) he allowed that workers pay their pension contributions from credit (negative saving); (iii) relying on a second extreme assumption, namely that the workers expect only a low share of the delivered benefits, he overlooked the possibility that the T-optimum (studied in Sect. 3.2) may be superior to the S-optimum, and depicted the pay-as-you-go system worse than it is. In this appendix, we try to correct these mistakes. (Just after the closure of the book, an anonymous referee called my attention to the fact that Andersen and Bhattachary (2011) has already published such an analysis without the critical tone.)

(i) Using the two-generation framework (see Sect. 15.5), $u(\cdot)$ is the age-invariant per-period utility function. If N_t is the number of workers in period t, then N_{t-1} is the number of the pensioners of the same period. Confining our attention to the representative period t, Feldstein's Lernerian social welfare function (see his (22)) is equal to

$$N_t u(c_t) + N_{t-1} u(d_t).$$

Introducing the time-invariant population growth factor ν, $N_t = \nu N_{t-1}$ holds, therefore the foregoing function is proportional to

$$u(c_t) + \nu^{-1} u(d_t).$$

But it obviously should be (cf. Docquier 2002)

$$V_t = u(c_t) + u(d_{t+1}).$$

(The two approaches are equivalent for stationary population and logarithmic utility functions, studied in Sect. 3.2!)

(ii) We have already studied the problem of slack and tight credit constraints and the corresponding S- and T-optima in Sect. 3.2, we need not dwell on it here. We only add that with longevity risk (Sect. 3.3), if the pensioner dies early, then there is no time to repay the credit she was given while working.

(iii) In addition to discounting the utility of future consumption, Feldstein's representative worker seriously underestimates the future pension benefit with a given factor, much less than 1.

Assuming fabulously high real interest rates, similarly strong discounting and very low expected-to-true benefit in (iii), Feldstein's neglect (ii) was not so important. However, considering his own more realistic parameter value-set, his treatment breaks down.

It is assumed that the worker earns 1 and pays a contribution τ. One period later, there are ν times as many workers as in one generation before, each worker earns g times as much as the previous generation did, therefore the public benefit is equal to $b = \nu g \tau$. Assume that the worker only expects a given part ($0 \le \alpha \le 1$) of her pension in return to her contribution: $\tilde{b} = \alpha \nu g \tau$. Let c and d be the worker's and pensioner's consumption, respectively, and s be her saving. Her true (3.1) and presumed consumption equations are modified by the growth effect:

$$d = \nu g \tau + \rho s \quad \text{vs.} \quad \tilde{d} = \alpha \nu g \tau + \rho s,$$

where $\rho > 1$ is the per-period interest factor. It will be helpful to introduce the *relative* interest factor, being the ratio of the interest factor divided by the economy's growth factor:

$$R = \frac{\rho}{\nu g}.$$

Then the triplet become

$$c = 1 - \tau - s \quad \text{and} \quad d = \nu g(\tau + Rs) \quad \text{vs.} \quad \tilde{d} = \nu g(\alpha\tau + Rs). \tag{D.1}$$

The worker's presumed lifetime utility [cf. (3.2)] is equal to

$$U(c, \tilde{d}) = \log c + \delta \log \tilde{d}, \tag{3.$\tilde{2}$}$$

where $0 < \delta \leq 1$ is the per-period discount factor. As a result, substituting (D.1) into (3.$\tilde{2}$) she maximizes the presumed reduced utility function

$$\tilde{U}[s] = \log(1 - \tau - s) + \delta[\log(\nu g) + \log(\alpha\tau + Rs)]. \tag{D.2}$$

The first-order condition

$$\tilde{U}'[s] = \frac{-1}{1 - \tau - s} + \frac{\delta R}{\alpha\tau + Rs} = 0 \tag{D.3}$$

yields

Lemma D.1. *For any given contribution rate τ, either the 'optimal' saving is positive and equal to*

$$s(\tau) = \frac{\delta(1-\tau) - \alpha\tau R^{-1}}{1+\delta} > 0 \quad \text{if} \quad 0 \leq \tau < \tau_R = \frac{\delta}{\delta + \alpha R^{-1}} \tag{D.4}$$

or zero otherwise.

Substituting (D.4) into (D.1), the corresponding 'optimal' consumption pair are equal to

$$c_S(\tau) = \frac{1 - \lambda\tau}{1+\delta} \quad \text{and} \quad d_S(\tau) = \nu g \frac{R\delta + \kappa\tau}{1+\delta}, \tag{D.5}$$

where

$$\lambda = 1 - \alpha R^{-1} > 0 \quad \text{and} \quad \kappa = 1 - \delta(R-1) - \alpha.$$

To obtain the socially S-optimal contribution rate in the corresponding interval, the government maximizes the social welfare function

$$V(\tau) = \log c_S(\tau) + \log d_S(\tau), \qquad 0 \le \tau \le \tau_R.$$

Due to dynamic efficiency, $R > 1$, hence $\lambda > 0$, therefore by (D.5), the worker's consumption $c_S(\tau)$ is always decreasing, but the behavior of pensioner's consumption $d_S(\tau)$ depends on the sign of κ, i.e., on (R, δ, α).

Dropping the denominators and the multiplier in (D.5), we have a simplified social welfare function

$$\tilde{V}(\tau) = \log(1 - \lambda\tau) + \log(R\delta + \kappa\tau).$$

The new first-order condition leads to

Theorem D.1. *The S-optimal contribution rate is equal to*

$$\tau_S^* = \frac{(\kappa - R\delta\lambda)_+}{2\kappa\lambda}. \tag{D.6}$$

Proof. If $\kappa > R\delta\lambda$, τ_S^* is the root of

$$\tilde{V}'(\tau) = \frac{-\lambda}{1 - \lambda\tau} + \frac{\kappa}{R\delta + \kappa\tau} = 0. \tag{D.7}$$

Otherwise,

$$\tilde{V}'(0) = -\lambda + \frac{\kappa}{R\delta} < 0.$$

∎

We suspect that Feldstein applied the extreme assumption (iii) [workers (almost) totally underestimate their future pension] to make room for positive S-optimal contribution rates and downplay the importance of the T-optimum to be discussed now.

Feldstein himself discovered T-optima in case of $\delta = 0$. But it is also relevant for $\delta > 0$ in the T-interval. Indeed, for $s = 0$, $c = 1 - \tau$, $d = \nu g \tau$, therefore

$$\tilde{V}(\tau) = \log(1 - \tau) + \log \nu + \log g + \log \tau, \qquad \tau_R < \tau \le 1,$$

i.e., the first-order condition remains the same as in Sect. 3.2:

$$\tilde{V}'(\tau) = -\frac{1}{1-\tau} + \frac{1}{\tau} = 0.$$

V' is positive in the interval $[\tau_R, 1/2)$—which is nonempty if and only if $\delta R < \alpha(\leq 1)$—and V' is negative in the interval (1/2,1), thus V reaches its maximum at $\tau_{\mathrm{T}}^* = 1/2$. The government has to choose that optimal rate out of τ_{S}^* and τ_{T}^* which provides the higher social welfare. We shall see that sometimes the S-optima are inferior to $\tau_{\mathrm{T}}^* = 1/2$, but otherwise superior to $\tau_{\mathrm{T}}^* = 1/2$. Depending on $(R[1], \delta[1])$, the welfare differences can be very large.

Turning to the comparison of S and T-optima, note that $\alpha = 0$ yields $\tau < \tau_R = 1$, eliminating the T-interval. But in our opinion, such assumptions beg the very problem of optimal public pension. On the other hand, for full anticipation of the benefit, i.e., $\alpha = 1$, $\tau_{\mathrm{S}}^* = 0$ and the role of the T-optimum cannot be neglected if $\delta R < 1$.

Using numerical calculations, Feldstein showed for a large set of parameter values that (at least in the S-interval) the S-optimal contribution rate is generally close or even equal to zero. He forgot, however, to compare the S-optimum welfare to that of the T-optimum, which played so important role in our Sect. 3.2.

We turn now to numerical illustrations. If T is the length of the period, say 30 years, then there is the simple transformation rule between per-period and annual factors:

$$\nu = \nu[1]^T, \qquad g = g[1]^T, \qquad \rho = \rho[1]^T,$$
$$R = R[1]^T \qquad \text{and} \qquad \delta = \delta[1]^T.$$

Turning to the numerical illustrations, we use Feldstein's annual population growth factor $\nu[1] = 1.014$ and wage growth factor $g[1] = 1.022$. In Table D.1, we use the original social welfare function of Feldstein, and depict the S and T-versions with his $\rho[1] = 1.08$, $\delta = 0.05$ (i.e., $\delta[1] = 0.9$) and $\alpha = 0.5$, for selected contribution rates. Note that for the S-curve (column 2), the maximum is reached at $\tau_{\mathrm{S}}^* = 0.2$ (italicized) with a value of 1.026, while for the T-curve (column 1), the maximum

Table D.1 The efficiency of three alternative systems: Lernerian welfare

Contribution rate	No saving	Saving	
		Positive/negative	Only nonnegative
0.0	0	1.000	1.000
0.1	0.825	1.021	1.021
0.2	0.978	*1.026*	1.026
0.3	1.045	1.018	1.045
0.4	*1.064*	0.998	*1.064*
0.5	1.045	0.965	1.045

Remark. $\delta[1] = 0.905$, $\alpha = 0.5$ and $R[1] = 1.08/1.036 \approx 1.04$ (Feldstein 1985, pp. 307 and 313–314)

arises at $\tau_T = 0.4$ (italicized) with a value 1.064. The true social welfare (column 3) is depicted as a maximum of the two previous columns.

Returning to our social welfare function and perfect foresight: $\alpha = 1$, in Table D.2, the annual relative interest factor $R[1]$ runs between 1.04 and 1.06 (corresponding to real interest factors $\rho[1]$ 1.077–1.098), while the annual discount factor $\delta[1]$ varies between 0.91 and 0.93, around the critical discount factor $\delta^*[1]$. Obviously, sometimes we surpass the limits set by ($A4$). We only depict 3×3 values of the S-optimal saving, the corresponding worker's and pensioner's consumptions and the relative efficiency of the T-optimum with respect to the S-optimum (no public component). In formula:

$$V(\tau_S) + 2\log \varepsilon_{T|S} = V(\tau_T),$$
$$\text{i.e.,} \quad \varepsilon_{T|S} = \exp\{[V(\tau_T) - V(\tau_S)]/2\}.$$

Note that for low enough but realistic relative interest factors and discount factors (e.g., $R[1] = 1.05$ and $\rho[1] = 0.91$), the pure public system is more efficient than the pure private one: $\varepsilon_{T|S} > 1$ ($A4$ holds). In the opposite case, the disproportional pensioner's consumption vs. the worker's consumption (e.g., Table 4.2) signals the unrealistically high relative interest factor ($A4$ does not hold).

Table D.2 The efficiency of public versus private systems: Samuelsonian welfare

Relative interest Factor $R[1]$	Discount Factor $\delta[1]$	Worker's, saving s^*	Worker's Consumption c_S^*	Pensioner's Consumption d_S^*	Relative efficiency, $\varepsilon_{T\|S}$
1.04	0.91	0.056	0.944	0.523	1.210
	0.92	0.076	0.924	0.710	1.049
	0.93	0.102	0.898	0.954	0.918
1.05	0.91	0.056	0.944	0.696	1.048
	0.92	0.076	0.924	0.946	0.909
	0.93	0.102	0.898	1.272	0.795
1.06	0.91	0.056	0.944	0.925	0.909
	0.92	0.076	0.924	1.257	0.788
	0.93	0.102	0.898	1.690	0.690

Remark. $\tau_T^* = 0.5$, $c_T^* = 0.5$ and $d_T^* = 0.5\nu g = 1.458$

Starting with Chapter 4 (with the exception of Chapters 10, 11 and Sect. 15.5), we shall generally work with realistic length ratios: $\mu < 1$, mostly $\mu = 0.5$.

Appendix E to Chapter 4. The Approximation Error in a Two-Period Life-Cycle Saving

In the bulk of the book, we approximate the annual life-cycle model with a two-period model, where the private life-cycle saving is approximated with a simple formula:

$$\mu^{-1} \rho s = d, \tag{E.1}$$

where s and d are the intensities of saving and private benefits, respectively; μ denotes the ratio of length of retirement to that of working and ρ stands for the per-period real interest factor. We shall assume away both population and productivity growth: $\nu = 1$ and $g = 1$.

To give the correct formula in an annual model with compounded interest, let integers R and D denote the *adult* ages in years at retiring and dying, respectively (the age at starting to work $Q = 0$), and $\rho[1] > 1$

denote the annual real interest factor. Then we have the following identity in present values:

$$s \sum_{i=0}^{R-1} \rho[1]^{-i} = d \sum_{j=R}^{D-1} \rho[1]^{-j}. \tag{E.2}$$

Using the formula for the sum of the geometric progression, (E.2) simplifies into

$$s \frac{1-\rho[1]^{-R}}{1-\rho[1]^{-1}} = d\rho[1]^{-R} \frac{1-\rho[1]^{R-D}}{1-\rho[1]^{-1}}$$

or equivalently,

$$s \frac{\rho[1]^{R}-1}{1-\rho[1]^{R-D}} = d. \tag{E.3}$$

Using

$$\mu = \frac{D-R}{R} \quad \text{and} \quad \rho = \rho[1]^{D/2},$$

the question is now how good the approximation $\rho[1]^{D/2}$ [cf. (E.1)] is for

$$\tilde{\rho} = \frac{\rho[1]^{R}-1}{1-\rho[1]^{R-D}} \mu$$

Table E.1 tabulates the exact and the approximate yield values for $D = 60$, $R = 40$ and varying $\rho[1]$. As the annual interest factor grows, the approximate yield lags more and more behind the exact yield: for annual interest rate 6%, the relative error is almost 18%.

Appendix F to Chapter 4. Heterogeneous Life Spans

As a prelude to Chapter 14, in this appendix, we consider an important case when not only the wages but also the length ratios are heterogeneous.

Table E.1 Exact and approximate yields

Annual, $\rho[1]$	Exact, $\tilde{\rho}$	Approximate, $\rho[1]^{D/2}$
	Interest factor	
1.01	1.355	1.348
1.02	1.847	1.811
1.03	2.534	2.427
1.04	3.496	3.243
1.05	4.847	4.322
1.06	6.746	5.743

As a starter, it will suffice to have a binary model with short (L) and long (H) life span coupled with low (L) and high (H) wages. To retain the basic structure, we assume that the ages of starting work and ending work are homogeneous but the ages at death are not. We assume that the proportional pension rule works with the aggregate length ratio.

There are two important special cases: (i) male (M) and female (F), where males earn more than females do but die earlier, i.e., (LH) and (HL) prevail and (ii) a unisex world, where low earners' (Poor) life span is shorter than high earners' (Rich), i.e., (LL) and (HH) prevail. The main point of our analysis is that in both cases, the aggregate public pension rule destroys the balance: in case (i), it produces a surplus; in case (ii), it produces a deficit.

In our simple model, there are two types, with index $i = 1, 2$, where $w_1 > w_2$ and μ_1, μ_2 with either $\mu_1 < \mu_2$ or $\mu_1 > \mu_2$. The aggregate length ratio, used in the calculation, is given as

$$\mu = f_1\mu_1 + f_2\mu_2. \tag{F.1}$$

In this case, the aggregate proportional public pension rule means that

$$b_i = \mu^{-1}\tau w_i, \qquad i = 1, 2. \tag{F.2}$$

The lifetime balance of type i is given as

$$z_i = \tau w_i - \mu_i b_i. \tag{F.3}$$

Substituting (F.2) into (F.3) yields the type-specific balances

$$z_i = \tau w_i - \mu_i \mu^{-1} \tau w_i = \tau w_i (1 - \mu_i \mu^{-1}). \qquad \text{(F.4)}$$

and the expected balance:

$$\mathbf{E}z = f_1 z_1 + f_2 z_2 = \tau \sum_{i=1}^{2} f_i w_i (1 - \mu_i \mu^{-1}). \qquad \text{(F.5)}$$

Introducing the deviation variables $\hat{w}_i = w_i - 1$ and $\hat{\mu}_i = \mu_i - \mu$, (F.5) simplifies to

$$\mathbf{E}z = -\tau \mu^{-1} \sum_{i=1}^{2} f_i (\hat{w}_i + 1) \hat{\mu}_i = -\tau \mu^{-1} \sum_{i=1}^{2} f_i \hat{w}_i \hat{\mu}_i. \qquad \text{(F.6)}$$

We separate the two cases and obtain the following theorems.

Theorem F.1 *(Males and females).* $\mu_M < \mu < \mu_F$ *and* $w_M > 1 > w_F > 0$.

(a) Males are losers and females are gainers:

$$z_M > 0 > z_F. \qquad \text{(F.7)}$$

(b) The expected balance is positive:

$$\mathbf{E}z > 0. \qquad \text{(F.8)}$$

Proof. (a) (F.4) implies (F.7).
(b) (F.6) implies (F.8). ∎

We shall illustrate the effect of male–female heterogeneity on a numerical example.

Example F.1. For the sake of simplicity, it is assumed that males and females have the same (unitary) length of contributions (including time spent by females with raising babies), the same population share $f_M = f_F = 1/2$ but have different remaining life spans $\mu_M = 0.45$ and $\mu_F = 0.55$ and wages $w_M = 1.1$ and $w_F = 0.9$, yielding $\mu = 1/2$ and $\mathbf{E}w = 1$. Working with $\tau = 0.3$,

$$z_M = 0.3 \times 1.1(1 - 2 \times 0.45) = 0.033$$

and

$$z_F = 0.3 \times 0.9(1 - 2 \times 0.55) = -0.027,$$

hence $\mathbf{E}z = 0.003$ is positive but negligible: 0.3% of the annual average wage.

We have a dual theorem.

Theorem F.2 (Unisex pensions with wage heterogeneity). *Assume $w_H > 1 > w_L > 0$ and $\mu_H > \mu > \mu_L$.*

(a) Long-lived workers (H) are gainers and short-lived workers (L) are losers:

$$z_H < 0 < z_L. \tag{F.9}$$

(b) The expected balance is negative:

$$\mathbf{E}z < 0. \tag{F.10}$$

We leave the proof to the Reader but present a second example.

Example F.2. For the sake of simplicity, it is assumed that the rich (H) and the poor (L) have the same (unitary) length of contributions (including the time spent with raising babies) but with the usual population share $f_H = 1/3$ and $f_L = 2/3$ and they have different remaining life span $\mu_H = 0.6$ and $\mu_L = 0.45$ and wages $w_H = 2$ and $w_L = 0.5$, yielding $\mu = 1/2$ and $\mathbf{E}w = 1$. Working with $\tau = 0.3$,

$$z_H = 0.3 \times 2(1 - 2 \times 0.6) = -0.12$$

and

$$z_L = 0.3 \times 0.5(1 - 2 \times 0.45) = 0.015,$$

hence

$$\mathbf{E}z = -\frac{1}{3} \times 0.12 + \frac{2}{3} \times 0.015 = -0.04 + 0.01 = -0.03,$$

is negative and not so much negligible: 3% of the annual average wage.

Waldron (2007) compared the male life expectancies at age 65 of the lower and of the higher income halves of the US population. He found that the pair (15, 16.5) in 1986 grew to (16.1; 21.5). Table F.1 displays Hungarian male data on the corresponding variables (Molnár and Hollós-Marosi 2015), for four groups of male pensioners of equal size with increasing benefits. We shall illustrate the four-class generalization of Theorem F.2 on these data.

Calculating the product of averages (as in Freudenberg et al. 2016) underestimates the expenditure and the relative error: $(\mathbf{E}(Tb) - \mathbf{E}T\mathbf{E}b)/(\mathbf{E}T\mathbf{E}b) = 0.025$, a surprisingly small number. Probably the distortion would grow if we had a finer resolution and if we extended the projection for the future where the heterogeneity of remaining life expectancy and of benefits will grow.

At the end of this appendix, we mention that the distortion discussed is closely related to Chebyshev's sum inequality (cf. Simonovits 1995 and Wagener 1996). This elementary inequality can be formulated as follows.

Theorem F.3 (Chebyshev 1882). *Let $I > 1$ be an integer, and let $(T_i)_{i=1}^I$ and $(b_i)_{i=1}^I$ be two increasing positive real sequence. Then the following*

Table F.1 Four male groups: benefits and remaining life expectancies, Hungary, 2012

Quartile, i	Relative benefit, b_i	Remaining LEXP60 (years), T_i
1	61.9	17.1
2	81.1	18.3
3	105.0	19.5
4	152.0	21.1
Average	100.0	19.0

Source. Molnár and Hollós-Marosi (2015, pp. 1268–1271, Tables 1–3) and private communication

inequality holds:

$$\frac{1}{I}\sum_{i=1}^{I} T_i b_i > \left(\frac{1}{I}\sum_{i=1}^{I} T_i\right)\left(\frac{1}{I}\sum_{i=1}^{I} b_i\right). \tag{F.11}$$

Remarks. 1. The dual of this inequality reads as follows: if $(T_i)_{i=1}^I$ is increasing and $(b_i)_{i=1}^I$ is decreasing, then the opposite holds:

$$\frac{1}{I}\sum_{i=1}^{I} T_i b_i < \left(\frac{1}{I}\sum_{i=1}^{I} T_i\right)\left(\frac{1}{I}\sum_{i=1}^{I} b_i\right). \tag{F.12}$$

2. The probabilistic meaning of this inequality is as follows: if the values of two positive discrete random variables with equal length are indexed in increasing order, then their correlation is positive. We shall apply this observation in Appendix G to Chapter 9.
The proof is so simple that it is worth presenting.

Proof. Introducing notation $x_{I+i} = x_i$ for $x = T, b$ and using the monotonicity of the series, we have the following n inequalities:

$$\sum_{i=1}^{I} T_i b_i = \sum_{i=1}^{I} T_i b_i$$

$$\sum_{i=1}^{I} T_i b_i > \sum_{i=1}^{I} T_i b_{i+1}$$

$$\ldots \qquad \ldots$$

$$\sum_{i=1}^{I} T_i b_i > \sum_{i=1}^{I} T_i b_{i+I-1}.$$

Adding up them and dividing both sides by $1/I^2$ results in (F.11). ∎

In Chapter 14, we return to this issue.

Appendix G to Chapter 9. Two Generalizations for NDC

This appendix contains two generalizations to Chapter 9: (i) replacing an idealized survival curve by realistic one and (ii) combining nonlinear NDC with fragmented labor career.

Realistic Survival Curves

We introduce a realistic survival function instead of that used in (9.4′). At the same time, we drop the age-dependent labor disutility, i.e., $\chi = 0$.

Presenting (9.4N) we have assumed that nobody dies between the minimum and the maximum retirement ages. Now we get rid of this assumption, and introduce the remaining life expectancy at age R, e_R (cf. Banyár 2012 and Simonovits 2015). In practice, e_R is a decreasing function with $e'_R > -1$, and in the interval $[R_{\mathrm{m}}, R_{\mathrm{M}}]$, it can be approximated with a linear function $e_{R+1} - e_R \approx \kappa$, where $0 < \kappa < 1$. For the United States, in 2003, $\kappa \approx 0.8$ (Arias 2006, p. 8, Table 1).

We can recalculate all our formulas by replacing $D - R^*$ with e_{R^*}. For example, (9.6N) changes into

$$\frac{b^{N'}(R)}{b^N(R)} = \frac{1}{R - Q} + \frac{e'_R}{e_R} \qquad (9.6\mathrm{E})$$

and the corresponding consistency rule for the linear approximation becomes $\alpha = \tau / e_{R^*}$ and $\eta = e'_R(R^*)/e_{R^*}$.

From Arias (2006), for $R_{\mathrm{m}} = 62$ years, $e_{R_{\mathrm{m}}} = 20.6$ years, we get the rough approximation $\eta = 1/20.6 \approx 0.05$, while the finer approximation gives at $R^* = 66$, $e_{R^*} = 17.6$ years and $e'_R(R^*) = 0.7$, $\eta = 0.7/17.6 \approx 0.04$.

Fragmented Labor Careers with NDC

Section 9.4 studied fragmented labor careers when the benefit function was linearized (9.4L). Here, we return to nonlinear NDC (plus the simplified life expectancy function) and show that the optimal retirement age is an increasing function of the nonfragmentation rate and the prescribed retirement age is a decreasing function.

We retain (9.14) for the employment length but drop the type index k:

$$S = \varphi(R - Q) \tag{9.14$'$}$$

and combine it with the appropriately modified NDC benefit function (9.5):

$$b(R) = \frac{\tau\varphi(R - Q)}{D - R}. \tag{9.5$'$}$$

Inserting (9.5′) into the discounted lifetime utility function (9.1) with the discount factor $\delta \in (0, 1]$ but without aging effect ($\chi = 0$), (9.7) reduced to

$$U'_R(\varphi, R) = \varphi[\log(1 - \tau) - \xi]$$
$$- \delta[\log\tau + \log\varphi + \log(R - Q) - \log(D - R)] + \delta\frac{D - Q}{R - Q} = 0. \tag{9.7$'$}$$

Luckily, we can determine the character of the dependence of the optimal retirement age R on the nonfragmentation rate φ. Neglecting the macrobalance, we prove

Theorem G.1. *If the nonfragmentation ratio is higher than a minimum, namely if*

$$\varphi > \frac{\delta}{\log(1 - \tau) - \log a}, \tag{G.1}$$

then the more fragmented the labor career, the lower the optimal retirement age.

Remarks. 1. The lower bound defines a nonempty interval if $\log(1 - \tau) - \log a > \delta$.

2. By (F.10), in an optimal NDC, the correlation coefficient between R and S is positive.

Table G.1 Fragmentation, optimal retirement age and employment length

Nonfragmentation rate, φ	Optimal retirement age (Year), $R(\varphi)$	Employment length (Year), $S(\varphi)$
1.0	62.6	42.6
0.9	62.3	38.1
0.8	62.1	33.7
0.7	62.1	29.5

Proof. In fact, by the theorem on the implicit function,

$$R'(\varphi) = -\frac{U''_{R\varphi}(\varphi, R)}{U''_{RR}(\varphi, R)}.$$

The denominator is negative (second-order condition) and the nominator is positive if and only if

$$U''_{R\varphi}(\varphi, R) = \log(1-\tau) - \log a - \frac{\delta}{\varphi} > 0.$$

This is equivalent to (G.1), i.e., $R'(\varphi) < 0$. ∎

We shall illustrate our result numerically in Table G.1.

At the end, we show the opposite case. This is an utterly simplified version of the seniority system. The government prescribes that every worker has to retire at an age where the ratio of his employment length to the retirement length is equal to $\sigma > 1$:

$$\varphi(R-Q) = \sigma(D-R). \quad \text{(G.2)}$$

Using $b = \beta w$, the equality of lifetime contributions and benefits implies $\tau\varphi(R-Q) = (D-R)\beta$, i.e., $\beta = \sigma\tau$. Hence, we have

Theorem G.2. *In a rigid system with (G.2), the retirement age is increasing and the employment length is decreasing in the nonfragmentation rate and are respectively equal to*

Table G.2 Fragmentation, prescribed retirement age and employment length

Nonfragmentation rate, φ	Prescribed retirement age (Year), $R(\varphi)$	Employment length (Year), $S(\varphi)$
1.0	60.0	40.0
0.9	61.4	37.2
0.8	62.9	34.3

$$R(\varphi) = \frac{\sigma\varphi Q + D}{\sigma\varphi + 1} \quad \text{and} \quad S(\varphi) = \frac{\varphi(D - Q)}{\sigma\varphi + 1} \tag{G.3}$$

Remark. By (F.11), in the rigid system, the correlation coefficient between R and S is negative.

Finally, we illustrate the rigid system numerically (Table G.2).

Following Czeglédi et al. (2017), Granseth et al. (2016) considered the time development of the male and female correlation coefficients in four countries: Hungary, Austria, Germany and Sweden. Though the foregoing eight indicators have evolved along very different ways, the Hungarian female correlation sunk as low as –0.7 in 2009, while the Austrian male indicator oscillated around +0.3 between 2003 and 2011.

Appendix H to Chapter 10. Approximation to the Raising Cost Function

In this appendix, we shall discuss the virtues and errors stemming from approximating the child raising function in the literature (also in Chapter 11). On the one hand, simplifications open more rooms for analytical calculations and enable us to prove directly some of our theorems above. On the other hand, they distort the analysis, causing significant qualitative and quantitative errors.

Earlier papers (van Groezen et al. 2003; Simonovits 2013) made the raising costs independent of the net income: $(\pi - \varphi)n$, making the (young) worker's consumption function linear in the fertility rate:

$$c = z - (\pi - \varphi)n, \qquad 0 \leq \varphi \leq \pi \tag{H.1}$$

and leaving the old worker's consumption $d = z = \hat{\theta} w + \gamma$ as was in Chapter 10. (There were no old workers in the papers mentioned above.) Comparing (H.1) and (10.2b), the differences are very large. Due to (H.1), the new reduced utility function is log-linear:

$$U[n] = \log(z(\pi - \varphi)n) + \zeta \log n + \log z, \tag{H.2}$$

therefore the new optimal wage-specific fertility rate is

$$n(w, \varphi, \gamma) = \frac{\zeta z}{\bar{\zeta}(\pi - \varphi)}. \tag{H.3}$$

Note that here the optimal fertility rate is counterintuitively an increasing rather than decreasing function of the wage and the basic income! Furthermore, for the maximal child benefit rate $\varphi = \pi$, the optimal fertility rate is infinite!

Taking the expectations on $n(w, \varphi, \gamma)$ in (H.3), $z = \hat{\theta} w + \gamma$, i.e., $\mathbf{E}z = \hat{\theta} + \gamma$, i.e., the current average fertility rate is given by

$$\nu(\varphi, \gamma) = \frac{\zeta(\hat{\theta} + \gamma)}{\bar{\zeta}(\pi - \varphi)}. \tag{H.4}$$

It is remarkable that the aggregate fertility rate is now independent of the wage distribution!

Rather than determining the balanced basic income, we introduce the difference between the tax rate and the basic income: $\lambda = \theta - \gamma$ (i.e., $\gamma = \theta - \lambda$). This is the part of the tax which finances the child benefits, shortly: the *tax rate for child benefit*. To shorten (H.4), we introduce notation $\omega = \zeta / [\bar{\zeta}(\pi - \varphi)]$, yielding

$$\nu(\varphi, \theta - \lambda) = (1 - \lambda)\omega. \tag{H.5}$$

(Note that for $\varphi = 0, \omega = n_0$.) Substitute (H.5) into the balance equation (10.9′):

$$(1 + \nu_{-1}^{-1})\lambda = \omega\varphi(1 - \lambda),$$

hence, the balanced tax rate for child benefit is equal to

$$\lambda[\varphi, \nu_{-1}] = \frac{\omega\varphi}{1 + \omega\varphi + \nu_{-1}^{-1}}.$$

Note that the balanced tax rate for child benefit λ is independent of the tax rate θ and is an increasing function of the child benefit rate φ. Therefore the balanced basic income is a decreasing function of the child benefit rate and any increase in the tax rate increases the income by the same quantity.

Substituting λ into (H.5) yields a simple fertility dynamics:

$$\nu = H(\nu_{-1}) = \frac{\omega(1 + \nu_{-1})}{1 + (1 + \omega\varphi)\nu_{-1}}. \tag{H.6}$$

To obtain the steady state, we substitute $\nu = \nu_{-1}$ into (H.6). The resulting quadratic equation

$$(1 + \omega\varphi)\nu^2 - (\omega - 1)\nu - \omega = 0$$

yields the steady-state fertility as the positive root

$$\nu^{\text{o}} = \frac{\omega - 1 + \sqrt{(\omega + 1)^2 + 4\omega^2\varphi}}{2(1 + \omega\varphi)}. \tag{H.7}$$

Finally, we could check the local stability under (H.6). As is well known, the dynamics is locally stable if $|H'(\nu^{\text{o}})| < 1$ holds. A simple calculation yields the condition of local stability:

$$\begin{aligned}|H'(\nu^{\text{o}})| &= \frac{\omega^2\varphi}{[1 + (1 + \omega\varphi)\nu^{\text{o}}]^2} \\ &= \frac{4\omega^2\varphi}{[1 - \omega + \sqrt{(\omega + 1)^2 + 4\omega^2\varphi})]^2} < 1. \end{aligned} \tag{H.8}$$

Table H.1 Child benefit rate and steady-state fertility rate: approximation

Child benefit rate, φ	Balanced basic income, $\gamma[\varphi, \nu^o]$	Steady-state fertility rate, ν^o	Contraction factor, $\vert H'(\nu^o)\vert$
0	0.300	0.816	0
0.04	0.283	0.906	0.009
0.08	0.259	1.015	0.020
0.12	0.226	1.150	0.034
0.16	0.180	1.323	0.052

Remark. $w_L = 1/2$, $f_L = 2/3$, $\theta = 0.3$

By geometric reasoning it could be proved that local stability here implies global stability.

In summary, we proved

Theorem H.1. *In approximation (H.1), the steady-state fertility rate is determined by (H.7) and it is locally (and globally) stable if (H.8) holds.*

We tried to give a quite general and plausible condition for (H.8) to hold but we must be satisfied with numerical simulations presented in Table H.1. We display the dependence of the approximated steady-state fertility rate as a function of the child benefit rate. As the child benefit rate rises from 0 to 0.16, the balanced basic income drops from 0.3 to 0.18 (the exact value is equal to 0.225 in Table 10.1) and the steady-state fertility rate rises from $n_0 = 0.816$ to 1.323 (the exact value is equal to 1.051). The approximation is hardly acceptable.

Appendix I to Chapter 11. Jump the Welfare Gap

In this appendix, we generalize the phenomenon *jump the welfare gap* already described in special pension models of Sect. 3.2, Chapters 5, 7, 8 and Sect. 11.3. Here we abstract away from young- and old-age consumption, and rather study ordinary and merit goods and assume that the individual underestimates the real utility of the merit good. Although private purchase (e.g., saving) is assumed to be more efficient than public one (e.g., pension contribution), workers are too myopic to care sufficiently for merit goods (e.g., to save enough for old age). This situation is modeled by an individual maximizing an additively separable utility function, where the merit good's real utility is discounted: the real utility is multiplied by a discount factor. Under normal assumptions, the individual buys less of the merit good than the government would like he did.

Therefore a paternalistic government chooses a transfer system (e.g., to finance a public pension system) to maximize a paternalistic utility function, where discounting is eliminated. Although one unit transfer is less efficient than a corresponding private purchase, but by its sheer size, it supplies enough merit good. Note that models of this type only justify public intervention by the distortionary effect of erroneous private preferences. But in real life, redistribution from the rich to the poor (e.g., Sect. 2.2) or simply supplying social insurance against bad luck (e.g., Sects. 3.3 and 3.4) can also justify transfers, but these items are neglected here. Due to the abstractness of the model, it concerns not only public pensions but also other transfers like public spending on health or education.

Peter Diamond suggested the following example (personal communication): Assume that people dispose of garbage infrequently—bothering their neighbors. The government introduces a more expensive garbage collection system. If the government collects garbage only a little more frequently than the private equilibrium, then the public system makes only things worse. It takes a large enough effort to make things better.

To avoid studying a trivial situation, we assume again that the discount factor is so low that the socially optimal transfer delivers higher welfare than the private system does. Then, we prove the following statement: the government needs to *jump the gap* of lower welfare arising for too low taxes. This result has two implications: (a) using only first-order conditions, one may end up with the second-best rather than the first-best social welfare; (b) if political opposition compels the government to choose a tax below the socially optimum, the society may end up with a lower welfare than not having tax at all.

Turning to the model, the foregoing quantities are generally positive real numbers, except if stated otherwise. The whole society is represented by a single individual, consuming one ordinary and one merit goods in quantities c and d, respectively.

The individual's original earning is equal to 1, he spends s on the merit good and can consume ρs, where $\rho > 1$. In addition, the government charges a tax t, increasing the consumption of the merit good to $\chi(t)$. We assume that $\chi(\cdot)$ is an increasing function in [0, 1] and $\chi(0) = 0$. In our mixed system, the consumption pair are as follows:

$$c = 1 - t - s \quad \text{and} \quad d = \chi(t) + \rho s. \tag{I.1}$$

The individual has an additively separable Cobb–Douglas lifetime utility function

$$U(c, d) = \log c + \delta \log d, \tag{I.2}$$

where δ is the discount factor, $0 \le \delta < 1$. Note that in the pension models, this is the usual time discount factor, but in other applications, it measures the private neglect of the consumption of merit goods.

We assume that the government and the representative individual play a Stackelberg leader and follower game: first the government (as the leader) chooses t and then the individual (as the follower) chooses s. Note, however, that making its decision, the government anticipates the individual's reaction. Inserting the consumption pair (I.1) into the individual utility function (I.2), the reduced utility function is equal to

$$U[s] = \log(1 - t - s) + \delta \log(\chi(t) + \rho s). \tag{I.3}$$

The optimality condition and the optimal intention $\tilde{s}$ are, respectively, equal to

$$U'[s] = -\frac{1}{1 - t - s} + \frac{\delta\rho}{\chi(t) + \rho s} = 0,$$

$$\text{i.e.,} \quad \tilde{s} = \frac{\delta(1 - t) - \rho^{-1}\chi(t)}{1 + \delta}. \tag{I.4}$$

If the solution is negative, then we replace it by 0: $s = \tilde{s}_+$.

At this stage, we allude to two concrete examples: the traditional pension model studied in Sect. 3.2 and the extended pension model with endogenous fertility in Sect. 11.2.

In the general case, the *separator* tax t_W is that tax at which the purchasing intention is just zero, i.e., the unique root to the implicit equation

$$\delta\rho = \delta\rho t_W + \chi(t_W).$$

We have the following classification: for $0 \le t < t_W$, the purchasing intention is positive; for $t_W < t < 1$, the purchasing intention is negative. Repeating: because of the existence of credit constraint, negative purchasing intentions become zero purchase, while positive intentions are preserved: $s = \tilde{s}_+$. We shall call t_W the *worst* tax.

We have now the following consumption equations:

$$c_S(t) = \frac{1 - t + \rho^{-1}\chi(t)}{1+\delta}, \qquad d_S(t) = \delta\rho c_S(t)$$
$$\text{if} \quad 0 \le t < t_W \qquad (\text{I.5} - S)$$

and

$$c_T(t) = 1 - t, \qquad d_T(t) = \chi(t) \quad \text{if} \quad t_W \le t < 1. \qquad (\text{I.5} - T)$$

We depict a situation, where the transfer *crowds out* the more efficient private purchase until the latter disappears: $c'_S(t) < 0$, i.e.,

$$\chi'(t) < \rho \quad \text{for} \quad t \in [0, t_W] \qquad (A1)$$

which is our first assumption.

To evaluate the social welfare of a system with tax t, we shall use the undiscounted *paternalistic* social welfare function

$$V(t) = \log c(t) + \log d(t).$$

To find its global maximum, we will separate the two cases of positive and negative intentions.

By $(A1)$, both $c_S(t)$ and $d_S(t)$ are decreasing functions in $0 < t < t_W$ (crowding-out effect), therefore, the corresponding local maximum is achieved at $t = 0$, a corner maximum.

Inserting $(I.5-T)$ into $V(t)$, and taking the resulting function's derivative in the second interval,

$$V'(t) = -\frac{1}{1-t} + \frac{\chi'(t)}{\chi(t)}, \qquad t_W \le t < 1.$$

We are interested in the sign of $V'(t)$, therefore, we introduce a simpler function

$$Z(t) = \chi'(t)(1-t) - \chi(t)$$

which has the same sign as $V'(t)$.

Note that $Z(1) < 0$. To have a unique root t^* (with $Z(t^*) = 0$) in interval $[t_W, 1]$, we assume (second and third assumptions) that

$$\rho\delta < 1 \qquad (A2)$$

and

$$Z'(t) = \chi''(t)(1-t) - 2\chi'(t) < 0. \qquad (A3)$$

Note that $(A2)$ implies $Z(t_W) > 0$ and $\chi'' < 0$ implies $(A3)$. Then $V'(t)$ is positive in interval $[t_W, t^*)$ and negative in interval $(t^*, 1)$, thus V reaches its local maximum at t^*, where

$$\chi(t^*) = \chi'(t^*)(1-t^*).$$

From now on, we confine our attention to interval $[0, t^*]$. The corresponding social welfare maximum is equal to

$$V(t^*) = \log c(t^*) + \log d(t^*).$$

Compare now the two optimal pairs of consumption:

$$c_S(0) = \frac{1}{1+\delta}, \qquad d_S(0) = \frac{\delta\rho}{1+\delta} \qquad (I.6-S)$$

and

$$c_T(t^*) = 1 - t^*, \qquad d_T(t^*) = \chi(t^*). \qquad (I.6-T)$$

To have a meaningful model, in addition to $c(0) > c(t^*)$ (due to myopia) we have to assume that $d(0) < d(t^*)$ (the aim of coercion). Inserting the formulas (I.6 – S) and (I.6 – T) into the second inequality, we arrive to our fourth assumption:

$$\frac{\delta\rho}{1+\delta} < \chi(t^*). \qquad (A4)$$

We are interested in that case when the socially optimal transfer system is superior to the private system:

$$V(t^*) > V(0).$$

Inserting the corresponding formulas into the last inequality results in (fourth-plus assumption)

$$\log(1-t^*) + \log\chi(t^*) > -2\log(1+\delta) + \log\delta + \log\rho. \qquad (A4^*)$$

It is easy to see that for any interest factor $\rho > 1$, there exists a critical discount factor $\delta_\rho < 1$, for which the two maximal welfares are equal to each other:

$$\log(1-t^*) + \log(\chi(t^*)) = -2\log(1+\delta) + \log\delta_\rho + \log\rho.$$

For $0 < \delta < \delta_\rho$, there exists a *neutral* tax $t_{\mathrm{N}} \in (t_{\mathrm{W}}, t^*)$ for which the social welfare is the same as at the private system. In formula:

$$\log(1-t_{\mathrm{N}}) + \log(\chi(t_{\mathrm{N}})) = -2\log(1+\delta) + \log\delta + \log\rho.$$

Note that in the special case of traditional pension model with $\chi(t) = t$, $t^* = 1/2$, assumptions ($A1$–$A4^*$) reduce to ($A1$): $1 < \rho$, ($A2$): $t_{\mathrm{W}} < 1/2$ and ($A3$): $-2 < 0$, ($A4$): $\delta\rho/(1+\delta) < 1/2$ and ($A4^*$):

$$-2\log 2 > -2\log(1+\delta) + \log\delta + \log\rho.$$

We have arrived to

Theorem I.1. *Under (A 1–A 4*), for any given interest factor* ρ*, there exists a critical discount factor* $\delta_\rho < 1$*, below which* $\delta < \delta_\rho$ *there exists a tax interval* $(0, t_N)$ *(with* $t_N < t^*$*) such that any tax of the interval delivers lower welfare than the no-tax system. To avoid this, the tax should jump the gap.*

Appendix J to Chapter 15. Dynamics of Pension Expenditures with Indexation

In a steady-state framework, Sect. 14.4 discussed the impact of indexation of pensions on redistribution for heterogeneous life expectancies. In this appendix, we shall present an approximation for the *dynamics* of pension expenditures with indexation. We shall use a cohort model with homogeneous life expectancy, where long periods are broken into years: $t = 0, 1, 2, \ldots$. We assume a stationary population where everybody starts to work, retires and dies at the same age: $0 < Q < R < D$. T denotes the number of years spent in retirement. We also assume that the new pension in year t is proportional to the past net wage, i.e.,

$$b_{0,t} = \beta_t v_{t-1}, \tag{J.1}$$

where $\beta_t > 0$ is the time-dependent total accrual rate and v_{t-1} is the net wage in the previous year. Here, the wage share in indexation ι denotes the share of the real wage growth which is awarded to the pensioners, $0 \le \iota \le 1$. Then, the net wage dynamics and the old pensions are given, respectively, by

$$\begin{aligned} v_t = v_{t-1} g_t \quad &\text{and} \quad b_{k,t} = b_{k-1,t-1} g_t^{\iota}, \\ t = 1, 2, \ldots \quad &\text{and} \quad k = 1, \ldots, T-1, \end{aligned} \tag{J.2}$$

where g_t is the time-dependent growth factor of real wages in year t.

By definition, the average benefit in year t is

$$\mathbf{b}_t = \chi \sum_{k=0}^{T-1} b_{k,t}, \quad \text{where} \quad \chi = \frac{1}{T}. \tag{J.3}$$

Inserting (J.1)–(J.2) into (J.3) yields a more appropriate formula:

$$\mathbf{b}_t = \chi \beta_t v_{t-1} + \chi g_t^{\iota} \sum_{k=1}^{T} b_{k-1,t-1}. \qquad \text{(J.4)}$$

We propose an approximation method for the average pension: knowing the initial values of the new and average benefits, we index the average (old) benefits and calculate the new average as

$$\tilde{\mathbf{b}}_t = \chi g_t g_{t-1} \cdots g_2 g_1 v_0 + (1-\chi)\tilde{\mathbf{b}}_{t-1} g_t^{\iota},$$
$$\text{where} \quad \tilde{\mathbf{b}}_0 = \mathbf{b}_0 \quad \text{and} \quad v_0 \text{ given.} \qquad \text{(J.5)}$$

This is a rather good approximation to $\mathbf{b}_t$ defined in (J.3) or equivalently in (J.4).

We shall consider two special cases.

Example J.1. The case of wage indexation is simple because then the benefits are independent of the date of start: $b_{k,t} = b_{0,t}$. Then $\tilde{\mathbf{b}}_t = g_t \tilde{\mathbf{b}}_{t-1}$, and the approximation is perfect.

Example J.2. Consider the case of time-invariant growth factor $g_t = g$. Then we have a closed-form solution for $\iota < 1$ as well:

$$\mathbf{b}_t = \beta v_1 g^{t-1} \frac{1 - g^{-T(1-\iota)}}{T(1 - g^{-1+\iota})} \quad \text{for} \quad \iota < 1. \qquad \text{(J.6)}$$

We display the dependence of $\mathbf{b}_0$ on the growth factor g and the wage share in indexation ι for selected values. $T = 20$ and $\beta = 0.7$. As the growth factor rises from 1 to 1.02 and the wage share in indexation drops from 1 to 0, the average benefit $\mathbf{b}_0$ sinks from 0.7 to 0.686 (Table J.1).

Turning to dynamics, we illustrate the approximation with a numerical example with parameter values $g = 1.02$, $b_{0,0} = \mathbf{b}_0$ and $\iota = 0.5$. Table J.2 displays the results. Indeed, the approximation is acceptable for small t's but gets worse and worse as t gets larger.

Table J.1 Average benefit, the growth factor and the wage share in indexation

Growth factor, g	Wage share in indexation (ι)		
	0	0.5	1
1.00	0.700	0.700	0.700
1.01	0.632	0.661	0.693
1.02	0.572	0.626	0.686

Table J.2 Old and new benefits, exact and approximate: $\iota = 0.5$

Year, t	Pension		
	New, b_t	Average exact, $\mathbf{b}_t$	Average approximate, $\tilde{\mathbf{b}}_t$
0	0.686	0.626	0.629
1	0.700	0.638	0.638
2	0.714	0.651	0.648
3	0.728	0.664	0.658
4	0.743	0.677	0.669
5	0.758	0.691	0.679
6	0.773	0.705	0.691
7	0.788	0.719	0.702
8	0.804	0.733	0.714

Correlations Between Output, Net Wage and Benefit

The latest economic history of Hungary is a good illustration of turmoil. Table J.3 presents the annual growth rates of the GDP, the real wage and of the real pension in Hungary, 1993–2015. We include the replacement ratios as well: $\hat{\beta}_t = \mathbf{b}_t/v_t$. Rather than commenting the quite erratic GDP and real wage dynamics, we confine our attention to the even more chaotic pension dynamics. There had been three phases of indexation in Hungary: wage, combined wage-price and price-indexed, shown in Table J.3. There were quite few years, when the indexation rules were followed: for example, 1993, 2001 and 2011–2012. As the comments of the last column show, in addition to these changes, there were very important discretionary measures overwriting the rules, due to elections (denoted by E), the introduction (2003–2006) and elimination (2009–2010) of the 13th month

Table J.3 Output, real wage and real pension dynamics: Hungary: 1993–2015

Year, t	Real growth rate of			Replacement rate, $\hat{\beta}_t$	Comment
	GDP $100(g_y - 1)$	Net wage $100(g_w - 1)$	Pension $100(g_\mathbf{b} - 1)$		
Wage indexation					
1993	−0.8	−3.9	−4.6	0.603	
1994	3.1	7.2	−4.7	0.594	E: change in PIT
1995	1.5	−12.2	−10.1	0.619	Change in delay
1996	0.0	−5.0	−7.9	0.593	
1997	3.3	4.9	0.4	0.563	
1998	4.2	3.6	6.2	0.578	E
1999	3.1	2.5	2.1	0.592	
Swiss indexation (half wage+half price)					
2000	4.2	1.5	2.6	0.591	
2001	3.8	6.4	6.6	0.591	+ raise
2002	4.5	13.6	9.8	0.573	E++ raise
2003	3.8	9.2	8.5	0.568	+ 1 week pension
2004	4.9	−1.1	3.9	0.600	+ 2 weeks pension
2005	4.4	6.3	7.9	0.611	+ 3 weeks pension
2006	3.8	3.6	4.5	0.623	E + 4 weeks pension
2007	0.4	−4.6	−0.3	0.668	
2008	0.8	0.8	3.4	0.691	
2009	−6.6	−2.3	−5.7	0.672	No 13th month benefit
2010	0.7	1.8	−0.9	0.651	E
Price indexation					
2011	1.8	2.4	1.2	0.647	
2012	−1.7	−3.4	0.1	0.670	
2013	1.9	3.1	4.5	0.678	Overindexation
2014	3.7	3.2	3.2	0.675	E+ overindexation
2015	2.9	4.3	3.5	0.668	Overindexation

Source. ONYF 2016, Table 1.3, p. 16

benefits, and the overestimation of inflation resulting in overindexation (2013–2015), respectively.

To discover some statistical regularity, first we report the arithmetic averages of the growth factors:

$$\mathbf{E}g_y = 1.021, \qquad \mathbf{E}g_w = 1.018 \quad \text{and} \quad \mathbf{E}g_\mathbf{b} = 1.019.$$

(The more appropriate geometric averages hardly differ: 1.02, 1.017 and 1.018, respectively).

Second, we present the standard deviations of the three growth rates, which are quite high:

$$\mathbf{D}g_y = 0.026, \qquad \mathbf{D}g_w = 0.054 \quad \text{and} \quad \mathbf{D}g_{\mathbf{b}} = 0.050.$$

The standard deviations of the growth rates of real wages and of the real benefits are close to each other and twice that of the output.

Third, we display the correlation coefficients of the three variables:

$$R(g_y, g_w) = 0.559,$$
$$R(g_w, g_{\mathbf{b}}) = 0.879$$
$$\text{and} \quad R(g_{\mathbf{b}}, g_y) = 0.681.$$

Allthe three coefficients are positive and quite strong. The strength of the first is weaker than the second, and the third lies between them.

References

Andersen, T. M., & Bhattacharya, J. (2011). On Myopia as Rationale for Social Security. *Economic Theory, 47,* 135–138.

Arias, E. (2006). United States Life Tables, 2003. *National Vital Statistics Report, 54:1,* National Center for Health Statistics, 1–40.

Banyár, J. (2012). Proposal for an Optimal Benefit Formula, (in Hungarian). *Szigma, 42,* 105–124.

Chebyshev, P. L. (1882). Approaching Integrals with Others (in Russian). *Communications of the Harkov University, 2,* 93–98.

Czeglédi, T., Simonovits, A., Szabó, E., & Tir, M. (2017). What Has Been Wrong with the Retirement Rules in Hungary? *Acta Oeconomica, 67*(2), 359–387.

Diamond, P. A. (2003). *Taxation, Incomplete Markets and Social Security, Munich Lectures.* Cambridge, MA: MIT Press.

Diamond, P. A., & Saez, E. (2011). The Case for a Progressive Tax: From Basic Research to Policy Prescriptions. *Journal of Economic Perspectives, 23*(4), 165–190.

Docquier, F. (2002). On the Optimality of Mandatory Pensions in an Economy with Life-Cyclers and Myopes. *Journal of Economic Behavior and Organization, 47,* 121–140.

Domonkos, S. (2016). Who Wants a Progressive Income Tax?: The Determinants of Tax Policy Preferences in Post-socialist Eastern Europe. *East European Politics and Society and Cultures, 30*, 127–151.
Feldstein, M. S. (1985). The Level of Social Security Benefits. *Quarterly Journal of Economics, 100*, 302–320.
Freudenberg, C., Berki, T., & Reiff, Á. (2016). *A Long-Term Evaluation of Recent Hungarian Pension Reforms* (Working Papers 2). Budapest: Magyar Nemzeti Bank.
Granseth, E., Keck, W., Nagl, W., Simonovits, A., & Tir, M. (2016). *Negative Correlation Between Retirement Age and Contribution Length?* (IE-CERS-HAS Working Paper, 33).
Mankiw, N. G., Weinzierl, M. C., & Yagan, D. (2009). Optimal Taxation in Theory and Practice. *Journal of Economic Perspectives, 23*(4), 147–174.
Mirrlees, J. A. (1971). An exploration in the Theory of Optimum Income Taxation. *Review of Economic Studies, 38*, 175–208.
Molnár, D. L., & Hollós-Marosi, J. (2015). Mortality of Old-Age Pensioners: Relation among the Amount of Pension, Age at Retirement and Mortality: Hungary, 2004–2012 (in Hungarian). *Economic Review, 62*, 1258–1290.
ONYF. (2016). *The Statistical Yearbook 2015 of the (Hungarian)*. Budapest: Central Administration of the National Pension Insurance.
Salanié, B. (2011). *The Economics of Taxation* (2nd ed.). Cambridge, MA: MIT Press.
Simonovits, A. (1995). Three Economic Applications of Chebyshev's Algebraic Inequality. *Mathematical Social Sciences, 30*, 207–220.
Simonovits, A. (2013). Savings, Child Support, Pensions and Endogenous (and Heterogeneous). Fertility, IE-CERS-HAS Working Paper 35.
Simonovits, A. (2015). Benefit-Retirement Age Schedules in Public Pension Systems. *Czech Economic and Financial Review, 65*, 362–376.
Simonovits, A. (2017). *How Did Feldstein (1985) Undervalue the Optimal Level of Social Security Benefits?* (IE-CERS-HAS Working Paper 22).
van Groezen, B., Leers, Th., & Meijdam, L. (2003). Social Security and Endogenous Fertility: Pensions and Child Benefits as Siamese Twins. *Journal of Public Economics, 87*, 233–251.
Wagener, A. (1996). Chebyshev's Algebraic Inequality and Comparative Statics under Uncertainty. *Mathematical Social Sciences, 31*, 217–221.
Waldron, H. (2007). *Trends in Mortality and Life Expectancy for Male Social-Security-Covered Workers* (ORES Working Paper 108). Washington, DC: US Social Security Administration Office of Policy.

List of Symbols

1. Common Symbols (with Few exceptions)

w = total wage (cost)
L = low
T = potential labor time
τ = contribution rate
$\hat{\tau} = 1 - \tau$ = net of contribution rate
(τ, θ) = conditional individual optimum
t = transfer rate (except Chapter 13 + Appendix C)
c = young-age consumption
b = pension
μ = length ratio
$u = U$ = utility function
f = relative frequency
β = accrual rate
γ = basic income
S = slack
$_{\mathrm{m}}$ = minimal
ν = population growth factor
I = number of types
y = income
N_t = number of (young) worker
[1] = annual factor

δ = discount factor
H = high
l = labor supply
θ = tax rate
$\hat{\theta} = 1 - \theta$ = net of tax rate
* = social optimum
$\hat{t}$ = net-of-transfer rate
d = old-age consumption
s = saving ($\tilde{s}$ = intention)
ρ = interest factor
V = social welfare function
$\mathbf{E}$ = expected value
ε = relative efficiency
ξ = labor disutility coeff.
T = tight
$_{\mathrm{M}}$ = maximal
g = productivity growth factor
i = index of a type
^{o} = special value
N_{t-1} = number of past workers

A. Simonovits, *Simple Models of Income Redistribution*,
https://doi.org/10.1007/978-3-319-72502-4

2. Introductory Tax Models

e = unreported income
J = cutoff index
t_i = net transfer paid
$\bar{\gamma}$ = maximal feasible basic income
θ_K^* = K-optimal tax rate
η = tax morale
W_J = J-minimum average wage
y_i = reported income
$\gamma[\theta]$ = balanced basic income

3. Introductory Pension Models

p = survival probability
X = random disturbance
ι = time preference rate
$\lambda = 1 - p^{-1}R^{-1}$ = efficiency difference
ζ = size of X

4. Two-Type Models

$R = \rho/(\nu g)$ = relative interest factor
τ_R = critical contribution rate
M = means-tested
V = voluntary (also in Chapter 8)
$\omega = w_{\mathrm{M}}/w_{\mathrm{m}}$ = wage ratio
$\lambda = 1 - R^{-1}$ = efficiency gap
$\bar{\tau}$ = maximal contribution rate
C = capped (see also Chapter 7)
ψ = cap-wage-ratio

5. Proportional Pensions (also Chapters 7 and 8)

f = wage density function
σ = density index
w_N = upper earning
δ_{m} = minimal δ
η = discount factor elasticity
F = wage distribution function
w_{m} = minimum wage
w_K = representative earning above cap
δ_M = maximal δ
ω = wage

6. Progressive Transfers

$\mathbf{w}$ = gross wage
$\mathbf{w}_i$ = gross age bend points
χ_i = progressive benefit rates
ι = cash-back
v_i = net wage bend points

7. Cap on the Contribution Base

$\bar{w}$ = cap
τ_w = critical value of τ
w_τ = critical value of wage

8. Voluntary Pension

z = voluntary contribution
α = matching rate
$\bar{z}$ = cap on voluntary contribution
m = total saving

9. Flexible Pensions

Q = starting age
R = retirement age
R_m = minimal retirement age
ξ = invariant labor disutility
ς = proportional adjustment
N = NDC
z = lifetime balance
S = contribution (employment) length
R_o = critical retirement age
D = age at death
R^* = normal retirement age
R_M = maximal retirement age
χ = variant labor disutility
ζ = actuarial adjustment rate
L = linear (benefit)
a = unemployment benefit
φ = 1–fragmentation coefficient
S_o = critical contribution length

10–11. Fertility and Pensions

p = absolute raising cost
φ = child benefit rate
ζ = relative utility of a child
t = transfer
E = quadratic equation
π = relative raising cost
z = narrow income
n = fertility rate
α = technical parameter

12. Political Economy

M = median type
$I = 2m - 1$ = number of types
e = type of ability
$\bar{w}$ = average wage
χ = benefit-ratio
ψ = factor of underestimation
Y = lifetime discounted income
τ_R = tax rate of retirees
w_M = median wage
F = distribution of ability
R = tax revenue
Ω = relative minimum earning
η = tax morale
$\mathbf{Y}$ = expected lifetime discounted income
τ_o = median tax rate

13. Imperfect Knowledge

ψ = underestimation of tax rate
$c = C(x)$ = young-age consumption
$\tilde{D}$ = mistaken D
q = loss of entry
Q = age at starting to work
R = retirement age
η = actuarial adjustment rate
ψ = underestimation of the DR credit
$d = D(x)$ = old-age consumption
α = plus efficiency
T = relative age at entry
D = age at death
R_m = minimal retirement age

14. Heterogeneous Longevity

Q = starting age
R = retirement age
$e_R(w)$ = w-dependent remaining LEXP
w_R = separator wage
α = weight of NDC
$e^{\iota}_R(w_{R-1})$ = indexed $e_R(w_{R-1})$
D = age at death
R^* = normal retirement age
e_R = average remaining LEXP
ζ = adjustment factor
ι = wage-share index
$e_R(\iota)$ = indexed e_R

15. Dynamic Extensions

t = time index
g_t = real wage growth factor
D_t = debt
E_t = primary balance
ι = wage share in indexation
a = pension wealth
λ = characteristic root
y_i = age-specific income
ρ_B = balanced interest factor
Y_t = output
$R = \rho/g$ = relative interest factor
d_t = debt ratio
e_t = primary balance ratio
$\mathbf{e}_t$ = traditional balance ratio
S = aggregate saving
ξ = undetermined coefficient
$s(\rho_{t+1})$ = young saving function
ρ_G = golden-rule interest factor

Appendices

Appendix A

$t(y)$ = tax–reported income
$y[w]$ = reported income
θ_1 = linear tax rate
$e[w]$ = wage-specific unreported income
$t[w]$ = tax paid
θ_2 = quadratic tax rate

Appendix B

x = volume of good 1
p = price of good 1
α = relative weight of good 1
$\kappa = 1/(1-\sigma)$
y = volume of good 2
q = price of good 2
σ = curvature of utility
$\varphi = \alpha/(1-\alpha)$

Appendix C

x = state of the system
t = step index
f, g = functions
q = contraction factor

Appendix D

t = time index
α = factor of underestimation
$R = \rho/(\nu g)$ = relative interest factor
κ = technical coefficient
$\tilde{d}$ = underestimated consumption
λ = gaplike coefficient

Appendix F

μ_L = short life span
μ_{M} = male life span
μ_{R} = rich life span
T_i = time spent in retirement
μ_H = long life span
μ_{F} = female life span
μ_{P} = poor life span
E = expenditure

Appendix G

e_R = remaining LEXP
σ = prescribed length ratio
κ = coefficient of RLEXP

Appendix H

λ = tax rate for child benefit
H = fertility transformation
ω = technical parameter

Appendix I

t_W = separator transfer
$\chi(t)$ = supply of merit good
t_N = neutral transfer

Appendix J

T = years spent in retirement
k = age
$\mathbf{b}_t$ = average benefit
ι = wage share in indexation
$\chi = 1/T$
$b_{k,t}$ = benefit at age k in year t
$\tilde{\mathbf{b}}_t$ = approximated benefit
R = correlation coefficient

Thesaurus

accrual rate is the ratio of the benefit to the wage.

actuarial adjustment rate is a positive number showing the annual (monthly) increase for delayed retirement or decrease for early retirement.

adjusted NDC is a Nonfinancial Defined Contribution formula, where the original formula is adjusted (A, B and C) to eliminate aggregate loss and reduce redistribution.

adverse selection occurs when only certain groups with adverse property choose the insurance designed for everybody.

basic income is a uniform (flat) income, paid to every citizen.

basic pension is a uniform (flat) pension, paid to every pensioner.

cap on pension contribution base is that value of the gross wage above which no worker pays additional contribution in a mandatory system and no worker receives matching in a voluntary system.

capped pension benefit is a pension benefit the value of which is limited from above by the cap on the contribution base.

child benefit is a transfer paid to a worker raising his/her children.

A. Simonovits, *Simple Models of Income Redistribution*,
https://doi.org/10.1007/978-3-319-72502-4

child benefit rate for the 1st, 2nd, 3rd etc. child is a rise in child benefit due to that child.
child support is a set of conditional or unconditional transfers paid to workers raising their children.
contribution rate (pension) is the rate at which (pension) contributions are paid with respect to the gross (or total) earnings.
credit constraint is slack/tight if the saving intention is positive/nonpositive.
critical value of a parameter is that number at which a qualitative change occurs in the behavior of a corresponding function.
subcritical value of a parameter is any number below the critical value.
supercritical value of a parameter is any number above the critical value.
decile ratio of incomes is the ratio of incomes earned by the top decile to that by the bottom decile of a population.
delayed retirement credit is added to full benefit for delayed retirement.
discount factor is a real number between 0 and 1 which diminishes the utility of next period consumption.
early retirement when somebody retires below the normal retirement age.
early(iest) retirement age is the minimal age when a healthy worker can retire.
earmarked tax is a virtual/real tax financing a special public expenditure.
earning-related (proportional) public pension is a system where the annual benefit is proportional to the lifetime wages.
farsighted worker does not discount the utility of future consumption.
fertility rate is the number of children (daughters) born by a woman (in the book).
flat pension is a uniform benefit, independent of the length of contribution and the wage.
flat-rate pension is a benefit, proportional to the length of contribution and independent of the wage.
flat-rate tax where the same marginal tax rate applies for all incomes.
flexible (variable) retirement is a system which—within a wide interval—allows the worker to decide on her retirement age.
fragmented labor career occurs when the paid working period is shorter than the difference between retirement and starting ages.

Gini coefficient is an income inequality index: it is equal to 1 minus the double of the area below the Lorenz curve.

growth factor is equal to 1+ the growth rate. In real life, we work with an annual factor, while in 2-period models, with a per-period one.

incentive compatibility condition is a condition which ensures that the employees of a given type will not choose a menu intended for other types.

income redistribution transfers goods, services and money from a certain group to another group.

indexation of pensions in progress is a rule which transforms last period (e.g., year) benefits into current benefits.

individual optimum is that choice of the vector of decision variables which maximizes the utility function subject to the constraints.

interest factor is equal to 1+ the interest rate. In real life, we work with an annual factor, while in 2-period models, with a per-period one.

intergenerational transfers redistribute incomes among various generations.

intragenerational transfers redistribute incomes among various income classes.

life annuity is paid from retirement until the pensioner dies.

life expectancy (at retirement) is the expected length of life span from birth (or retirement).

Lorenz curve is the curve showing the share of incomes received by the poorest x percent of the population, $x = 1, \ldots, 100$.

mandatory pension is paid to every citizen, who mandatorily participates in the system, it can be public or private.

marginal accrual rate is a positive number showing the relative rise of the benefit for an additional year of employment with fixed retirement age.

matching rate is a positive number; the government matches voluntary contributions by this rate.

means-tested pension is paid only to those pensioners whose other incomes are below the critical income.

mechanism design is a mathematical method to find the socially optimal reward scheme subjected to incentive compatibility conditions.

mixed pension system is a combination of public and private pension systems.

moral hazard occurs when the existence of the reward scheme influences the behavior of the employee.

nonfinancial defined contribution system (NDC) is a proportional public pension scheme where the remaining life expectancy at retirement is explicitly taken into account.

normal retirement age is that age where the retiring worker receives full benefit, calculated without deduction for early retirement or delayed retirement credit.

old-age dependency ratio is the ratio of the number of old-aged to that of the working aged.

Pareto distribution is a probability distribution where the probability of a worker earning more than w is proportional to a power of w, e.g., to $1/w^2$.

pay-as-you-go pension system is an unfunded public system.

pension contribution (or payroll tax) is paid by the workers for obtaining pensions after retirement.

pension credit is a combination of the flat and the mean-tested pensions.

pension rules connect the length of contribution, the retirement age and the lifetime average earnings to the per-period (annual) benefit.

period in the book is generally a long homogeneous time interval, where the worker works (unit length) and the pensioner is retired (compressed length).

per-period growth factor = annual growth factor raised to the power of the period length.

per-period interest factor = annual interest factor raised to the power of the period length.

personal income tax (PIT) is paid by the person (typically by a worker) after her income (typically earnings).

population aging is a process where the old-age ratio rises in the long-run.

private pension is paid by a private pension fund to a retiree, typically proportionally to the accumulated pension wealth, it can be mandatory or voluntary.

progressive PIT is a personal income tax where there are at least two marginal tax rates and they increase with incomes.

proportional (earning-related) public pension is proportional to the lifetime contribution.

public pension is paid by the public to a retiree.
Rawlsian social welfare is equal to the lowest individual utility.
relative efficiency of A w.r.t. B (compensating variation) is that number by which multiplying all incomes in B, the social welfare of the modified B becomes equal to that of A.
replacement rate is the ratio of pension benefits to wage.
saving (here private pension contribution) is net income less consumption.
seniority pension is paid to workers with long enough contributing period who retired below the normal retirement age and its value is not reduced for early retirement.
separatrix is a curve/surface in the parameter plane/space which separates the S-domain from the T-domain.
shortsighted worker discounts the utility of future consumption.
slack credit constraint holds where the lifetime saving intention is nonnegative.
social insurance achieves health and retirement risk community of the citizens.
social optimum is that choice of the government parameter vector which maximizes social welfare.
social welfare is an appropriate average of transformed individual utilities.
survival probability is the chance that an individual survives from the start to the end of a given period.
tax evasion occurs when the citizen partially or fully evades paying taxes.
tax (personal income) is paid by the citizens to the government to finance public expenditures including income redistribution.
tax rate (marginal) is a positive number determining the marginal rise in tax in terms of the similar rise in income, constant in an income bracket.
tax morale influences the citizen's readiness to pay her due taxes.
tight credit constraint holds where the negative lifetime saving intention is transformed into zero saving.
total dependency ratio is the ratio of the number of dependents to the number of working aged.
total fertility rate is the estimated number of children having the same mother.
transfer rate is the sum of the pension and the tax rates.

transfers are paid by citizens to the government (negative transfers are received).

undeclared (unreported) income is that part of the income which the citizen hides from the authorities.

underreported income is the full income less the undeclared income.

unfunded public pension system pays annual benefits from annual contributions.

utilitarian social welfare is the arithmetic average of the individual utilities.

variable retirement (→ flexible retirement).

voluntary pensions are paid to those retirees who voluntarily contributed to their pension accounts before retiring.

wage share in indexation is a number between 0 and 1, showing the share of wage dynamics in pension indexation.

Index

A. Simonovits, *Simple Models of Income Redistribution*,
https://doi.org/10.1007/978-3-319-72502-4

R

The manufacturer's authorised representative in the EU is Springer
Nature Customer Service Centre GmbH, Europaplatz 3, 69115 Heidelberg,
Germany. If you have any concerns regarding our products, please
contact ProductSafety@springernature.com

Printed and bound by CPI Group (UK) Ltd, Croydon, CR0 4YY
30/09/2026
02225653-0011